W9-BHG-262

CASHING IN
ON THE
AMERICAN DREAM

CASHING IN
ON THE
AMERICAN
DREAM

HOW TO RETIRE AT 35

Paul Terhorst

BANTAM BOOKS
TORONTO · NEW YORK · LONDON · SYDNEY · AUCKLAND

CASHING IN ON THE AMERICAN DREAM
A Bantam Book / August 1988

Grateful acknowledgment is made for permission to reprint lyrics from "It's Alright Ma, I'm Only Bleeding" by Bob Dylan, copyright © 1965 by WARNER BROS. INC. All rights reserved. Used by permission.

All rights reserved.
Copyright © 1988 by Paul H. Terhorst and Vicki Terhorst.
Book Design by Nicola Mazzella.
No part of this book may be reproduced or transmitted in any form or by any means, electronic or mechanical, including photocopying, recording, or by any information storage and retrieval system, without permission in writing from the publisher.
For information address: Bantam Books.

Library of Congress Cataloging-in-Publication Data

Terhorst, Paul.
  Cashing in on the American dream.

  1. Finance, Personal—United States. 2. Retirement income—United States. 3. Middle age—United States. 4. Retirement—United States. I. Title.
HG179.T43   1988   322.024'01   87-47888
                ISBN 0-553-05289-6

Published simultaneously in the United States and Canada

Bantam Books are published by Bantam Books, a division of Bantam Doubleday Dell Publishing Group, Inc. Its trademark, consisting of the words "Bantam Books" and the portrayal of a rooster, is Registered in U.S. Patent and Trademark Office and in other countries. Marca Registrada. Bantam Books, 666 Fifth Avenue, New York, New York 10103.

PRINTED IN THE UNITED STATES OF AMERICA

BP   0 9 8 7 6 5 4 3 2

Vicki and I dedicate this book to our friends Mike, Vilma, Melanie, and Paul.

Acknowledgments

I would like to thank:

Edward Shaw, Maria Shaw, Ricardo Rybak, and Tati Rybak, for helping me figure out how to retire at age 35.

Antonia Anderson, Pat Bell, Robin Bell, Joe Drescher, and Karen Drescher, for encouraging me to write about it.

Cliff Naughton, Jerry Bowles, Eric Ehrmann, and others, unfortunately too numerous to mention, for criticizing drafts of this book.

Eileen Fallon, of Barbara Lowenstein Associates, and Peter Guzzardi, of Bantam Books, for their conviction that this material would interest others.

Robin Bell, for suggesting the title.

Contents

PART 1

RETIREMENT AT AGE 35 IS FOR REAL

1.

It Takes Less Money than You Think

I was sitting in the transit lounge of Heathrow Airport in London when the notion of very early retirement first came to me. I was on the way home from a business trip to Europe, dozing off in my chair, when I overheard two guys talking about someone.

"He did a couple of dope-smuggling deals in Mexico," one of them said. "Very big. But it was risky, so he got out and bought real estate in San Diego County. He's retired now—lives on a ranch down there, breeding horses and hunting."

There I was, tired, successful, lonesome for my wife, Vicki, peeking out the corner of my eye at two guys in designer jeans and lizard-skin cowboy boots. They had Halliburton cases at their sides and smoked cigarettes I didn't recognize. They were talking about someone my age who had retired.

I wasn't a drug dealer, just a certified public accountant. I was 33 years old, a partner in a major accounting firm. Ahead lay a future of big challenges and big money. But I began toying with the notion that if I could come up with a way to live off what I already had, I'd never have to work again. I could retire decades before becoming eligible for Social Security. I could travel, read, learn, and relax rather than continue to grind away at the job.

It took me two years from that day at Heathrow to figure out a way to retire. At age 35 I did it—with class. The formula in this book tells how you can do it too.

All my life I had wanted nothing more than a piece of the corporate action. At age 5 I played at my desk for hours at a time. When I was 7 I begged for a file cabinet for Christmas. My parents and teachers told me I could be anything I wanted to be, and I believed every word of it. When I was in high school my hero was Jonas Cord of *The Carpetbaggers*. As I recall, Jonas failed in his private life, but I viewed that as a minor miscalculation. As they say, money may not buy happiness but it sure takes the sting out of being unhappy.

I didn't just dream about money and power and expense-account living—I planned for it. Before starting my career I got an M.B.A. from Stanford Graduate School of Business. After Stanford I went for the gold and loved every minute of it. Seven years later, at age 30, I was one of the youngest partners in the history of Peat, Marwick, Mitchell & Co., the international accounting firm. By 1984 I had a huge office, a leather chair, and a view of a polluted river. Someone brought me coffee, someone else made my phone calls, and a highly trained staff did the work. I was so high up in the world that instead of talking on the phone in intervals, I talked on the phone all day long. I played golf at the best clubs and flew to places like London, Rome, Miami, and Rio de Janeiro.

In late 1984, a few months shy of my 36th birthday, I hung up my pencil. I retired before I had my first pair of bifocals, before the gold watch could tick away my best decades. I didn't win a lottery, have a rich uncle, or rob a bank. I didn't make a fortune in real estate, catch a run in the stock market, or invent a new toy. I wasn't a millionaire. All I had were some savings, equity in my home, and a few minor investments. But I decided to stop working and get on with a new phase of my life. I'd earned my fair share. However, I'd seen enough compulsive gamblers in Las Vegas to know that the house will take back what you've won and more than even the score. I became convinced that my decision wasn't irresponsible or degenerate. I simply wanted more time to myself before it was too late to get out. I wanted a good life, not a good job.

In our society it's considered normal to work during the best years of your life. You work when you're young, healthy, and vital. You work when your mental powers are sharp, your mind inquisitive. You work when you still have a family at home and your kids need you the most. You give the best years of your life to your career and the last few years to yourself.

Are we crazy or what?

When we get to be a broken-down 62, or even a healthy 62, we retire. We finally begin a life we can call our own. We buy a Hilton Head condo, sign up a Mayo Clinic doctor, and talk shop with a clique of retirement-ghetto friends.

You don't *have* to resign yourself to that kind of fate. You can discover in your 30s or 40s that you've got more going for you than the upward spiral that so often ends in messy divorce, with kids, shiny cars, adult toys, and a country home as bargaining chips.

A long time ago we had no choice but to work a lifetime. Things were simpler then. A man worked fifty or sixty hours a week, from age 15 to the day he died, and earned barely enough to support his family. Cars were American, field-goal kickers had last names you could pronounce, and three-hour phone calls to Europe were only a glint in some crazy person's eye.

Today's M.B.A.s, lawyers, and high-tech scientists earn megabucks from the start. Even after discounting for inflation, what you earn in a few years is more than grandpa and grandma spent in their entire lives. Work fifteen or twenty years and you may make enough money to last a lifetime. Most young people keep working past age 35, 40, or 45 and pile up wealth. But if you're prepared to make it happen, the forty-year career can go the way of vacuum tubes, mono records, and domestic oil supplies.

Some say America is changing from a smokestack to a service economy. Others are less kind. They say America's economy is falling apart. Big labor has lost its ability to protect the rank and file. Japan and Korea are changing the way we think and work, and the British-style Fleet Street hype has taken over TV and most of the press. Huge numbers of college students struggle to read and write. They graduate without having learned to think or decide. Product quality is an impossible dream in many industries, and the focus on current earnings per share plagues even the most farsighted planners. All that's left, it seems, is to work hard and make money.

I believe most young managers respect the system. They know it's a long shot, but they still hope to wind up in power by the time they're 50. But today, unlike a few decades ago, one needs more than the right M.B.A. or the ability to put a smile on the boss's face. The surplus of baby boomers means that the system will be less and less able to make room for good people at upper levels. We need to find new opportunities for sharp, hardworking people who leave the corporate structure.

Up to now, those outlets have been second careers, the Peace Corps, turning a hobby into a business, and the like. Those outlets give you at least some money to live on. The route I describe in this book offers more freedom. The dramatic feature of my plan is that you live the rest of your life without earning another dime. You let your equity sweat for you. You can have the incredible luxury of looking at life as a brand new ball game, nearly without economic restraints, while you still have a keen mind and active spirit.

It sounds scary, and it is scary. But once you decide to get out of corporate life—taking your fair share but no more—you'll be part of a unique group that can say they've met the challenge and moved on to lusher fields, a group that will have taken advantage of a possibility that only the richest, most varied country in the world can provide.

This book tells how you can do it *now*. If you follow the formula, it could be the best thing that ever happened to you.

STRESS KILLS

All Peat Marwick partners are required to have an annual physical exam. I used to have my annual physical every three years. When I went in for the physical in early 1984, the doctor didn't know of my plans to retire.

As I recall, the doctor looked up from the illegible notes he had made during the exam and said, "You're in great shape, Paul. Everything's normal."

I frowned and tilted my head. "Everything? With all the stress in my job? All the traveling I do? All the salt in my diet? Additives? Red dye number two?"

He looked back at my file, then shrugged. "You could lose a couple of pounds. Five, maybe."

I observed his beefy frame, easily thirty pounds overweight. I decided against a wisecrack. It was my physical, not his.

I said, "Heartbeat okay? Vital signs strong? Blood pressure normal? I eat a lot of salt."

"Within the normal range."

"So my job hasn't affected my health at all?"

The doctor looked at me patiently and shook his head. "Not at all." Then, trying to be helpful, he smiled and said, "Wait a couple of years."

My doctor knows. My wife knows. Every New York City cabdriver knows. Every money-driven lawyer, IBM salesman, and art dealer knows. Life in the fast lane can be dangerous to your health. Tennis and golf, hiking and skiing, and unnatural sex help a little. Travel, booze, massage, meditation, Club Med, and rediscovering God give us a respite. But stress takes its toll. Ulcers, back pain, high blood pressure, and "substance abuse" plague compulsive achievers in their 30s and 40s.

Life in the fast lane can ruin more than your health. Marriages these days last an average of eight or nine years. Half of America's children live with one parent or the other, but not both. How many families collapse because parents absorb tension on the job and take it out on those waiting at home?

I started working at Peat Marwick in San Francisco in 1972. When people with money in San Francisco hang it up, they can drive two hours down the California coast to Carmel. Carmel has a cool climate and ocean breezes. It has more golf courses than Harvard has M.B.A.s. A house on the water near Carmel can strain even the fattest budget. Houses seem to be built for two people but on the assumption that they want to lose each other. An architect once told me the problem is how to design a nine-thousand-square-foot house that has a decent place to read.

In short, Carmel is the perfect place for the reasonably rich to retire.

For years I watched partners from San Francisco's most elite firms put away their briefcases, get a new set of golf clubs, and move to Carmel. They were going to play eighteen holes with their wives in the morning and eighteen with the guys later on. They were going to relax and enjoy the money they had worked so hard to save.

And some of them did—for six months or so. Then they had heart attacks and died.

The numbers back up the anecdotal evidence. Life expectancy for American men ranks only twenty-fourth in the world, partly because we have so many fatal heart attacks so early in life. Life expectancy for women ranks much higher, ninth in the world. But American women seem determined to fill the jobs that appear to be killing men. Today women set corporate policy, defend clients in lawsuits, cut into brain tissue in operating rooms, and run cities. Unfortunately, according to cardiologist Meyer Friedman and nurse Diane Ulmer, "The incidence of coronary heart disease is increasing rapidly among women." In *Treating Type A Behavior—And Your Heart* (Knopf, 1984), Friedman and Ulmer report that Type A professional and business women—those who hurry the most and get annoyed the quickest—suffer from coronary heart disease *seven times* more frequently than Type B women.

Nancy Mayer, in *The Male Mid-Life Crisis* (NAL, 1970), says that the body's ability to withstand stress may be finite. She reports that Dr. Hans Selye "first identified the stress syndrome that causes a chemical rallying of the body's defenses . . . Stress is a drastic wearing force, he found, and once each man's 'adaptation energy' is expended it cannot be replaced. . . ." If Selye is right, and our stress is work-related, we're literally wearing ourselves out on the job.

Today's executive men and women will most likely succumb to fast-lane killers like heart disease, cancer, stroke, emphysema, diabetes, and cirrhosis of the liver. None of those killers were among the top ten causes of death at the turn of the century. Grandpa's grandpa died of less esoteric diseases like diarrhea, typhoid, cholera, tuberculosis, and smallpox. That was before organization man, the gray flannel suit, and the information war. Before antismoking laws. Before three-Perrier lunches. Before softer-than-soft toilet tissue that feels like Wonder Bread on a roll. Before television.

Have you ever been to an old folks' home? An old folks' home provides harsh evidence of society's failure to provide a decent environment for aging for many people. You'll find it isn't an old folks' home at all. It's an old ladies' home. The one I visited had seventy-eight women and two men. Neither of the men came out to see me. Perhaps they were back in their rooms wondering what the hell they were doing there.

I asked the matron why there were so few men. She looked at me suspiciously. "You really want to know?"

I nodded, not at all sure I really did.

She said, "Women come here to live. Men come here to die."

When today's old people were my age, the idea of living to work was coming into its own. Vance Packard's 1959 study *The Status Seekers* (McKay) glorified and exposed the ad world and the ugly side of corporate life. William Whyte wrote *The Organization Man* (Simon & Schuster) in 1957. Whyte's story now has its terrible final chapter. When the organization man can't work, he has no reason to live.

Having seen what lies ahead of you when you hang up your boots—or when you're forced out at age 55—do you still think you need more money before you can afford to retire *now?* Why wait for golden years you may not live to enjoy? Maybe you can't afford *not* to retire now.

HERE'S THE FORMULA

Part 1 of this book reveals the formula that can turn your retirement dream into a here-and-now reality. The formula has three parts. First, you'll find out how much money you need, how to invest, and how to spend. Next, you'll see how to kick the work habit. Finally, you'll get some ideas about what's out there and how to get started in your new life. Follow the formula and you'll never snooze through lukewarm coffee and bad cognac at your retirement dinner.

The rules you need to follow aren't conventional; neither is retiring after only ten or fifteen years of work. But they're simple rules, far more simple than the rules you've followed up to now. I've set out the rules in big block letters so you won't miss them. The three-part formula in part 1 is:

Do your arithmetic
Do some soul-searching
Do what you want

Part 2 expands on this formula. It tells how to make the formula come alive for you. It presents real-life case studies, tells how to save on taxes, looks at retiring with kids, and suggests a few lifestyle changes that can save hundreds of thousands of dollars. Someone once said it's not ideas that change things, but tactics. Part 2 of this book helps you come up with tactics that fit your style. All that's required on your part is a little imagination.

Later on, when you're 55 or 65, if you want to you can "unretire" and go back to work. We used to work and then retire. This book suggests you work, then retire, then consider going back to work. Under this plan you devote your middle years to yourself and your family. During those years your mental and physical powers reach their height. You can explore, grow, and invest your time in what's most important to you. You can enjoy your children while they're still at home. Later, after you've lived the best years for yourself, you can go back to work if you want to. The choice will be up to you.

Pro athletes never plan forty-year careers. Martina Navratilova, Fernando Valenzuela, and Magic Johnson know their playing years are numbered. My work life lasted twelve years. To me, twelve years seems the minimum for a solid, proper career. But for football players, twelve years is the brilliant career of a superstar. Bob Griese, Herschel Walker, and Walter Payton may play twelve years. But most athletes burn out before they ever hit their Thirties Crisis. They may continue to dream of a chance to play in a Super Bowl, haggle over one more contract, or enjoy another headline. But their bodies scream at them to quit.

A tackle graduates from Ohio State and gets a signing bonus from the Raiders. For two years he draws a six-figure salary to play preseason games, beat up on special teams, and learn the playbook. In his third year he begins to start. Al Davis connects the name with the face, the fans and press talk about his quickness, and opposing players respect his talent. Our man plays three or four more years. During that period his salary doubles and then doubles again. He also makes big money on promotions and endorsements. But the travel, late nights, long workouts, mental strain, and injuries slow him by a fraction of a second. He begins to dread that inevitable Sunday when a younger player starts in his place. A season later he's washed up, as useless as a water boy without a pail.

But our man hired an agent to help him make deals, invest, and prepare for retirement. When his playing career ends he can live the rest of his life on interest and dividends from his investments. He may choose to buy a car dealership or open a saloon. But he may also choose to travel, relax on the beach, or organize a Special Olympics for retarded children.

We executives probably think we're smarter than the average jock. Most of us handle our own investments. But who's to tell *us* when to retire? Should we retire in our early 30s, like Sandy Koufax? In our 40s, like Pete Rose? Or in our 60s, like our fathers, grandfathers, and great-grandfathers? If a washed-up Raider can't decide to retire, Al Davis decides for him. Do you want your company to decide for you? Or do you want to step down on your own, with dignity, when you're still young and clearly in command?

This book is the first attempt to do for executives, screenwriters, models, stock jockeys, whiz kids, and mad marketeers what agents like Irving Marks do for highly paid jocks. Start thinking like athletes and you may wind up retiring at the same age they do. And you've got a big advantage. Their legs are shot. You can go back to work if you feel like it.

HOW MUCH MONEY DO YOU NEED?

A few years ago I was a quiet power in the moneymaking system. Each year I passed judgment on the financial health of billions of dollars of balance sheet assets. I was what we called an "audit engagement partner." That means that for my clients I had final authority and responsibility for signing the Peat Marwick name to the numbers we audited. In plain language, it means that no matter how many other partners might give advice and help, it was my personal ass that went squarely on the line behind the Peat Marwick name. If I made a mistake, we could be sued for millions. If I believed the numbers presented an unfair picture, I refused to sign the opinion. In that case, people could lose face, lose their jobs, or even lose their minds.

With that kind of pressure I kept a pretty sharp pencil. And in 1984 I decided to put that pencil to a different sort of task. I decided to check out how much money one needs to retire at age

35. How much money would my wife, Vicki, and I need to live off interest income for the rest of our lives?

I found that a net worth of as little as $100,000 can be enough. That's *total* net worth, including home equity, IRAs, and cars. Retiring on $100,000 is bare-bones retirement, and chapter 11 tells how to do it. Chapter 11 also discusses a recent Census Bureau report on wealth. The report implies that more than half the families in America may be within striking distance of $100,000 of net worth.

But to retire on $100,000 you have to be willing to make sacrifices. After a few years of retirement you may have to take on part-time work, for example. When I retired I refused to sacrifice anything important. I wanted to travel, keep up my hobbies, go to the theater, and go out to dinner. I wanted to do those things forever, not just for five years or so. How much money would I need for that?

I figure $400,000 is enough, but that $500,000 is more comfortable for most of us. Again, that's total net worth, including home equity. If you have kids you may need a bit more than that (see chapter 9), depending on how many kids you have and how old they are.

A net worth of $500,000 may seem like far too little. But if you convert that net worth to cash and put it in the bank at 8 percent interest, you have a gross annual income of $40,000—which is more than some 75 percent of American families make. Interest rates move around, so your income could be slightly higher or lower, but that kind of money ought to be plenty to live on.

This book tells how to retire with an income of $40,000 or so a year. You'll have somewhat less than that after you pay income taxes and set aside something for inflation. You'll live without the addictive trappings that hook you to the good life. Without a house the size of the Taj Mahal and without first-class hotels when you travel. Without a Mercedes and without tax shelters. Without private schools for the kids. Without a ski cabin and his and hers lawns. But you won't have to drink ordinary scotch, thank God. You won't have to go without his and hers coffeepots. You'll be able to travel the world, staying in center-city hotels and doing all the tourist things you want to do. You'll be able to party all you want, get to know your kids before they're grown, and maybe even bring joy back to your marriage and avoid becoming another statistical casualty. You'll be spending based on your needs rather than on what you can "afford."

And you'll never work another day in your life—unless you want to. You may even find you need a new way to define "work."

MILLIONS COULD RETIRE RIGHT NOW

How many young Americans have $400,000 or $500,000 of net worth and can retire like I did? Would you believe something like 4 million?

I looked it up. The U.S. government has statistics on every·thing. The number of nongay drinkers of cheap white wine who find it's not required that they use a deodorant. The increase in Spanish-surnamed modern females without hangovers who sleep late on Wednesdays even though the alarm goes off. I don't believe it either. But the Federal Reserve Board really *does* say they have a handle on net-worth numbers, and they break them down by age. I had to massage their data and make a few guesses. But it turns out that nearly 2.5 million of America's 70 million households are headed by people under 55 years old with a net worth of $250,000 or more. After allowing for single heads of households, that's about 4 million people with close to the target net worth of $400,000. Those 4 million people have the luxury of continuing to work only if they feel like it.

I suspect that most of the 4 million people got their wealth the same way I did, by getting a good education, working hard, and having a little luck. That's what's so great about opportunities in America. Four million people—the population of a city the size of Chicago—have earned so much money so early in life that they can hang 'em up after only a dozen years of work. That doesn't happen in other countries.

If you're anything like I was before I retired, your personal balance sheet may show a net worth of $400,000 or $500,000. You have to update the value of your home, but you get there. You're one of the 4 million. If you're not, chapter 10 tells how to build your net worth over the next several years. But having $500,000 of net worth doesn't mean you have $40,000 in interest income, does it? Hell no. That net worth is tied up in your house, your car, your investments, and your sensible life insurance program. And anyway, you couldn't possibly live on $40,000 a year, right? You've got two career earners in the family, both busting their asses, knocking down a combined $100,000 a year, and your December Bloomingdale's bill was so high you could barely afford to tip the doormen at Christmas.

I know. I was there. But my accountant's instincts drove me to do some more arithmetic. I figured out that Vicki and I were spending about $50 a day on our basic living expenses. That's $50 a day for food and clothes, the maid and dry cleaning, movies and dinner out. It included vacations, golf club dues, guitar lessons, gifts, a cigar now and then, and French cognac. I call that the money we spend on *us*.

There's nothing tricky about this. It's called the $50-a-Day Rule, and you'll read about it in chapter 8. It's a universal truth, as it turns out. Like the law that every bus station everywhere in the world has a cheap Chinese restaurant nearby; or that when you spill on your tie, it's your favorite tie; or that all accountants are dull.

Fifty dollars a day is an average, not a daily, quota. On trips to New York or Paris you'll need to budget to stay even close to $50 a day. But in Paraguay or Bangkok or even West Texas you'll find it's hard to spend that much money—unless you're more kinky than my accountant's mind can imagine.

THE $50-A-DAY RULE

A friend first told me about the $50-a-Day Rule. (Some of the players in this book are composites, and details have been changed.) He was 42 years old and chief financial officer of a Houston-based oil company when his work life unraveled. The new chairman was acquisition-minded and hammered on the financial staff. Two people on my friend's staff suffered heart attacks; one of them died, and the other was forced to retire. A third had bleeding ulcers; a fourth had high blood pressure.

My friend saw what was happening. "It was crazy," he told me a few years later. "I traveled three days a week to check out companies we wanted to buy. I'd call the office from my hotel room and talk for hours. When I was at home in Houston I'd put in fifteen-hour days. My secretary went into hysterics a couple of times when I gave her things to type. I began to get used to people crying at the office. The place was a zoo."

He tried jogging and working out to relieve the stress. For emotional support he leaned on his wife and 14-year-old son. He tried to replace his spent staff with better people. But he could see himself slipping. He began to drink, have funny stomach pains that puzzled doctors, and wake up sweating at four in the morning. By five o'clock on workdays he was as irritable as a saber-tooth tiger with a toothache.

At about that time, he inherited the house he was living in. Also at about that time, his last healthy department head quit. My friend decided enough was enough. He went to see the chairman, with the idea of quitting, and came out with a one-year leave of absence. He rented out his house for $2,000 a month, pulled his daughter out of school and his wife out of the doldrums, and flew off to Europe.

The three of them learned firsthand that the English heat their buildings to freezing, that the French bathe only every three months or so, that the Spanish hoard information, and that most of Italy stays closed most of the time. They made new friends, got a more rounded view of life, and learned to swear at waiters in three languages. They grew as a family. My friend remembered how to laugh without having a couple of pops at the bar beforehand. His stomach pains went away and he started doing sit-ups in hotel rooms instead of lifting weights at a gym.

At the end of the year the family returned home. My friend was a new man. He knew he could handle his old job but he had little desire to do so. Pushing numbers seemed irrelevant. He felt more like starting something new.

Before going to the office to discuss it with his boss he put together some figures and discovered his family's net worth had *increased.* They had spent $1,600 a month in Europe—just over $50 a day. But they had rented out their home for $2,000. After taxes and expenses they had cash left over to cover inflation. The best year of their lives had cost them nothing.

My friend called his old boss and resigned. He bought a small apartment, moved in the furniture, and planned their next trip. He still wanted to start a new business venture, but he had no idea what it was. He decided to enjoy himself until he found out.

DON'T WORK FOR YOUR ASSETS

The $50-a-Day Rule says the money we spend on *us* is only $50 a day. That's $18,000 a year. But you're spending more than $18,000 a year, aren't you? A hell of a lot more. Off the top come income taxes or some of those tax shelters that seem to cost more than the taxes. With what you have left you pay the mortgage. You pay condo expenses, property insurance, and property taxes. You make car payments and car insurance payments. You have car repair bills, gas bills, oil and lube bills, parking fees, and parking tickets. That's on two cars plus a recreational vehicle or two. Then there are all those toys: cameras, home stereo and video equipment, expensive but rarely used ski and camping equipment, computers, motorcycles, and his and hers swimming pools. In short, after paying to keep the world safe for democracy— paying the retroactive tribute for the privilege of having the freedom to make all that money—your income goes to maintain your assets.

I know. I was once in the same place. Instead of my assets working for me, I was working for them. I call that the money I spend on *them* rather than the $50 a day on *us*. And I ask myself, how in the hell did I get into this mess?

How many others are trapped like I was and want to get out?

In chapter 4 I offer detailed advice on how to convert your net worth into assets that work for you—so you can stop working for them. It tells how to avoid slow death from the two great killers: the big house and the fast car. Hard assets create expenses. When you retire, you want your equity in liquid assets that can sweat for *you*. You'll find you need to sell your two-story house and pay off the mortgage. Rolling over the equity in your home can be smart when you're working. You defer capital gains tax and deduct interest and property taxes. But payments on a place the size of South Fork can break someone living on $40,000 a year. Chapter 4 tells how to sell the house and get off the treadmill, minimizing taxes along the way.

Chapter 4 goes on to explain how to invest the proceeds in staggered one-year certificates of deposit to protect against a drop in interest rates and earn high cash income when rates go up. It's a boring way to invest. But the CDs will throw off plenty of money for you to live on. They're guaranteed. You'll never spend a single agonizing minute thinking about your investments. You'll never have to collect rent, prepare a complicated tax return, or check up on the market for rare coins, Picasso prints, or Japanese yen.

When I retired I went to see my broker to tell him my plans. Like any good investment counselor, George listened to what I wanted from my investments and to my strategy for getting there. Then he tried to pick holes in it. That's his job, and he's good at it. What about inflation? What about putting 20 percent to 50 percent in common stocks? What about playing with 10 percent in high-risk assets? At the end of the hour he was convinced that my plan made sense for me. Now George rolls the CDs when they come due.

As I said before, the advice in chapter 4 goes against conventional wisdom. Sage old men say never sell a piece of real estate. I say sell. Business schools say look for a 20 percent threshold return. I say take CDs at 8 percent or whatever. Wall Street writers say put between 20 percent and 50 percent of your net worth into stocks. I say forget the stock market. Accountants say buy tax shelters. I say reduce your income so you don't have to worry about taxes.

Although the rules may be counterintuitive, they're easy to understand. They're designed for a life of freedom. Follow them and you'll have money to wander around the world, play golf, or buy a new guitar. You'll have money to eat at ethnic restaurants, go to jazz clubs at two in the morning, and take your kids to Yankees' games.

Here are some rules we've already discussed:

Live on $50 a Day
Turn hard assets into cash
Buy one-year insured CDs

I'll talk more about these and other rules later on. On p. 220 you'll find all the rules in a handy summary. If you want to skim the book—you haven't retired yet, and I know how busy you are—just look at the rules. Follow the rules and you'll probably retire before your parents do. Almost certainly you'll retire before your friends even think about it.

2.

You *Can* Kick the Work Habit

So maybe you're starting to believe you might be able to live on $40,000 a year. During college and the first years on the job you lived on a fraction of that. Remember those times? Gas cost 25 cents a gallon and gas station attendants spoke English. Spiro Agnew pleaded nolo contendere with honor. Detroit pushed big cars.

In many ways your life was better back then. Sure, it was great to make a few bucks. A few bucks helped a lot in the first few years of marriage and family life. But somewhere along the way things got distorted. The concept of family faded away. Economic security, once based on savings and parental support, changed when the Treasury started cranking the presses into overdrive, and advertising persuaded baby boomers to squeeze out every last dollar for image-based purchases. Social values shifted when 20-year-olds who protested against Vietnam, racism, and poverty grew up and dropped out into the world of vacation condos, status cars, and exclusive golf clubs.

Deep down you know you can live without the new BMW, the beach house, and $35 hamburgers; without Valiums, two divorces and their $90,000 lawyer's fees, and feeling slightly self-conscious in a not-yet-upscaled Burger King.

But can you live without the job itself? Without a secretary to do your bidding? Without the challenge of making a buck in a market that's turned against you? Without the power, responsibility, and sense of getting something done? Without going to the office every day? Without two-hour meetings, career counseling, and that first cup of coffee at your desk each morning?

Before retiring I had lunch with a 50-year-old friend who had been eased out of the law firm he had founded. He felt disoriented and frustrated. Money was no problem—he had inherited quite a stash—but the office had been his life. A few years before, he had told me that stress on the job had ruined his marriage and caused a mild heart attack. He had willingly paid the price—until now. Now he was so frightened of the future that he had trouble choosing from the menu, not to mention putting together a new life for himself.

He panicked when I told him I was going to retire at age 35.

"Don't do it," he told me. "You'll be cut off. No one will call. No one will ask your advice. Hell, you won't even get any *mail*. You laugh, but I know what I'm talking about. It's a problem."

Just before making the final decision to retire, I went to New York on business. After a day at the Peat Marwick office on Park Avenue, I ran into a young acquaintance. He had designed dresses for years, bouncing from one job to another in New York's Seventh Avenue garment district. When his dresses didn't sell, he was out the door faster than a Federal Express package. The jobs paid well when he had them, but he needed every dime to keep up with high New York prices. He lived in a fifth-floor walkup that the landlord figured was worth about the same as the King Ranch in Texas. A drink in the bar around the corner cost the same as a day's pay in most countries in the world. (In chapter 5 I review living costs in the United States and around the world. I give you a list of U.S. cities where you can live well on $50 a day. New York is not one of them.)

He had heard about my plans to retire. "But don't you have a job that pays a lot of money?" he asked. "A job with prestige, security, and plenty of vacation? With a big accounting firm or something?"

I nodded.

"And you're going to quit?"

I began to feel funny, but I nodded again.

"Why would anyone ever quit a good job?" he asked incredulously.

I mumbled something about personal choice and looked away. I felt clobbered. Here was a guy breaking his back to achieve what I already had. If I was doing the wrong thing, after a short time I would be back pounding the pavement like him. His eyes told me I didn't want that to happen.

Later that night I agonized over the decision one more time.

I had started with Peat Marwick in 1972 making something less than $14,000 a year. I worked hard, got good raises, and became a valued contributor. Now I lived in the best part of town, paid a maid to watch TV, and bought $500 suits. The future looked so bright I was even thinking of flying first-class on *personal* trips.

Why would I gratuitously give up something I had worked so hard to achieve? I was under no illusions. If after a few years I had to go back to work, I could never get as good a job. I wouldn't have to throw Tupperware parties or drive a Good Humor truck, but I would almost certainly have to take a big cut in pay. At business school we called the top jobs "golden handcuffs." Golden means you have a good job, make good money. Handcuffs means you're tied to it: you'd never be able to make as much money doing something else.

But what kept hammering in my head was that Vicki and I could live without the big income. After converting our assets to cash and investing in CDs we would earn over $40,000 of interest each year. Under the $50-a-Day Rule we lived on only $18,000 a year. The balance would more than cover inflation and taxes. I'm an accountant, right? I went over and over the numbers. A net worth of $400,000 or $500,000 doesn't *seem* like enough. But pencils don't lie. I *knew* I didn't need any more money.

So the only reason to work was for nonfinancial rewards. Does that make any sense?

It can for some people.

A HARD-DRIVING SUCCESS WITH A SOUTHERN DRAWL

According to *Forbes* magazine, Sam Walton was the richest man in America in 1987. The article says he's 69 and has over

$8.5 billion of stock in Wal-Mart, the company he founded. Whatever he wants to buy, with $8.5 billion he can buy a lot of it. He's so rich he could outspend a Saudi prince *before* OPEC lost its grip on the oil market. He can live wherever he wants, do whatever he wants, and spend whatever he wants.

So what does he want? More work, that's what. He works eighteen hours a day. He's a true role model for the American work ethic.

He lives in Bentonville, Arkansas, in a rustic ranch house that's comfortable but not spectacular. His passion, outside of Wal-Mart, is quail hunting, what else? At the beginning of the season he waits in line in the local Wal-Mart to buy shotgun shells. Then he heads off with his hunting dogs in his 1979 Ford pickup.

Associates say he's not much interested in what he's worth. He doesn't spend much on himself—probably $50 a day, just like Vicki and I do.

If you asked Sam Walton why he works, he probably wouldn't talk of money. I'm guessing now, but he'd probably say he's having a ball at Wal-Mart. He'd say he still gets a kick out of socking it to the competition. He'd say he loves playing the game and the thrill of winning.

Sam Walton stopped working for money a long time ago. So did Armand Hammer, Lee Iacocca, Lawrence Tisch, and Frank Sinatra. So did 4 million others, according to the Federal Reserve Board numbers we mentioned in chapter 1. Those millions of people work for power, prestige, status, and a sense of belonging. They work for "attaboys." They play the game and they like winning. They identify with their jobs. In a very real sense they are what they do—and they love it.

But we can't all be Sam Walton or Armand Hammer. We'd like to stay charged up and turned on like we were when we were 25. But most of us reach a plateau, when we know we have little chance of getting another promotion. And we're vulnerable to new waves of baby boomers challenging us from below. Head hunters say we're most vulnerable from age 42 to 50. Before that we're not making enough money for anyone to notice. After that we can be eased into a retirement program. But between 42 and 50 we're most likely to be fired in a 10 percent or 20 percent across-the-board cutback.

Even if you get a big break by age 50, you still face the Peggy Lee Syndrome. The syndrome gets its name from the song Peggy Lee made famous: "Is That All There Is?" Peggy Lee Syndrome hits many of us at age 40 or so, when we look back on our lives and know we missed something. At the same time we look forward and find that, whatever it is, we're going to continue to miss it in the future.

Has it happened to you? Can you believe it *could* happen to you?

In *Passages* (Dutton, 1976), Gail Sheehy's book about life's turning points, Sheehy says that midlife crisis is inevitable. "Whatever rung of achievement he has reached, the man of 40 usually feels stale, restless, burdened, and unappreciated." The game was fun, but the fun part is over. The rest of one's career, in the absence of a sharp change, becomes a burden rather than a new challenge. You feel like a cheerleader with your team losing 63 to 7 in the fourth quarter.

Most of us respond by redoubling our efforts. Instead of telling our job "goodbye, *ciao*, it was fun while it lasted," we put our heads down and dig. We figure the job bores us because we're not giving it enough. That's like saying the milk went sour because we didn't tell it we loved it.

Jokes about reaching midlife crisis are funny but they're also uniformly bleak. Dean Martin says you drink so much that falling in the street is the only time you get any rest. Your cufflinks double as curb feelers. Your idea of the great outdoors is playing bridge in a smoky room with the window open half an inch. You decide to discuss the facts of life with your teenager and he starts with, "Sure, what would you like to know?"

Midlife crisis, with different names, has been around for centuries. Grandpa and grandma got restless too. What's new in the 1980s is not the crisis but the wealth that offers young people a way out of it. The Census Bureau reports that the real net worth of U.S. households has *tripled* during the past thirty-five years. For the first time in history, millions of young Americans own a home, a couple of cars, and have money in the bank. For those millions, very early retirement is a viable way out of the pain of midlife crisis.

If you have a modest nest egg, you can opt for bare-bones retirement. Chapter 11 tells how to make it work. If you have a slightly bigger stash, say $200,000 or $300,000, you can retire well. If you have $400,000 or $500,000, like I did, you can retire with class. And if you're lucky enough to have millions, like my friend Big Bill, you can retire to a life of luxury.

THE MAGNATE WHO QUIT

Big Bill is an insurance magnate. He's shrewd, cautious, hard-driving, quick to analyze people, and a terror when he's mad. He spent the first twenty years of his adult life in penny-ante deals. He scratched to pay bills. But he was content, raising five kids and spending weekends with his family aboard a small cabin cruiser.

When he was 42 years old he did his first big deal. It almost ruined him. But next time around he hit a home run. It led to another and then another. By the time he was 50 he had more money than snake-oil salesmen have promises.

Big Bill says he changed after he got power and money. At work he became uptight and suspicious. He drove himself, always riveted on bigger and better deals. He began screaming at servants. He drank more, and after the third drink he started bragging.

Big Bill decided he didn't like his changed self. At age 50 he decided to hang 'em up and spend some of his millions. He bought a sixty-five-foot yacht and headed for Mexico and the Caribbean. He has plans to cross the Atlantic and spend three years in the Mediterranean.

Big Bill is a new man. He's playful and quick to laugh. He radiates goodwill and excitement about the future. "I've learned to enjoy life again," Big Bill told me one afternoon. We were in a peaceful bay in Curaçao, swilling martinis on the yacht's upper deck. "I fix things around the boat. I've always enjoyed doing that, but never had the time. I would just complain when someone else did the job badly. Now I do it myself. When we cruise, I take the helm. I go all night if I want to, without worrying whether I'll be fresh enough to fly back to the office the next day. It's wonderful.

"At first I was reluctant to retire because the money was so good. Twenty years ago I worked six months to make ten thousand dollars. Now with just a few phone calls, it seems, I can make millions. But life is more than being rich. Besides, I'm rich already." At this last, a broad smile covers his face.

Big Bill knew when to quit. His partners, by contrast, seem to be afraid to quit. They made the same deals as Big Bill, and they are all as rich as he is. But they continue to grind.

"I really believe my former partners want to be the richest men in the world," Big Bill told me. "They're so rich now they haven't the slightest idea how much they're worth. Still, they work harder than ever. They're going into new areas, things they know nothing about. They're a bundle of nerves. Two are getting divorces, two have had heart attacks. I think they all have ulcers. They rarely have a talk with their grown kids that doesn't end in a shouting match. All they get for it is more money. And they've already got all the money they need."

Big Bill's partners present one extreme and Big Bill the other. You may find a happy medium. But most of us keep working until we're 55 or 60 regardless of whether we need the money, enjoy the job, or would like to do other things.

DON'T TOUGH IT OUT

Big Bill does exactly what he wants with his life. You don't have Big Bill's millions, but you may have enough to retire. The only difference between you and Big Bill is that while you may have just enough to retire, he has more than enough. Big Bill replaced work with a yacht. You can't afford a yacht. But perhaps you can afford $50 a day. In chapter 8 I show how two people can put together a retired life that costs $50 a day. In chapter 9 I show how two people with children can put together a retired life that costs on'y slightly more than $50 a day. And in chapter 11 I discuss bare-bones retirement—how to live well on even less than $50 a day.

But you have to decide to get out of the rat race now. Toughing it out where you are can lead to trouble. You may end up like Big Bill's partners on a smaller scale. Gail Sheehy writes in *Passages:*

> Most middle managers know they are a dime a dozen.
> A man in this familiar state, feeling unappreciated and
> unutterably valueless, often keeps the tears inside; they

are shunted into ulcers and covered by accumulations of overweight . . . Anyone who challenges him to reconsider his priorities—a wife, a friend, a management consultant—becomes the enemy. He may try every form of self-delusion, retreat into drinking or hypochondria, cast his wife as a monster, abandon his family, almost anything to forestall looking into the mess inside.

When I turned 35 I hadn't reached the state Sheehy describes. But I had just been offered a lateral transfer. When the regional partner told me about the job, he emphasized that careers can seem to go flat at times. "You don't always go up," he told me at lunch. He moved his hand across the table in an upward motion. "Sometimes you go like this," he said. He moved his hand horizontally across the table before going up.

General Motors, Procter & Gamble, Exxon, and other companies announce new top executives every now and again. The new executives are nearly always people in their 50s or 60s who've spent thirty or more years with their companies. I wonder how those executives, the top 1 percent, stuck it out. And I wonder how the other 99 percent, those who reached plateaus and worked for decades more with little or no career growth, stuck it out. As the Bob Dylan song says, "He not busy being born is busy dying."

I decided that my career was keeping me "busy dying." I opted for the exciting challenge of a new life.

THE COMPANY WILL GET ALONG WITHOUT YOU

It's curious that executive crisis is independent of what level of success you've achieved. You may be chairman of Peat Marwick or junior partner of a small firm. You may be the top guy in IBM, the second guy, the one-hundredth guy, or the ten-thousandth guy. You may have two secretaries, one, or none. You may make big bucks or chump change. It doesn't matter. Somewhere, sometime, you're going to reach your personal career plateau. When you get there, some people will be higher than you and some lower. In this sense all managers are middle managers. Even a chief executive feels he's in the middle, sandwiched between customers, suppliers, stockholders, directors, government, and the organization's needs.

Remember the bathtub test? I learned it early in life—after toilet training but before I learned that "nice guys finish last." The bathtub test goes like this: "Fill a bathtub with water. Put your fist in the water and then pull it out. The size of the hole you leave is how important you are." I remember doing the bathtub test as a kid. I remember being almost surprised by the obvious fact that there's no hole at all. I felt like crying. "I'm not worth *anything?*"

I finally realized I *am* worth something, to myself and to my family and friends. But in the larger scheme of things, the bathtub test holds. I remember hearing a talk by Reginald Jones when he headed General Electric. After his formal remarks someone asked, "How many employees do you have at GE?"

Mr. Jones's reply, as best as I can recall, was, "Three hundred eighty thousand."

"So do you think there's any slack in there?"

Mr. Jones laughed. Indeed there was slack in there. People could leave, even hundreds of people could leave, and GE would continue its course without the slightest waver.

We tell ourselves the company might make more mistakes without us. We convince ourselves that we're indispensable. We can't say that about anyone *else* in the company. The boss could leave, the boss's boss could leave, and their replacements would be just as good or better. *We're* the only indispensable ones. We shove the bathtub test to the back of our minds, along with other ideas like "go visit Aunt Margaret" or "stop smoking."

Why do we do it? Because we want to feel important on the job. We want work to give us a sense of fulfillment. At times it does. But research shows it doesn't happen very often.

RIDING THE JOB IS RIDING A LOSING HORSE

In 1978 *Psychology Today* polled its readers about their jobs. *Psychology Today* readers are more highly educated, professional, and better paid than the national average. The 23,000 readers who responded said that the five most important aspects of their jobs were:

1. The chance to do something that makes you feel good about yourself
2. The chance to accomplish something worthwhile
3. The chance to learn new things
4. The chance to develop your skills and abilities
5. The amount of freedom you have on your job

Unfortunately, what we want out of our jobs and what we get from them are two different things. Thomas J. Peters and Robert H. Waterman, Jr., wrote the bestseller *In Search of Excellence* (Harper & Row, 1984) about American companies. They found that most of us "desperately need meaning in our lives and will sacrifice a great deal to institutions that will provide it to us." But Peters and Waterman concluded that the infrastructure of most American companies is almost consistently unable to provide meaning or any sense of worth to its employees.

One interesting side of being an auditor is that you get to peek into other people's business. I got an inside look at well-managed companies and not-so-well-managed companies. I toured big plants and small plants. I saw healthy balance sheets and sick ones. I saw top managers, middle managers, and people who just played at managing. Many of the people I met said that firing a loyal employee was the most painful thing they did. But every executive I know accepts firing as a part of his or her job.

Not so in Japan. The Japanese view people as permanent capital, to be protected and nurtured, rather than as a discretionary cost to be chopped at signs of falling market share. According to Peters and Waterman, this view goes a long way toward explaining the productive, loyal Japanese work force. Some American companies have tried to adopt something similar to the Japanese view. But those companies are exceptions.

A partner once told me that the inexorable project life cycle explains America's institutional traps. Any project must pass through five phases. Phase 1 is *enthusiasm and commitment*. In this phase of the project we're turned on and geared toward success. Early on in our careers we may spend years in this phase. But senior people know that enthusiasm and commitment at some time give way to *disappointment and disillusionment*. Yesterday's new idea becomes today's black-and-white TV.

Disappointment and disillusionment usually last only a short time before companies begin *the search for the guilty*. Here we decipher old memos, distance ourselves from the project, and start ordering doubles at the Fifty-Fifty Club. Our hands shake more and we gain weight. If we're lucky we come through relatively unscathed and join in phase 4, *the punishment of the few*. Like phases 1 to 3, phase 4 is inevitable. Blood flows until, in phase 5, we reach every middle manager's dream, the *"distinguishment"* *of the uninvolved*. In this final phase, those who managed to avoid being associated with the project—or any project—seem more intelligent, more capable.

The project life cycle sounds uncomfortably like a career life cycle. The focus on short-term results, unbounded legal liability, antibusiness bureaucracy, laissez-faire trade policy—these and other worries push "people problems" far down the line. The old AT&T defined managing as "getting things done through people." But that didn't stop ravenous government lawyers from devouring the company. Silicon Valley high-tech companies say they have a "policy" of never firing anyone. But they make abrupt policy changes when a couple of their top products suddenly lose their margins.

To protect yourself, the rule is:

Look for meaning in yourself, not in your job

The only sure way to avoid the pain of the bathtub test is to look inward—rather than at the bath water—to gauge your self-worth. You may have to remind yourself to do it. But you'll be rewarded with a happier retirement and a more fulfilled life.

BUT I LIKE MY JOB

Some of us seem untouched by the career life cycle. We seem to find meaning in our work, even in a system that is manifestly unable to provide it.

I recently talked to a turned-on friend who runs his own business—selling replacement parts for high-tech measurement devices—without any employees. He works at home and keeps the inventory in his garage. His main job is order-taking, which he does by answering the phone. He sells a couple of million dollars' worth of parts each year and manages to put an incredible

40 percent of it (pretax) in his bank account. Between phone calls he plays with his two small children. He loves chatting with his customers, his suppliers, and anyone else who happens to be around.

"Why the hell should I retire?" he asked me when I suggested it one day. "I'm in the prime of my career. I'm at peak earning power. I'm having a ball."

My friend has felt that way for years, and he may never change. Sam Walton probably feels the same way. If you're like them—having a ball in what is still a richly rewarding job—you're probably smart to stay where you are. But look down the road a few years. Circumstances change. Chances are that the Peggy Lee Syndrome will pop up sooner or later. Even if you skate through executive crisis, you'll probably retire *some*day. And when you do, you'll want your new retired life to be as fun and exciting as the old.

LIFE AFTER WORK

This chapter's second rule is:

Enjoy your career and then move on

I look back on my work years with pride. I gained confidence and insight. I played the game and won my share. That success makes me one up on the playboy who inherited his wealth. I can go to the luncheon club, look at the guy across the table, and know I can do what he's doing. I've already done it. The only difference between him and me is the number of years of play.

After twelve years of work I had a good income and a full complement of executive trappings. I met with big people about big deals involving big bucks. But as the song in *A Chorus Line* goes, "that ain't it, kid." I wasn't getting many jollies at the office. New experiences were fewer and farther between. Old challenges suddenly became chores. The next move up was years away. Problems seemed stupid rather than interesting. I felt I was slugging away just to keep even. I saw myself trudging rather than skipping down the hall to the office.

A wealthy chief executive I know puts it this way: "If you don't have people dumping on you *all the time*, you're not far enough along in your career. People don't dump on the poor." When I first heard that, several years ago, I decided I could tough it out with the best of them. But as I thought about it in 1984, I figured I had been dumped on long enough. There *had* to be a better way.

I figured it was time to move on.

The inner need was like a seismic fissure deep in the rock under a ski run. Resort owners treat the fissure by dynamiting the mountain. The blast causes a mild, controlled snow slide but releases pressure on the rock. The alternative—to do nothing— may work for a while. But sooner or later there'll be an avalanche and almost certain disaster.

When you reach the anxiety of midlife plateau, you're the fissure in the rock. You can blast yourself into a new mountain. Or you can suffocate in the crushing avalanche of middle management, hoping for the vaguely defined big break somewhere down the line.

KICKING THE WORK HABIT

How hard will it be to cash in your chips when the time comes? To schedule that final meeting with the boss? To walk out of the office for the last time?

Let me put it as simply as I can. It may be the hardest thing you'll ever do.

You'll recall that the three-part formula for retiring is:

Do your arithmetic
Do some soul-searching
Do what you want

Of the three, the second was by far the most difficult for me. Vicki and I spent almost two years making the decision. We went over it and over it, with friends, psychologists, and almost everyone else we could confide in. We were *certain* we were making the right move. But I was terrified before the final jump. I felt alone and vulnerable. I dreaded the consequences if I was wrong.

But the big day finally came and I went for it. The talk with the boss lasted only a few minutes. As predicted by the bathtub test, the boss took my resignation in stride. I was just one more incident in his busy day.

When I left the office I felt like a free man for the first time in twelve years. For the next few days I was euphoric, tingling with pleasure. Then one Friday night about two weeks after I resigned, Vicki and I went to a dinner party with a group of friends. The men there were executives I had known for years, and we toasted my retirement. But the champagne didn't sit right. Halfway through dinner I lost my appetite. By the time the others had finished I felt nauseated. During dessert I asked Vicki to take me home.

I spent most of the night vomiting. At one point I asked Vicki to take me to the hospital. She resisted, telling me to try to sleep. The next day, Saturday, I couldn't keep down any solid food. I went to see a gastroenterologist.

"Have you been under any extraordinary stress lately?" he asked after I told him my symptoms.

I gritted my teeth and spit out a simple "yes." I'm sure my eyes told him how much I meant it. Thank God he didn't ask me to go into detail.

"I think you've got an ulcer," he told me. "Either that or a very nervous stomach related to the stress you're going through. I want you to go get an X-ray on Monday."

The X-ray showed nothing, and by Tuesday I was back to normal. The whole incident had been stress-related, a purely psychosomatic response to kicking the work habit.

My fleeting stomach problem was a small price to pay for my entry into the new world. Vicki and I have been happier in retirement than we ever thought possible, better than planned or hoped. I heartily recommend it. But don't kid yourself. Unless you're Superman, kicking the work habit may be one of the most agonizing moves you'll ever have to make. Only the tremendous opportunity of the new life makes it worthwhile.

Retirement isn't the only way out of executive crisis. You can arrange a long-term leave of absence. You can try changing jobs. You can pour yourself into fund-raising, a Little League team, or public service. But retirement offers a sharp break, the chance to go out a winner and start a new game with a head start. If you don't have enough money to retire, see chapter 10, "Building Your Net Worth." If you already have $100,000 to $500,000 of net worth you can retire now. But before you make a move you should answer the question posed in the next chapter: "But what will I do?"

3.

Life After Work—What You Can Do

We've seen that the job can be a lousy place to search for meaning in life. So what's the alternative? Where *can* we find meaning?

WORK ISN'T ALL BAD

Before retiring I struggled with this question more than with any other aspect of my new life.

Work isn't all bad—it beats being bored. When you leave the nine-to-five you've got to come up with something better. Whatever it is, it has to do more than the job did in helping you find meaning in life—even if the job didn't do very much.

"What time do you plan to get up in the morning?" envious friends would ask before I retired.

"Anytime I want," I answered. But behind my cocky response lay uncertainty. Just what the hell would I get up *for?* Jane Pauley has pretty hair, and Bryant Gumble a soothing voice, but would I drag my ass out of bed and watch *Today* at seven if I had nothing to do at nine? Morning meetings are dull, but nothing compared to *As the World Turns*.

Shortly before retiring I visited Los Angeles, my home town.

You've heard of Los Angeles. Woody Allen says Los Angeles's most important cultural achievement is that, in a car, you can turn right on a red light. Calvin Trillin says there's a theory that sooner or later anything in America that's any fun at all will be ruined by people from California. Raymond Chandler called Los Angeles a city with no more personality than a paper cup. Matt Helm, the jaunty, cynical secret agent created by Donald Hamilton, says that "Southern California drivers are a courageous lot. You might even call them reckless—perhaps life has lost its meaning down there without any real air to breathe."

Anyway, I told a cousin in Los Angeles that I was retiring. "I couldn't do that," he announced. "I'd go crazy if I had to sit on my butt all day."

Just what the hell *do* retired people do from Monday to Friday, while everyone else fights freeway traffic, drinks institutional coffee, and goes to meetings?

IMAGINE BEING RETIRED

Before retiring I insisted on having a clear picture of what my days would be like. I wanted to spell out my new life with the precision of last year's budget. What would I do in the morning? Would I put on a suit and go to the club for lunch? Would I memorize key lines from deodorant ads on TV? Would I take vacations? This last was very bothersome. After all, when you're retired you don't have any compulsory activity to vacate *from*. (I later found that I enjoy vacations as much as ever.)

I struggled with those questions before retiring, but I never came up with a typical day, month, or year. Instead, I made a list of activities, interests, places to visit, and the like. I listed things I *might* want to do rather than things I *would* do. I worked on the list over a six-month period before retiring. Making a might-want-to-do list is the only way I know to get a handle on "but what will I do?"

The time to start your list is right now, while you're still working.

A TO-DO LIST

Pilots check out their planes with lists. Housewives shop with them, and a certain kind of boy refers to them when building model cars. If you're like me your to-do list at the office has become a should-do list, as in "things I should do but really don't want to do." Your list tells you how far behind you are. You charge around the office all day like Walter Payton. But at the end of the day your to-do list stretches just as long or longer. The list reminds you that last summer's time-management course changed your behavior hardly at all.

But no matter how much you may hate your to-do list at work, I believe a good list in retirement helps chart your course. Imagine yourself retired, sitting in front of a TV rerun of *My Mother the Car*. You're as absorbed as a 7-year-old in church. You're desperate for something to do but nothing comes to you. The solution is to pull out the to-do list, choose something, and get cracking. Remember, you've listed the things you *want* to do, not things you have to do or should do.

Make a to-do list

The list should be as specific as possible. But settle for general ideas when specifics don't come to mind. You'll have plenty of time for specifics later.

Your list may look something like mine: ride bikes, learn yoga and TM, play golf, cook. Set up a daily routine, keep a notebook, read, go to the library, write a new novel, edit the old novel, write a business article for a newspaper, write letters to friends, learn to speed read. Write computer programs, learn to play the sax, join a hospital board. Go to the club for lunch, see friends, go to theater, concerts, movies, and ballets. Go to the beach, travel. Spend more time with Vicki.

It's less exciting than, say, the kind of list a kinky sex manual might recommend for planning an orgy. And even with a good list, you'll still have a couple of days as dull as a Phi Beta Kappa newsletter. But during my first year of retirement I went over the list every few weeks. "Join a hospital board" led me to inquire and decide I couldn't do much as a board member. The hospital near me is so mismanaged that Alfred Sloan himself couldn't help. I need that kind of challenge like I need my old accounting books. "Learn to play the sax" led me to sax lessons. I now play with friends in a nine-piece modern jazz band and, on occasion, with a bar piano player.

Your list should have a second section with interests rather than things to do. Mine has academic interests like history, anthropology, geography, philosophy, and physics. I also list industries that fascinate me: airlines, farming, computers, television, and pharmaceuticals. Farming, for example, led Vicki and me to arrange a six-day visit to a cattle ranch in Argentina. Later, we accompanied a wine-connoisseur friend on a two-week trip through the Argentine wine country. We liked Argentina so much we decided to retire there. (In chapter 5 I talk about setting up in a foreign country.)

If you have kids, you need a list of things *they'd* like to do, given that Mom and Dad will have more time. Getting your kids' ideas on paper will help you choose activities that are fun for them *and* you.

Traveling is a big part of most retirements. You can wander through Morocco, Algeria, Tunisia, or Egypt; study tribal history in Bali, Thailand, Sri Lanka, Malaysia, or Singapore; compare agricultural methods in Greece, Turkey, Bulgaria, and Russia; learn about Eastern religions in India, China, and Tibet. You can learn firsthand that Mexicans seldom cook spicy food, that the French like to be rude, that Japanese businessmen get drunk in public, and that restrooms in Lima don't have towels to dry your hands. You can also learn new ways to cook, dance, dress, and even think.

Closer to home, a retired dad can buy season tickets to the Dodgers, Raiders, and Lakers—or whoever the local teams may be—and actually take the kids to the games. You can get into keeping the stats. Learn how many times Willie McCovey stole second off the pitcher, how many spitters Don Drysdale threw per nine innings, and how many products Pete Rose endorsed in his career.

The mind at age 40 absorbs knowledge quickly. Dedicate yourself and you can become one of the world's experts on Martin Luther, Isaac Newton, Ty Cobb, acid rain, tribal customs, ocean currents, or naval warfare. You and your kids can collect or build model soldiers, guns, planes, or trains. You can give talks comparing Kierkegaard to Nietzsche, Sartre to Malraux. You can become a roving private ambassador or a specialist in young African nations or maritime law.

Use your imagination. Suppose your boss walks in tomorrow and gives you a three-year sabbatical. Let's say the company has a special program to enable key workers to recharge their batteries. You're to spend the three years enjoying yourself, doing anything you want. What would you do? Bosses who grant three-year sabbaticals are about as common as big-hearted loan sharks who forgive and forget loans. But think about what you'd do for three years. And remember you can do it on your own, without the sabbatical, if you follow the rules in this book.

When you retire you have time to pursue any or all of your interests. You can even go to the club and talk about business if you want to. When you're living on $50 a day, going to lunch with someone on an expense account is a splurge. Those banquets, cocktail parties, and Christmas bashes that used to be a chore are fun when you don't do them every week. It's okay for *you* to live on $50 a day, but thank God *they* don't. You were almost rich once, gave it up of your own volition, and now live simply. But that doesn't mean you don't want a taste of those fast-lane perks every now and again.

WHAT DO YOU REALLY DO AT WORK?

Your to-do list will help promote an exciting, vigorous retirement. But getting retirement off the ground takes a little time. When you started your career no one gave you much responsibility. It took you a couple of years on the job before you gained any expertise. Retirement starts the same way. During the first few years you'll tend to dabble, to let your mind wander, to dream a little. Gradually you'll settle down to four or five things that turn you on. You'll start to pursue them with a passion you never thought you had in you. Your life will open in ways you never imagined.

The immediate problem, though, is to get through the transition. Your list may give you things to do, all right, but nothing really *important*. At times your entire *life* will seem about as important as last week's weather. There's a surefire way to cheer up, though. Ask yourself this key question: "What did I do at work all day that was so goddamn important?"

Ask yourself right now what you *do* at work—as opposed to what you *think* you do. If you're ready to retire you'll find that what you do doesn't amount to much. We've already seen that "I earn money" is a lousy answer. Chapter 8 ("Life on $50 a Day") and chapter 11 ("Bare-bones Retirement") tell how to live well on the money you already have. "I earn money" can't justify working when you don't need the money.

We've also gone over the bathtub test. We may think we're making a contribution. But someone can replace us as easily as a magician replaces a silk scarf with a bunny. Most associates will forget we were ever there. Only our secretaries and therapists will know for sure.

Before I retired I was asked to speak at a high-school Career Day. I told a couple of jokes, talked about public accounting, and asked for questions. One of them was, "What do you physically *do* at work?"

I thought it over and answered as best I could: "I talk on the phone all day, just like everyone else I know."

I think the kids got the point. Maybe "talk on the phone *all day*" isn't precise. You also go to meetings. You make budgets, remake them, cut them by 10 percent, then forget about them until review time. You read memos, write memos, lose memos, and ignore memos. You approve expense accounts. You complete your personal evaluation form each year. But when you get off your high horse, and remember the bathtub test, "I talk on the phone" pretty much describes your business day. Almost anything you do in retirement seems more important than that.

Remember that work was just talking on the phone

ALTERNATIVE VIEWS OF LIFE

You're a candidate for retirement when you have enough money to retire. The ideal amount is $400,000 or $500,000, and you may be 35 or 45 when you get there. At that point you can "stop working and start living."

But what is "living"?

Before I give you an answer that works for me, let me tell you a little about two answers that didn't.

A decade or so ago I hadn't even thought about "what is living?" I came out of the Stanford M.B.A. program a custom-made bowling ball and hurled myself down the alley of life. I rolled through the first career years on a clearly defined trajectory, gaining momentum along the way. I call this the "keep your head down" approach to life. The only rough period I recall was when I turned 29 and had a Thirties Crisis.

I hit my Thirties Crisis the way a bowling ball hits the headpin. Suddenly I didn't sleep well and woke up feeling nauseated. Doctors took stomach X-rays but found nothing. During the day I had a vague sense of uneasiness. I worried about earthquakes in China and plane crashes in Honduras. I worried about being unable to pronounce the names of Arab leaders.

One night after a Peat Marwick training session I found myself having a drink with my mentor—the one who would soon sponsor me for partnership. I'll call this person Harriet. I think we were arguing a disputed play in the Super Bowl when I said, "I'm not doing so well."

"What's the problem?"

"Thirties Crisis."

"What kind of crisis is that?"

"You know. Your typical Thirties Crisis."

"What kind of crisis is that?" Good listener, Harriet.

"Whither are we wandering? What am I doing here? What's life all about? What's the meaning of our day-to-day existence?"

Harriet listened for a while longer, then nodded gravely and said, "You know, Paul, you never find the answers to those questions. But after a while the questions go away."

We had a good laugh. But Harriet was right, thank God. After a few months I was back to normal. Normal, that is, if a life of hard work can be called normal. But those tricky questions were buried. The "keep your head down" or "wait for the questions to go away" approach had passed its first test.

But eventually those questions came back, and I began searching for alternative approaches to life. One is "wait'll you die." The movie *Caddyshack* has some funny lines about this approach.

In *Caddyshack* comedian Bill Murray plays the demented greenskeeper Carl. Barely able to maintain himself, Carl lives on the fringes of adult struggle. He makes the Roman emperor Nero look stable. Carl talks to himself. For fun he whacks off the newly budded flowers in front of Bushwood's clubhouse. He uses plastic explosives to kill gophers. Carl lusts after matronly lady golfers as if they were Dallas Cowboy cheerleaders in heat.

In one scene Carl tells a young co-worker about the time he caddied for the Dalai Lama in Tibet. "Big hitter, the Lama," says Carl. "Long. So the round's over, and the Lama's going to *stiff* me. So I tell him, 'Hey, Lama. How's about something . . . you know . . . for the effort. You know.'

"So the Lama says, 'There won't be any money. But when you die, on your deathbed, you will achieve total consciousness.' "

Carl gets a self-satisfied, superior smirk on his face. "So I've got that going for me. Which is nice."

Carl's "wait'll you die" approach works for disturbed greens-keepers and many others as well. But for me, "wait'll you die" seems as unsatisfying as "keep your head down." I need a more positive approach.

GO FOR RESPONSIBLE PLEASURE

When I retired I had the sensation of moving from the "real" world to a more playful, almost make-believe world. The world hadn't changed, only my point of view. When my job was the center of things, work was a given, like certain accounting principles. I took my job seriously and viewed life from the vantage point of an executive. That was the "real" world.

But what happened when I left the job? It was like going from Newtonian to modern physics. Newton explained the "real" world of gravity and its effect on planets. Modern physicists, on the other hand, explain a playful, make-believe world. In it particles don't behave as they ought to. Particles move around based on probabilities rather than "natural" laws. They change size when they move, they jump around in sudden, quantum leaps, they can even be in two places at the same time.

Newtonian differs from modern physics in its frame of reference. Modern physicists know that some things are "true" from one perspective but not another. I remember an example from the college physics course I took a couple of centuries ago. Suppose clocks and sticks start moving very fast—approaching, say, the speed of light. Funny things start to happen. Moving clocks run slow and moving sticks get shorter. But the clocks and sticks haven't changed, only our frame of reference has.

When you retire you change your frame of reference. You move from a world with work at the center to a playful, almost make-believe world with your life at the center. In my case I adopted an attitude of "go for responsible pleasure" instead of "go for the corner office." From my new vantage point, if something makes me happy and it's not irresponsible, it's important in my life.

It takes a little imagination to take off your work hat and try on "responsible pleasure" before you retire. It's not a change from "wrong" to "right" any more than Newton was "wrong" and the new physics "right." But the change in point of view is essential if you choose to retire in midlife.

Responsibility comes first. Someone once said that being an adult is being responsible. That makes sense to me. Otherwise, I suppose, kindly people in starched white jackets would have to take care of us. But for my purposes "responsible" sets the bounds of behavior. I try not to hurt anyone. I treat my body and spirit with respect. I don't do drugs or booze to excess. I don't let myself get fat or lazy. I work hard at whatever I do. I try to treat myself seriously but not take myself too seriously.

For most of us, being responsible is second nature. We're solid citizens, dependable parents, loving mates, and tough executives. We take to responsibility the way a rhinoceros takes to mud. The idea of living for pleasure, on the other hand, makes us squeamish. We profess to believe that pleasure is good, that happiness is what we want in life, but somehow we feel guilty when we enjoy ourselves.

MASOCHISM, THE AMERICAN WAY

The American way often amounts to masochism rather than pleasure. When we fail at something we're told to tough it out rather than stop, reevaluate, then switch to something we're good at. Masochism and sadism turn us on, whether in movies, cockfights, or a grinding, bone-wrenching football game or ride on the Lexington Avenue express. I'm not talking about the leather parlors near New York's piers or on San Francisco's Polk Street, but about healthy, well-rounded American masochism.

Our forefathers called it self-denial. Philip Grevee, a colonial history scholar, wrote a book about our past called *The Protestant Temperament* (Knopf 1977). You won't find Greven's book on many yuppie bookshelves. But it goes a long way toward explaining why pleasure brings guilt and suffering brings pleasure.

Greven found that our "evangelical" forefathers lived with total hostility to the self. They searched for ways to abase, deny, and destroy their sense of self-worth and selfhood. Some of these evangelicals left diaries. Their entries are a long way from what a pubescent girl might start with "Dear Diary." One man said, for example, that "the very thought of any joy arising in me . . . is nauseous and contemptible to me."

Not all early settlers were evangelicals. A second group— Greven calls them moderates—weren't quite as stern. (Genteels, a third group, developed later in the eighteenth century.) John and Abigail Adams were moderates. Greven says that "both John and Abigail Adams felt most comfortable when denying themselves something they desired or enjoyed." Adams became president of the United States, but for him "a life in . . . politics was actually a form of self-denial, for it kept him from his beloved wife and children and his house and farm."

John Adams drove himself so hard he had to go to New England to restore his health. While up there he wrote in his diary, "I feel guilty. I feel as if I ought not to saunter and loiter and trifle away this time. I feel as if I ought to be employed for the benefit of my fellow men."

We don't have to go back three hundred years to find people who believe struggle is good and taking life easy is bad. Take Lee Iacocca. He became president of Ford and then got fired. "Should I pack it all in and retire?" he asked himself. "I was 54 years old. I had already accomplished a great deal. I was financially secure. I could afford to play golf for the rest of my life. But that just didn't feel right."

Iacocca is neither colonial nor Protestant. But Iacocca seems driven by the work values Greven describes. After Ford he looked around for another hole to fill. He found it in Chrysler, probably the most punishing job in the country at the time. For Iacocca, taking on Chrysler "felt right."

The Chrysler story has a happy ending. Iacocca turned Chrysler around and wrote a book about himself. He's a hero, America's favorite businessman. In his autobiography he's a very appealing guy. But what hole can he fill now? He headed the 1986 Statue of Liberty committee and got fired again. In his world, you've got to continue to dig. But what happens at the end of a lifetime of digging?

Colonials looked to hard work for that sense of suffering they valued so highly. Their work ethic has survived in even better shape than masochism. J. Paul Getty, for example, was taught that "an individual had to work to justify his existence." Getty retired at age 24, during World War I, and spent the war years playing and enjoying himself. But he finally concluded he was "wasting time" and, although he was already a millionaire, at age 26 he went back to work.

We "new breed" types are supposed to have a new work ethic. It includes "duty to oneself" as well as the job, and even admits to a little pleasure. If you're a baby boomer, when you went to college people said you were part of a "Me" generation. I suppose that means we think masochism is bad and pleasure is good. But the cultural pull Greven describes is strong. In a 1970s' survey of college students, when asked whether they would continue working if they were to inherit enough money to live comfortably without a salary, seven out of ten said yes, they would still work. *Redbook* magazine, in a national survey of women aged 18 to 35, found that 80 percent said they would continue to work even if money were no problem. State lottery winners prove the point. In many cases after becoming rich, the winners take a short vacation and then go back to work.

CHANGING ATTITUDES

If you're a candidate for retirement at age 24, like J. Paul Getty, or at age 35, like me, you need to modify your work ethic. The work ethic helped build America. We're proud of the work ethic in our heritage. But retiring at age 35 with the work ethic intact is like an alcoholic's entering a rehabilitation center with a suitcase full of Chivas Regal.

The *Oxford American Dictionary* defines the work ethic as "a belief in the moral and sociological importance of work." But that same dictionary gives eight definitions of "work." We most often think of the fifth definition: "what a person does to earn a living; employment." But the dictionary's first definition is "use of bodily or mental power in order to do or make something." When you retire at age 35 you begin thinking of this broader first definition. Work is what you do with your life, what you accomplish over time. A work ethic that keeps you anchored to an office, filling out forms, making schedules, and reading reports is too narrow. Helping a friend, reading a poem, or learning how to cook are all part of "work" as well.

When you modify the old work ethic you should also get rid of the guilt that goes with it. Any number of self-help books tell you how to do this. They have names like *I'm Okay, You're Okay, Reality Therapy,* and *Your Erroneous Zones.* Books help you be your own best friend, help you be number one, and help you say no when you want to say no.

The books call guilt excess baggage. You can continue to haul it around or decide to shed it. The choice is yours, but to retire at 35 you have to shed it. Don't worry; there are enough Jewish mothers, evangelicals, and Woody Allen characters to pick up the slack.

Here are more rules:

Go for responsible pleasure
Modify the work ethic
Live without guilt

Erma Bombeck calls guilt the gift that keeps on giving. My advice is to give it back. Try to live for responsible pleasure rather than out of a sense of guilt. Life is too short to fill it with things other people want us to do.

TOWARD A NEW LIFE

Your own replacement for the work ethic may turn out to be personal growth, spiritual well-being, or inner peace rather than responsible pleasure. Whatever it is, it should be immediate, here and now.

Cook because you enjoy cooking, not because you enjoy eating. Go to Rome to look at churches and ruins, not to take pictures to show the neighbors. Go to Argentina to drink wine and eat steaks, not to be the only one on your block to go to Argentina.

Play golf for the fresh air and companionship, not to lower your handicap. Play with your kids to have fun with your kids, not to show them how to behave when they get to be adults.

With this approach you never have to answer the question, "What are you going to do with it?" As in, "Why are you learning to play drums? I mean, what are you going to do with it?" Or in, "Why are you going back to school to study Eastern religions? What are you going to do with it?" Or in, "Why study French cooking? You can't afford the calories. And what are you going to do with it?"

With a "do it now" attitude these questions don't come up, because the answer's always the same: "I enjoy it. It's fun. I'm growing."

When you enter the Metropolitan Museum of Art in New York, the sign says: PAY WHAT YOU WISH, BUT YOU MUST PAY SOMETHING. When you retire, the rule is:

Do what you wish but you must do something

The idea is to live, not to dissipate time. With a to-do list and a little imagination you'll soon be just as short on time as you are now. But with a difference. You'll be doing exactly what you want to do, when you want to do it. Your time—and your life—will be your own, all day long, every day of the year.

You'll never get the feeling that life is passing you by. It's not!

Here's a recap of this chapter's rules:

Make a to-do list
Remember that work was just talking on the phone
Go for responsible pleasure
Modify the work ethic
Live without guilt
Do what you wish but you must do something

To decide what to do when you retire, just follow the rules. Within a few months you'll look at people who go to the office every day and wonder why they do it.

PART 2

HOW TO GET
STARTED

4.

Make Your Assets Work for You and Save on Taxes

So you make $70,000 a year but think twice before planning a lavish night on the town? You and your spouse pull in a combined $130,000 a year and your last vacation blew your savings? You have $400,000 of net worth but the last time your property taxes went up you felt the pinch?

Chances are you have "mortgagitis"—inflammation of the mortgage. You're not alone. What Americans go through to own big homes makes a junkie needing a fix look circumspect by comparison.

To retire at age 35 you need to unload that great financial burden you call home. Upscale Americans spend 33 percent of their spendable income on housing. That 33 percent is more than any other item in the budget. Get housing costs under control and you've freed up a bundle. For many, retiring is as simple as turning housing *costs* into cash *income*.

Convert home equity to cash

Sounds crazy, right? Of all the rules in this book, this one most goes against the grain. Your home gives tax shelter. It hedges against inflation and goes up in value. What you've made by trading up over the years is the only reason you're reading this book. It's why you have $100,000 or $400,000 of net worth. Anyone who tells you to cash out must have a couple of dead spark plugs.

HOME OWNERSHIP: THE GREAT AMERICAN RIPOFF?

On San Francisco's Russian Hill you can rent a $300,000 condo for about $1,200 a month, $14,400 a year. You can also buy the place. If you buy, you put $50,000 down and get a $250,000 mortgage. You forfeit $4,000 a year interest on your down payment and pay $27,000 annual interest on the mortgage. Insurance, taxes, condo fees, and upkeep come to $10,000. The total cost to own is $41,000 a year, or approximately three times the cost to rent.

So why would you ever want to buy rather than rent?

For one thing, you can deduct interest and taxes. The federal tax rate is 28 percent. The California rate, net of federal benefit, is about 8 percent. At those rates, the annual cost to buy the Russian Hill condo can go from $41,000 to about $30,000.

But you're still paying twice as much as renters. Is there any other reason to buy?

Some say the condo will go up in value, like in the California real estate boom of the late 1970s. People became millionaires, it seems, simply by moving once in a while. If you're one of the lucky few who bought in Los Angeles in 1975, Manhattan in 1977, Cape Cod in 1981, or Boston in 1983, you made a pile.

But those were booms. If you bought an Illinois farm in 1979, a San Francisco condo in 1981, or a Houston tract house in 1984, you got stuck with a white elephant.

Perhaps the most likely scenario is somewhere between catching a boom and getting stuck with a white elephant. Suppose, for example, you bought a house in Atlanta in 1980. The place cost $100,000 and you spent $22,000 on the down payment and closing costs. Six years later you sold for $150,000. You figure you made $50,000—not bad on a $22,000 investment.

But you forget the interest you could have earned on that

$22,000. You forget that every month for six years you paid mortgage, taxes, insurance, repairs, and other costs. Renters who plan to buy know their monthly outlay will go up. Landlords who rent a newly acquired mansion to others know they'll most likely have to plunk down cash, sometimes a lot of cash, to keep current. Rents alone seldom cover the mortgage and other expenses on a new real estate investment.

Suppose you had rented instead of bought that Atlanta house in 1980, and that the $22,000 went into bank CDs instead of a down payment. Your net monthly outlay to rent would have been $500 to $1,000 less than to own, depending on the Atlanta rental market, your tax bracket, and other factors. Let's suppose you'd saved $500 a month and put it into bank CDs. Investing that way is about as sexy as a medieval Mass. But with compounding over those high-interest-rate years, you'd have something like $100,000 in cash by 1986. That's a gain of $78,000 rather than $50,000. And your money would be in the bank, earning interest, rather than tied up in a house that costs money to maintain and money to sell.

If you bought a house in Atlanta or elsewhere in 1980 you did better or worse than in our example. Similarly, if you bought in 1975 or 1985, rather than in 1980, you did better or worse than in our example. That's because timing makes such a difference. Anyone who can lie with statistics knows the importance of choosing one's base year. Choose carefully enough and you can make the South Florida land boom of the 1920s look like the crash of the 1930s. As they say, there are liars, damn liars, and statisticians.

People sometimes hit the real estate jackpot. They buy a $50,000 house that goes to $200,000 in a couple of years. Vicki and I know many San Franciscans who made hundreds of thousands of dollars on their homes between 1975 and 1979. It was wild. Invite six people for dinner and by the end of the evening all six would have recited their litany. "Three years ago we bought a cute but discreet doghouse in Palo Alto for $40,000. Last week a doghouse down the street, smaller than ours and chewed by a Great Dane, went on the market for $300,000. A neighbor told me there were three offers the first week." If you didn't have your own story to tell, you could always talk about someone else: "My brother bought a tract house in Livermore . . ." or simply, "I know a guy who bought . . ."

But when the boom was over Vicki and I noticed something curious. Everyone who had made a pile on his home had traded up to a bigger home. We noted this phenomenon almost without exception. The old house may have had five hundred square feet or five thousand. The old house may have been in a good neighborhood or in the best neighborhood. The old house may have been adequate for their needs or not. But it seems to be a universal law: when a young man's house goes up in value, he buys a bigger house. The bigger house creates bigger monthly payments. The spiral goes on forever—or at least until the housing market flattens out.

WHAT WE SPEND ON OUR HOMES

What happens to housing costs when people have been in the spiral for a few decades? In 1986 the Bureau of Labor Statistics reported on how the richest 20 percent of Americans spend their money. Based on 1982–1983 data, the bureau found that the median top-20-percent family earned $57,267. After taxes, savings, and payments into retirement plans, those families spent $30,623. Here's how they spent it:

Housing	$10,188	33.3%
Transportation	6,950	22.7
Food and drink	5,302	17.3
Other	8,183	26.7
Total	$30,623	100.0%

Housing takes a third of our income, and that percentage is going up. The Federal Reserve Board figures that new home buyers pay 30 percent of their income on mortgage interest alone. They pay thousands more to replace the roof, paint, fix leaky pipes, put up new wallpaper, hang the chandelier, put a wall around the yard, clean the pool, rake the leaves, and sweep the driveway. They pay taxes and insurance. With what's left over it's a wonder they can buy the baby a rattle.

A 47-year-old woman I know owns some apartments and wanted to retire. "Can I afford it?" she asked. "My net income from rentals is $35,000 a year. That should go up steadily."

I said, "Anything more than $18,000 a year is just mad money."

"Are you sure?" she asked. "I have expensive tastes. I ski with my kids, go to the opera, eat at fine restaurants, travel. Can I do all that on $18,000 a year?"

I said, "Easy. Doing those things is what retirement is all about. But you're mistaken about one thing. What you want to do is cheap, not expensive. What's expensive is a $3,000-a-month mortgage payment."

She agreed. "That's what I figured. To keep my rent down, I'm going to move into a small flat in one of my buildings. That way I pay no rent at all. I forfeit the $300 a month a tenant would pay. But $300 is nothing."

The last time I saw her she had a different sort of question. "My son and I are going skiing for two months this winter. Which do you recommend: Austria or Italy?"

FUZZY BLANKETS

Many people know they're spending too much on their homes. They may even admit their homes make little sense as investments. But those are purely financial matters, and I suspect finances are beside the point. People buy homes because of an emotional need. Having a home of one's own is part of the American dream. Our home is our security, a fuzzy blanket for those too old for the real thing.

For many people, the emotional need to own a home borders on a fixation. I know. I'm one of them. It's easy to figure where it comes from. I can hear my mother now: "Buy a home as soon as you can. That way you build equity. Otherwise all you get is a bunch of rent receipts."

Mom got a lot of things right. For someone starting a career and struggling to get ahead, she may still be right. Many young people lack the self-discipline to save. Buying a home, in effect, forces them into a scheduled savings program. They're sure to get a piece of the action if another boom comes along. Perhaps most important, buying a home instills a sense of growing up. Pride of ownership helps many young people get serious about their lives for the first time.

But what propels us along life's path at age 25 can hinder us at age 35. It's one thing to buy a $25,000 starter and make a few bucks when the value goes up. It's another to trade up to an $800,000 Beverly Hills shack. Maintaining and paying off the mortgage on an $800,000 house does more than force you into a scheduled savings program. It can force you into living like the poor.

Many of us feel a need to own our homes. But let's not get carried away. Vicki and I own a modest apartment in Buenos Aires, Argentina; you'll read about it in chapter 5. It satisfies my emotional need until I can work through it. It's worth maybe $20,000. I can afford a fuzzy blanket that costs $20,000. You can afford it too. What you can't afford are mortgage bills so high that financial markets tremble when you're late with a payment.

HOMES PAST AND FUTURE

You're a 40-year-old New York lawyer, Miami realtor, or Denver oil man. That one-bedroom condo you bought fifteen years ago was a fuzzy blanket that helped you mature. Later, the big house served as a secure place to raise kids, relax, watch TV, and feed the multitudes. Over the years you've made $200,000, $500,000, or more by trading up on your homes.

But whatever your home has meant in the past, when you retire you look to the future. Your home was a super investment? Great. But it may be a lousy investment now. And you don't need super investments. All you need are safe, high-yield, trouble-free CDs that throw off enough cash to live on. Your home helped impress customers? Great. But when you retire you won't have any customers. You needed lots of space to feel comfortable? Great. But you're about to embark on a new adventure. What you require from your living space will change. To process that change, you need an open, uncluttered mind more than a mansion that costs a pile. You need freedom rather than the security a big house can seem to give.

For those with $400,000 to $500,000 of net worth, the choice is simple. Do you want a big house with the right address or life without work right now? If you grind away at the office for two or three more decades you may be able to afford both. But in most cases, to retire young you have to choose.

The following chapter describes some exciting places where

you can live cheaply. But when you sell your expensive crib you're bound to feel you're giving up something. Decide for yourself which you prefer: an expensive house and the job that goes with it, or a modest living space and time to do something new with your life.

CONVERT HOME EQUITY TO CASH

Tax laws let you defer capital gains taxes on the sale of your residence. All you have to do is roll the gain into another house within two years.

Builders, lenders, escrow agents, realtors, and title insurance companies love the law. It's one more way to bind us to the trading-up spiral. Mothers who believe that "homeownerness" is next to godliness love the law. With that kind of support, Congress is about as likely to close this loophole as they are to ban apple pie. (The 1986 Tax Reform Act was the most comprehensive tax change since 1954. Yet, the home-rollover benefit sailed through Congress intact.)

So when you sell your home you pay the tax and buck the system. That costs some real, out-of-pocket tax dollars. If you have a $100,000 gain on the sale of your home you'll pay roughly $28,000 of federal tax. You'll also pay a couple of thousand dollars in state taxes. It hurts.

But there are a couple of things you can do.

First, you can smooth your taxable-income stream. Smoothing is not income averaging. Rather, when you smooth you avoid reporting a large taxable income in any one year. That lets you take full advantage of lower tax rates on lower income. For example, in 1988 a married couple filing jointly must pay a 5 percent extra federal tax on income between $71,900 and $149,250. With smoothing you try to keep your income below $71,900 and avoid the extra tax. Without smoothing, and assuming you run your taxable income to the full $149,250, you pay an extra $3,868.

One way to smooth is to sell your home in a low-income year. That way the gain stands alone, rather than on top of a lot of other income. Remember, you'll have plenty of low-income years after you retire. Another way to smooth is to sell your home in a year in which you have losses from other sources—sale of stock, for example. Net the gains against the losses and you reduce taxable income.

Another way to smooth is to defer interest income in the year you sell your home. For example, suppose you retire and sell your home in March 1989. Your 1989 taxable income will be quite high, with three months' salary, severance pay, and gain on the sale of your home. To avoid piling taxable interest on top of an already high base, you should defer interest income to 1990. Simply tell your bank to give you one-year CDs with principal and interest due at maturity in 1990. Since you're not entitled to the interest until 1990, you don't pay tax until 1990.

With smoothing you can sometimes avoid the 5 percent tax surcharge and save a small amount of state taxes. Deferring nets you a year of interest on the tax due. You'll want to smooth and defer if you can. But those are fairly minor matters in the scheme of things. It's more important to get a good price on your home than to try to postpone the sale until next year. It's more important to choose a bank that offers good rates than one that offers to defer income.

Another trick is to defer the gain on the sale of your home for two years. Rather than saving you money, deferring the gain is likely to cost a few bucks. But it will save you plenty of mental anguish. Saving on mental anguish, in turn, might save you a fortune in therapy fees, Dalmane prescriptions, massages, liquor, and "I'm guilty" gifts to your spouse.

The two-year deferral works like this. Suppose you retire and sell your home in 1989. In your 1989 tax return you compute your gain on Form 2119, *Sale or Exchange of Principal Residence*. But you pay no tax on the gain at that time. Instead, you state that you plan to replace your residence within the two-year replacement period. Thus, you avoid writing that big tax check in the year you retire. Instead, you have up to two years to change your mind. You may decide to buy another mansion and get back on the treadmill. I doubt you'll want to do that. But if you do, you won't have paid any tax dollars.

When you decide that you can live without a fuzzy blanket, pay the tax. Amend your tax return in the year of sale, 1989 in our example, using Form 1040X. Send your check to the IRS for the tax due plus interest (9 percent at the time of this writing) during the interim period. (If you send a check for the tax but not the interest, IRS computers will bill you for the interest.)

The IRS interest rate varies, but it's slightly higher than you can get on one-year CDs. Since you'll probably use the standard deduction after you retire, you can't deduct the interest you pay to the IRS. On the other hand, the IRS taxes your CD interest income. So this deferral scheme will cost you some money. You'll want to cut the deferral period and pay the tax as soon as you decide you'll live without owning a home.

You don't have to use the deferral period at all. You can write the tax check to the IRS in the year you retire. If you wind up buying a new home within the two-year period, you amend your old return and get your money back. But when you retire your entire life turns upside down. The last thing you need to make yourself do is write a big check to the IRS. Give yourself a break and postpone paying the tax. Sometime down the road, when you're well grounded in your new life, you can face the IRS. What you gain in peace of mind is worth a little interest expense.

In order to make it easier on yourself, I suggest a mental trick. When you cash out of your home, set money aside to pay the tax on the gain. Put the money in a separate CD in a bank or savings institution you don't use for other accounts. When you calculate your net worth, leave the earmarked CD out of the total. When it comes time to write the check to the IRS, it will be easy. You'll already have the money set aside; your net worth will stay the same.

CONVERT OTHER ASSETS TO CASH

You should convert your home equity to cash. You should also:

Convert other assets to cash

Here again we're going against conventional wisdom. The norm is to diversify your assets. You invest in hard assets like rental property, a beach house, or railroad cars. For liquidity you buy stocks, options, bonds, and Ginnie Maes. We'll look closer at stocks and other investments later on. But they usually involve risk, or hassle, or both. Neither risk nor hassle has any place in the retired good life. You're better off to convert your assets to cash and buy high-interest CDs.

What about furniture, paintings, rugs, antiques, jewelry, gold, home entertainment centers, cars, and recreational vehicles? Those are either investments you can use or simply things you enjoy owning. But how important are they to your retirement?

Henry David Thoreau had something to say on the subject. "Most of the luxuries, and many of the so-called comforts, of life are not only not indispensable, but positive hindrances to the elevation of mankind."

As far as I'm concerned, Thoreau was weird. He may have been a genius and all that. But he chose to spend over a year and a half, including a freezing winter, alone in the woods near Concord, Massachusetts. Anyone who chooses to do that must be wrapped up with some very loose string.

But Thoreau broke life down to its basics. He concluded that what we are, what we do, and how we live mean more than what we own. I think most of us would agree with that. But Thoreau went further. He said that owning a lot of things actually *prevents* us from focusing on who we are and what makes us happy.

My proposal stops short of Thoreau's near-total abstinence. First, I recommend you review each of your major personal assets to see if it has been or is likely to be an important part of your life. If you answer "yes," keep it. Vicki and I, for example, kept our piano and word processor when we retired. Second, ask if you bought the asset to satisfy your drive to acquire, to enhance your ego, or to impress your friends. If you did, sell it or give it away. I suspect most vehicles fall into this category, but we'll talk about vehicles in chapter 8. Third, ask which of your remaining assets have a ready market and are likely to bring in a worthwhile sum. If you have any of those, sell them.

Assets tend to complicate our lives. We insure, store, haul, clean, repair, maintain, and talk about them. We feel guilty if we don't use them or notice them. If you have any assets that don't fit into the three categories above, my advice is to give them to charity or sell them—regardless of how much they're worth. If you can't force yourself to do it now, perhaps you'll be able to do it after a year or two of retirement. If Vicki and I don't use an asset for three years, we presume we should get rid of it: TVs, books, chairs, paintings, clothing, and kitchen appliances. We give those assets to friends or to charity. We enjoy giving and feel we're simplifying our lives.

LET'S LOOK AT AN EXAMPLE

Statistical Abstract of the U.S., published by the Department of Commerce, profiles the asset mix of top wealthholders. Based on these figures, John and Mary Doe's $435,000 net worth breaks down like this:

Residence, net	$129,000
Corporate stocks	101,000
Cash	58,000
Bonds	27,000
Notes and receivables	22,000
Other	98,000
Total	$435,000

With this asset mix, John and Mary Doe work for their assets. Nearly a third of their net worth is in their home. Rather than throw off income, the home costs money to maintain. Corporate stocks—perhaps received as part of a key-man compensation scheme—rarely pay good dividends. Other assets include cars and furniture as well as tax shelters and speculative deals that provide little income. John and Mary Doe each earn, say, $65,000 a year. After Social Security, unemployment, and other payroll taxes they have a combined gross income of over $120,000. With that much money they think they should be living well. But day in and day out, they spend to maintain their assets. With what's left over they can barely afford a pizza.

Let's suppose John and Mary follow the advice in this book and retire in 1988.

First, they read chapter 8 and start trying to live on $50 a day. Because of the big house, cars, and other expensive assets that soak up cash, their current living costs are way above that. At times John and Mary feel that what they spend on parking alone could keep Brazil current on its external debt. But once John and Mary start to shed assets, they'll find they need less to live. Little by little they'll get down to $50 a day.

Next, John and Mary put the house up for sale. We suppose it takes a few months to find a buyer, and that the closing is set for January 1989. John quits work in December 1988, telling his boss he's having a hard time giving his all to the job. He plans to rest, write, and travel for a time before looking for new work. John has been with the company many years and it's almost Christmas. The big boss gives him six months' severance pay.

In January 1989, John and Mary close the sale of the house and move to a small apartment in a cheaper section of town. They get a break on the rent because John's brother owns the building. (Chapter 5 tells how and where you can rent for $200 a month or less.) John and Mary enjoy fixing the place up a bit. They learn that one painter can paint the entire apartment in a few days. In the mansion they had before, painters arriving reminded them of the charge of the light brigade.

In June 1989 there's a cutback at Mary's company. The company offers four months' severance pay for people with Mary's seniority. She takes it, and the Does are retired. They begin to sell their cars and other household assets that can bring in cash. In this example we assume they sell half of their "other assets."

Beginning in 1990 John and Mary sell their stocks and bonds and buy one-year bank CDs. In March 1990, the Does file their 1989 tax return. They defer the tax on the gain on the sale of their house. That gives them until 1991 to change their minds and buy another house. They buy a two-year CD for $35,000 to cover the tax bill two years hence.

By early 1990 John and Mary have converted their assets to cash. How much will they have paid in taxes? What will be their net worth?

Income and related income taxes are as follows. ("Earned income" is net of payroll taxes, including Social Security taxes, and taxes on income used to pay those payroll taxes.)

	1988	1989	1990	1991
Earned income	$150,000	50,000		
Gain on home		99,000		
Gain on stock			50,000	
Interest	14,000	20,000	35,000	45,000
Total	164,000	169,000	85,000	45,000
Tax due	$ 53,000	21,000	22,000	50,000

Total tax over the period is $146,000. Tax on the gain on sale of the home is $34,000. John and Mary pay it in 1991 by amending their 1989 return and adding $6,000 interest.

John and Mary's cash flow from 1988 to 1991 is:

CASH IN	
From salary/severance	$200,000
From sale of home	129,000
From sale of stocks, bonds, notes	150,000
From sale of other assets	49,000
From interest income	114,000
Total	$642,000
CASH OUT	
Living expenses	$84,000
Taxes (as shown above)	146,000
Total	$230,000
Net increase in cash	412,000
Add: Beginning cash	58,000
Total cash for retirement	$470,000

JOHN AND MARY DOE ARE RICH

Before they retired John and Mary had a total net worth of $435,000. After they retire and convert their assets to cash, their liquid net worth jumps to $470,000 and they have $49,000 of "other assets." They paid $146,000 in state and federal income taxes. Nobody likes to pay taxes. But taxes arise when we convert assets to cash, and we have to convert assets to cash to lower our living expenses and put cash in the bank. The benefits—lower expenses plus interest income—pay the taxes and then some.

I had to make assumptions to do the above example. I assume a state tax rate, net of federal benefit, of a flat 6 percent. I ignore the benefit of itemized deductions in 1988, when the Does still own their home. Assuming John and Mary have IRAs included in stocks and bonds, I ignore the benefit of tax-free IRA income. I assume that net equity in their home includes $30,000 of their own money (down payment plus costs and improvements) and a $99,000 gain. I assume that CDs pay 8 percent. I assume a $50,000 gain on sale of stocks, bonds, and notes. I assume the Does live on $50 a day, or $18,000 a year, after they retire. In 1988, while they're working to maintain their assets, I assume they need $30,000.

Those assumptions simplify the example and seem reasonable at the time of this writing. You may want to change the assumptions based on your personal situation. But don't get too fancy about it. Refining assumptions too far is like using razor-sharp knives to cut butter. Just assume a few simple facts that fit your circumstances. In most cases, you should be pleased with the results of the conversion process.

With nearly half a million dollars in the bank, John and Mary Doe are retired and rich. Rather than work at the office, they work on a to-do list of things they've dreamed of doing. Rather than scrimping to pay the mortgage and taxes, they fly around the world on bargain airfares. Their idea of a tough decision is choosing the right wine for dinner. With half a million dollars in the bank they can enjoy retirement for the rest of their lives.

And all they did was convert their assets to cash.

YOUR NEW INVESTMENT STRATEGY

Once retired, like John and Mary Doe, you have a ton of cash. You need a clear, easy-to-follow investment rule that provides enough money for you to live. Here it is:

Buy one-year insured CDs

Buy your CDs in chunks of $50,000 or more. Most banks and savings institutions give you their best rate on $50,000 and above. Put each CD in a different institution, so as not to go over the $100,000 FDIC or FSLIC insurance limits.

To find the best rates for your CDs, check the ads in local papers and *The Wall Street Journal*. You can also check milk cartons, supermarket bulletin boards, and bathroom walls, although I've found those sources to be less helpful. When you see an institution offering good rates, buy a CD. Be careful, though.

You must make certain your CDs are insured by the FDIC or FSLIC. Beware of guarantees by state or private insurance groups. The FDIC and FSLIC are U.S. government agencies that insure deposits up to $100,000. The U.S. government itself has a moral obligation to step in if those agencies lack funds to cover losses.

Buy the CDs to mature every month or two throughout the year. To set this up during the first year or two, you may need to go out fourteen or sixteen months or whatever to line up your maturities. After the initial period, you simply roll each CD for one year when it becomes due.

Suppose, for example, you have $500,000 including a $50,000 IRA. First you sell the investments in your IRA and buy a one-year CD with the proceeds. Then divide another $50,000 of your net worth between your checking and money-market accounts. That's your liquid money for day-to-day expenses. The third step is to take the remaining $400,000 and buy eight one-year CDs of $50,000 each. Stagger them so that one CD matures every month or two throughout the year. On four of the CDs, roll the principal and interest at maturity. That keeps your capital roughly intact for inflation. On the other four CDs, roll the principal but ask to have the interest deposited in your money-market account. That's the money you'll live on during the year.

Vicki handles the investments in our household. She takes an hour or two each month to record CD numbers, check bank statements, modify standing instructions, and the like. When we travel, often for months at a time, she forgets about it entirely. No problem. Nothing requires day-to-day or even month-to-month control.

When we travel we get cash advances on VISA or MasterCard for the dollars or foreign currency we need. Our bank pays the monthly VISA and MasterCard bills by automatic debits to our money-market account. Every so often, interest on a maturing CD is credited to our account. It's all a little scary, even after four years of retirement. We travel for four or five months, helping ourselves to the money we need at the nearest bank. The bank may be in Boston or Madrid, Los Angeles or Vienna. At the end of our trip we return home. We find our net worth has increased. We find all the paperwork is in order, that nothing needs our attention. It's almost as if our lives go on without us, whether we intervene in them or not.

It reminds me of the joke about the guy who took a cash advance on his VISA to pay his MasterCard bill. When the VISA bill came, he paid it with a cash advance on his MasterCard. He paid the next MasterCard bill with another VISA advance, and so on for several months. He finally wrote both VISA and MasterCard. "Why don't you two mail your bills to each other and leave me out of it!"

Every January Vicki adds our bank and CD balances and checks that the total went up by inflation during the year. So far it has—with a few thousand dollars to spare.

Choose CDs over other investments because they're simple and secure. There's no work, no analysis, and no decisions to make. The CDs are backed by a U.S. government agency, making them nearly risk-free.

Why one-year CDs instead of a longer or shorter maturity? Banks normally pay one or two points higher on one-year CDs than on money-market accounts. If a money-market account pays 6.5 percent, for example, a one-year CD in the same bank is likely to pay about 8 percent. That difference adds up over time.

Going longer than one year, however, exposes principal to a run-up in rates. Suppose you go out three years. Market rates could jump in three years from, say, 8 percent to 12 percent. You'd be stuck with a low 8 percent yield throughout the three-year period. Rates could go down over the three years. That means you're stuck with annual rollovers at lower rates. But when rates go down it's usually because inflation goes down. Your money will go farther at the lower rates, so you give up little or nothing in purchasing power.

In summary, one year is long enough to get higher yields than money-market accounts. One year is short enough to keep up with market changes.

What about other liquid investments? In my view, none of them are as simple or secure as CDs. Bonds expose principal to a run-up in rates. Shrewd speculators may make money on stocks, commodities, and options. But few young retirees have the skill or want to devote their time to those risky investments. Zero-coupon bonds, municipal bonds, and Ginnie Maes are similar to bonds in that market value goes down when rates go up.

Some suggest you hire professionals to help you with trickier investments. You can buy into funds that specialize in stocks, bonds, options, or whatever. You don't have the expertise to evaluate tax-free municipal bonds? Buy into a tax-free fund. Those who run the fund take care of buying and selling, finding the best prices, hedging against a run-up in rates, and the like.

The problem with funds is commissions and fees. When you buy into the funds you pay a commission. Those who manage the funds charge a management fee for doing so. When those fund managers buy and sell for the fund's account, the fund pays commissions. The triple whammy can cost 3 percent or 5 percent or more. That cost amounts to a reduction in your yield. If you're not careful, the advertised yield of 10 percent or whatever can translate to much less than that, especially if you move in and out of the funds fairly often.

If you're lucky, or shrewd, or both, you can make good returns on real estate, Ginnie Maes, stocks, foreign exchange, and other investments. Retired friends think my CD plan is too conservative. But CDs throw off the money you need to live without risking your capital. Why fool around with something that can cost you money if it doesn't work out?

REAL INTEREST RATES

We've had huge swings in interest rates since 1980. I assume a one-year CD rate of 8 percent in this book. I use 8 percent consistently and it seems as good a choice as any. But in 1981 one-year CD rates rose to 17 percent and higher. In early 1987 rates fell to 7 percent and lower.

But those swings from 17 percent to 7 percent tell only part of the story. To know what we can spend we must compare interest rates with inflation. "Real" interest refers to the excess of interest over inflation. If interest is 8 percent and inflation 3 percent, the real rate is 5 percent. (To be precise, the real rate is 1 plus 8 percent divided by 1 plus 3 percent, less 1, or 4.85 percent. But simple subtraction—interest less inflation—serves the purposes of this discussion.) Real interest is what we have left after we set aside enough additional cash to keep our capital intact. It's the amount young retirees can spend on taxes and living expenses.

The history of real rates divides into two parts: pre-1980 and post-1980. Before 1980 the Federal Reserve Board's Regulation

Q strictly limited the amount of interest banks could pay on deposits. With Regulation Q, real rates generally hovered around 2 or 3 percent. During periods of high inflation, real rates went negative.

But the Fed and Congress started to deregulate our financial markets in the late 1970s. Deregulation occurred in phases, but by 1980 the process was nearly complete. I remember opening my first money-market account, called a Merrill Lynch Redi-Credit Account, in 1980. You may have done the same. For the first time in modern history, money-market accounts offered high yields to the American saver. And real rates skyrocketed.

The following table shows real rates during the deregulation era. "Interest" is the one-year CD rate at mid-year. "Inflation" is the U.S. consumer price index for food. I use the food index, rather than the composite index, to reflect how we spend under the $50-a-Day Rule. (The composite index is heavily weighted for home and car costs; those are minor expenses under the $50-a-Day Rule.)

YEAR	RATE	INFLATION (food)	REAL RATE
1980	15%	8.6%	6.4%
1981	17	7.9	9.1
1982	14	4.0	10.0
1983	11	2.1	8.9
1984	13	3.9	9.1
1985	9	3.2	5.8
1986	8	3.7	4.3
1987	8*	4.0*	4.0
		*estimated	

Why did real rates go up after deregulation? With deregulation, rates are set by markets. The Fed can influence but not control those markets. And remember that the U.S. government has an insatiable need for money. So do merger-makers, Third World countries, and others. That demand puts constant pressure on credit markets, and real rates tend to stay high.

The table shows that real rates have fallen over the last three years. By 1987 real rates were about 4 percent, lower than at any time in recent history. Our experience with deregulation says they'll go back up, especially if we get another bout of inflation. Real rates in highly inflationary countries, like Brazil and Argentina, jump to 30 percent or 50 percent or more as inflation increases.

HOW CD PERFORM

Our CD income should cover inflation and pay our taxes. We can spend what's left over. The following table shows what's left over with either $400,000 or $500,000 in net worth, assuming interest rates at 8 percent and inflation at 2.5 percent:

NET WORTH	$400,000	$500,000
Gross income at 8%	$ 32,000	$ 40,000
Less taxes	3,850	5,280
Net income	28,150	34,720
Less inflation	10,000	12,500
Spendable income	$ 18,150	$ 22,220

Gross income is the 8 percent interest rate times $400,000 or $500,000. Similarly, inflation is the 2.5 percent inflation rate times $400,000 or $500,000. The resulting inflation amount maintains capital against loss of purchasing power. Taxes are based on the 1988 federal tax rates as set by the 1986 Tax Reform Act. State taxes are assumed to be 10 percent of federal taxes, after you move to a low-cost state (see chapter 5).

With $400,000 of net worth you pay $3,850 in taxes, set aside $10,000 to keep your capital intact, and spend up to $18,150. With $500,000 you can spend up to $22,220. You need only $18,000 to live under the $50-a-Day Rule. With $400,000, you have about $18,000; with $500,000 you have money to spare.

Look at what you're paying in income taxes: $3,850 or $5,280, depending on your net worth. That's less than you've paid in decades. You've finally hit on life's best tax shelter: stop working. That eliminates earned income. Your income tax plummets and you pay no Social Security taxes at all. In 1987, self-employed Social Security taxes came to $5,387 for high earners. That's more than your *total* income tax after retirement.

And you'll still collect Social Security benefits when you reach
age 62. After paying for ten years you're fully vested.

In the example above, real rates were only 5.5 percent. That's
quite low by historical standards during the postderegulation era.
There's more money to spend if we return to the days of higher
inflation and higher real rates. The following table shows what you
can spend with interest rates at 17 percent and inflation at 8 percent:

NET WORTH	$400,000	$500,000
Gross income at 17%	$ 68,000	$ 85,000
Less taxes	14,300	19,800
Net income	53,700	65,200
Less inflation	32,000	40,000
Spendable income	$ 21,700	$ 25,200

Under this scenario you pay more in taxes. But you've also
got more to spend on yourself: $21,700 or $25,200, depending on
your net worth.

Note that the difference between $400,000 and $500,000 of net
worth translates into a difference of only $3,500 in spendable income.
In the first example the difference was $4,070. And with either
$400,000 or $500,000, in either example, you can live according
to the $50-a-Day Rule. So $400,000 is plenty of money to retire.
But most of us want to be conservative in our plans; $500,000 is
a more comfortable figure because it gives us a cushion of $100,000.
We can eat into that cushion if something goes wrong.

What can go wrong? Suppose CD rates drop to 6 percent and
inflation jumps to 4 percent. That's a real rate of only 2 percent,
far lower than anything we've seen in the postderegulation period.
Because of the constant, growing pressure on credit markets, it's
doubtful that real rates will stay that low for very long. But it
could happen, and here's what we'd have:

NET WORTH	$400,000	$500,000
Gross income at 6%	$ 24,000	$ 30,000
Less taxes	2,200	3,300
Net income	21,800	26,700
Less inflation	16,000	20,000
Spendable income	$ 5,800	$ 6,700

It looks pretty bad, right? You need $18,000 a year to live and you have only $5,800 or $6,700, depending on your net worth.

But let's take a closer look. Your interest income is $24,000 or $30,000. That's far more than you need to live. Your only concern is that your capital grows less than inflation. How bad is that?

It could mean trouble if your capital erodes, say, fifteen years in a row. But you can withstand some bad years with your $100,000 cushion. If you don't have a cushion, your $400,000 will be worth less and less. But you can stand a little of that, too. You're simply amortizing your capital over your lifetime. And as you get older you'll get a helping hand from other sources. If you're vested in your company's pension plan, for example, you'll start receiving checks at age 55 or 60. You may inherit some money, maybe even a lot of money. Pension plans and inheritance can bail you out if your capital erodes too far. And Social Security kicks in at age 62.

SOCIAL SECURITY

If you're a very early retiree, it's futile to try to guess what your Social Security check might be. For one thing, Congress changes the Social Security laws every year. It's hard to predict next year's changes. It's impossible to predict the cumulative changes over the next ten or twenty years. And remember that tens of millions of baby boomers will reach old age about the same time you do. It's a cinch that Congress will delay eligibility dates, say from age 62 to 65, and reduce benefits.

So, very early retirees can make only a wild guess as to the amount of their Social Security checks. But if you've paid the maximum Social Security tax for, say, twenty years, you'll likely receive a healthy benefit. It matters little whether you retire young or continue to work.

In studying the Social Security system, I've found it helpful to break it into two parts. Part one is a tax. Part two is a welfare and retirement program. As we'll see later, the amount of your retirement benefits bears some small relation to the tax you've paid in. But it's far more helpful to view the two parts—taxes and benefits—as independent.

Part one is taxes. If you're self-employed and made $43,800 or more in 1987, you paid $5,387 in Social Security taxes. If you're an employee and made $43,800 or more, you paid $6,263 in Social Security taxes. Part of that $6,263 came out of your paycheck. The other part went directly from your employer to the IRS. For that part your employer avoids the bother of running the amount through your paycheck. But don't kid yourself. Your employer looks at total cost, including salary, taxes, and benefits, when he figures what you take out of the company. To justify your job, you have to "earn" both the employer and employee portions of the tax, regardless of bookkeeping tricks meant to conceal the fact.

If you and your spouse each earned $43,800 in 1987, the employer and employee combined to pay $12,500 in Social Security tax. Not only is $12,500 a huge amount in most budgets, the tax itself is horribly unjust. The Social Security tax is a regressive tax. It falls most heavily on the poor. Historians tell us that, in eighteenth-century France, only the poorest 20 percent of the peasants paid tax. The wealthy got exemptions of some sort, just as those making over $43,800 in 1987 were exempt from further Social Security tax. The French tax system ended with the French Revolution. In the United States today the tax system is less skewed than in eighteenth-century France. But with respect to Social Security taxes, the poor and middle class pay a higher percentage of their income than do the wealthy.

So why do Americans put up with a regressive tax? It's probably because we feel we're getting something for our money. That we're "contributing" to our own retirement. That we all benefit "equally" and we all should pay.

But what we pay is *not* a contribution, it's a tax. That tax money pays retirement benefits to *today's* retirees. Whether there's any money around when *we* retire is another question.

Fortunately, after you retire young you'll have no earnings. That means you'll pay no Social Security tax. But what about benefits? What's the effect of very early retirement—and avoidance of Social Security tax—on your ultimate retirement benefits?

That's a good question. A very good question. Unfortunately, the answer is shrouded in mystery.

To try to find the answer I checked the *Social Security Handbook*, published by the Social Security Administration. I found the *Social Security Handbook* to be the single most abstruse document I've ever read. Compared to the *Social Security Handbook*, the *Internal Revenue Code* reads like a light, breezy, human-interest piece. I'm an accountant. I not only understand annual reports, I used to help write them. Difficult pension footnotes in annual reports can bring grown SEC lawyers to tears. But annual reports are child's play compared to the *Social Security Handbook*.

Unable to understand the handbook, I called the Social Security Administration. The person who answered the phone masqueraded as a recording. Phone companies try to make recordings that sound like real people. I got a real person that tried to sound like a recording. Whatever I asked, the recording said, "We calculate based on your highest earnings."

I asked, "How are retirement benefits calculated?"

The recording said, "We calculate based on your highest earnings."

I asked, "Are all earnings or only covered earnings, up to $43,800 in 1987, used in the calculations?"

The recording said, "We calculate based on your highest earnings."

I asked, "How many years of earnings are required in the calculation?"

The recording said, "We calculate based on your highest earnings."

I asked, "Who's going to win the World Series?"

The recording said, "I beg your pardon?"

I said, "Never mind."

I suppose the recording was meant to be reassuring. But I later learned that the recording was covering up for somebody. That somebody—the only one who really understands retirement benefits—is a massive computer. The calculation is far too complicated for mere human minds to grasp.

Still, I persisted. After checking libraries and taking another crack at the handbook, I was able to piece together a framework.

First, I learned that if you've paid Social Security tax for ten or more years, you're fully vested. That means you'll get 100 percent of your calculated benefit at age 62 or 65, even if you retire young. Second, your calculated benefit is based on your "average earnings" up to the maximum—i.e., $43,800 in 1987. (The computer adjusts for changes in the maximum over the years.) In making the calculation, the computer throws out your lowest five years. So at least five zero-earning years are "free" in that they don't reduce your "average earnings".

But here's where it gets tricky. What happens to your "average earnings" and related benefits if you have more than five years of zero earnings? Do *all* the low years get thrown out, like the phone recording says? I never got a clear answer to that question. I could have tried to go straight to the computer. But I was told that the computer refuses to see anyone under age 60. You can hardly blame it, given the law's propensity to change.

So I took the worst case and assumed that "average earnings" go down as a result of factoring in the zero-earning years. And I found that, the way the computer sees things, your retirement benefits go down proportionately far less than "average earnings."

By way of illustration, suppose you have fifteen zero-earning years after throwing out the five freebies. And suppose your "average earnings" are reduced by taking the zero years into account. Instead of receiving, say, $1,100 a month from Social Security, you and your spouse may get only $800 or $900.

Remember that these numbers are solely to illustrate the calculation. Congress will change the law. Earnings, taxes, and benefits change with inflation. If you have a working spouse, the calculation changes. So I may be overly optimistic or pessimistic in my illustrative numbers.

But the point is clear. You'd never *choose* to pay Social Security tax just to increase your retirement check. By working an extra twenty years you'll pay, say, $150,000 of additional tax, depending on how high Congress pushes the rates. That $150,000 can double or triple with compounding over twenty or more years. If your spouse works too, your combined additional Social Security tax may approach a million dollars. Paying that much tax is a ridiculous way to get an extra few hundred dollars, or even an extra few thousand dollars, of Social Security benefits each month. Other things being equal, you're better off to retire young and avoid the tax.

Some actuaries say that the Social Security system is broke. That we shouldn't count on a dime when we reach retirement age. And I could be wrong about real interest rates. Real rates could drop and stay low "forever." Your company's pension plan may pay peanuts. Your parents and Aunt Joslyn could cut you off without a dime. You could wind up at age 55 with $400,000 of nearly worthless dollars. What happens then?

I guess you'd have to go back to work.

WORK, RETIRE, GO BACK TO WORK

The chances of being forced back to work for financial reasons are remote. Too many bad things have to happen for too long a time. You may *choose* to go back to work. Chapter 7 gives examples of retirees who make money, sometimes a lot of money, after retiring. But if you follow this book's formula, most of you will never work another day in your life unless you choose to do so.

Still, financial disaster could strike. When that happens you'll probably have a good sum in CDs, enough money to carry you a few more years. But you'll recognize that because of low real rates, unusually high expenses, or whatever, you'll have to get a job.

First, you'll want to remember to take your time looking for work. It took you time to decide to retire. Give yourself a decent amount of time—six months or a year—to reload the work habit. You'll have lived without a paycheck for years. You should be able to last another six months or so.

Second, recognize that the $50-a-Day Rule will have become a way of life. Even if you go back to work, you'll spend less than you did during your earlier, fast-track career days. So you can accept a lower salary than before and still have plenty of money to live well.

When you look for a job, *don't* consider that you're still a lawyer, engineer, personnel manager, surgeon, editor, marketing rep, or whatever you were before you retired. You'll be in your 40s or 50s. It's hard enough for "old-timers" to get a job. And you'll have been out of the labor force for years. Your knowledge will be out-of-date. Headhunters will talk to you the way undertakers talk to the bereaved. Headhunters try to steal stars from name companies rather than take chances on "has-beens" who were foolish enough to take time off.

So, instead of trying to pick up where you left off, repackage yourself. Create a second career, taking advantage of what you learned and the people you met during retirement. Start with a list of what you did in retirement. Then decide how to take advantage of that in starting a second career.

A man retires and, among other things, gets involved with community affairs. He sets up a coordinating group for block associations, raises funds for a new civic auditorium, and pushes for an urban bicycle freeway. When he goes back to work, he looks for a job in state or local government. He begins his job search by calling those officials who helped him with his projects.

A woman retires and, for fun, writes a weekly column on child rearing for the local newspaper. When she goes back to work, she converts her column to a daily and tries to syndicate.

A couple retires and moves to Brazil. When they go back to work, they try to get a license to represent American products in Rio de Janeiro or São Paulo.

The best book I've seen on how to repackage yourself is Richard Bolles's *What Color Is Your Parachute?* (Ten Speed Press, 1987). Now in its umpteenth edition, the book helps you focus on what you want to do rather than on "just getting a job." *What Color Is Your Parachute?* tells how to contact others to help decide where you might fit in. Once you know what you want to do, why you want to do it, and what you have to offer, you interview better and impress people more. You'll get the job not because of your resume but because of your enthusiasm, insight, and sense of direction.

If and when you go back to work, you'll have grown spiritually and intellectually. You'll have enjoyed your kids while they were young, pushed a lot of stress out of your life, and seen the world. You'll have gained insight that can help you enjoy life more. You may wish you could stay retired. But you'll be excited about the possibilities of a second career.

5.

Control Your Living Costs

Why do you live where you live?

My uncle first taught me to think about that question. My uncle is a strong, skilled carpenter. He works fast and hard, and when he's finished a job it's done right. His buildings will be around decades after he's gone, and he's proud of that. My uncle is fairly quiet by nature. He'd rather listen than talk. But when he gets around to saying something, it's usually worthwhile to pay attention.

When we were small, living in Los Angeles, my uncle would tell us about a winter he spent in Ohio. He'd tell us about snow, how it turns to slush and then freezes. He'd tell us how he had to jump start his car when it was too cold for the starter to turn over. He'd put his hands in front of his mouth and breathe, explaining that to breathe properly in extreme cold you had to do it that way; otherwise your breath would freeze in your mouth and you'd never get it out. I'd be wide-eyed, straining to imagine what it would be like. It seemed a grisly horror story.

My uncle always finished the Ohio story the same way: "There I was, stuck in Cleveland for two months. I couldn't wait to leave. But everyone else was *choosing* to live there. They were living there *of their own free will*."

That was the end of the story. We'd shake our heads at how peculiar some people can be. I always had the impression that my uncle could pretty much figure things out. But how people in Ohio can choose to stay where they are was something he never understood.

When I was a little older I lived briefly—but not briefly enough—in Grand Rapids, Michigan. I observed firsthand what my uncle had described. I decided to ask people why they lived there. Maybe I could enlighten my uncle after all those years.

To my surprise, I found that most people had never thought about why they lived where they lived. After some stammering they'd glare at me and say, "We've lived here a long time."

So why *do* you live where you live? Chapter 4 focused on the huge amounts you pay for housing. This chapter talks of how and where you can live for less. To retire you must control your living costs. To control your living costs you must know what you need in terms of living space. To start you thinking about it, I've prepared a list of questions. Choose the answers that best describe your present situation.

1. What do you like most about your living room?
   a. There's a cozy, well-lit reading chair.
   b. There's a comfortable seating area to chat with friends.
   c. It shows off your expensive furniture and paintings.
   d. A B-1 bomber could fit nicely in the corner.
   e. You can't answer because you haven't found it yet.

2. What is the ratio of telephones to televisions in your home?
   a. One to one.
   b. Two to two.
   c. It depends on whether you include broken phones and black-and-white televisions.
   d. You're not sure you can find them all.
   e. You can't figure it out because higher math is your weak suit.

3. What troubles you most about your kitchen?
   a. It's slightly too small.

    b. You never know what can go in the dishwasher and what can't.

    c. It takes a mechanical engineer to work all the gadgets.

    d. Your children are always playing football in it.

    e. You can't answer because the maid won't let you in.

4. What do you have in your backyard?

    a. You don't have a backyard but there's a park nearby.

    b. A table, chairs, and barbecue.

    c. A self-mowing lawn.

    d. A sauna, swimming pool, tennis court, basketball court, stables, and jogging track you seldom use.

    e. A private golf course.

5. What do you like best about your neighborhood?

    a. You can walk to stores, restaurants, and the bus stop.

    b. You have warm, friendly neighbors.

    c. You're on the nonsmoking side of the street.

    d. It's only a three-hour drive to the office.

    e. It's so expensive that the others on the block can't afford it either.

When you retire you have simple answers to these questions. Vicki and I, for example, prefer warm climates where we can live outdoors most of the year. We like to be near a shopping area with good public transportation, preferably in a city center. We like a small backyard, apartment patio, or balcony where we can put a table, chairs, and barbecue. Our living room should have a well-lit reading chair and comfortable places to sit. Our kitchen should be big enough for someone to cook or clean up. We require only one television, telephone, refrigerator, microwave, toaster, kitchen sink, and dining table.

You may have other ideas about your living space. But to retire, you should know exactly what your needs are. That way you can search for a place that has the essentials and not one thing more.

I recently heard a banker give a talk on mortgage-loan policy. In the 1970s his bank had a rule that no more than 25 percent of income could go toward housing costs. If the monthly payments were more than that, the bank wouldn't make the loan. Now the bank makes loans to people who spend 35 or 40 percent or more on housing costs.

So what do they cut out of their budgets to pay for their homes? "We've looked into that," the banker said. "We've found that people go out to dinner less, and that they go to cheaper restaurants. They rarely go to the movies. They stay at home during vacation time and on holidays. With a big color TV, VCR, swimming pool, large backyard, and maybe a tennis court, who needs to leave home?"

My mentor, Harriet—you met Harriet in chapter 3—agrees: "I'm so busy during the year I don't have time to relax at home. When August comes I head for my backyard rather than the beach. I swim and play ball with my kids. At night we rent a movie and watch it in the living room. Or maybe I read *The Ascent of Man* or something else I never have time for. And I'm close to the office. I get my mail every day, return phone calls, catch up on business reading. On weekends I can entertain clients."

When you retire at age 35 this scenario changes. You no longer need a spacious refuge at the end of a grueling day because you have easy, fun-filled days. You no longer need a special place to spend August with your kids because you have time for your kids all year long. You no longer need a formal area to entertain clients because you don't have any clients. You no longer need an office at home; you don't need an office at all.

When you work, your home becomes the center of your personal life. When you retire, your home is almost an afterthought. You travel more, party more, go out to eat more. Home is simply a pleasant place to be part of the time.

It would be great to retire and still afford the big house in Newport Beach or the condo in Chicago's near-North Side. You'd like to have a pool, patio, barbecue, and tennis court. But most of us have to give up the mansion to retire.

The rule is short:

Move

MOVING

Around 1900 my grandfather came from Holland and wound up in Buffalo, New York. He worked as a railroad carpenter by day and took English lessons from the dishwasher at night. He enjoyed the work and managed to save some money. But he hated the cold in Buffalo. To hear Grandpa tell it, penguins near Buffalo can get frostbite if they don't scurry for cover during a cold snap.

One night the dishwasher told Grandpa about a place where it never got cold. Grandpa checked that he understood correctly. "Here in the U.S.?" he asked.

The dishwasher nodded. "Place called Los Angeles."

"You can get there by train?" Grandpa wanted to know.

"You can, but don't even *think* about doing it. With weather so good, the place is overcrowded. You'll never get a job."

That night Grandpa looked in the mirror and said to himself, "Grandpa, why in the hell are you living in Buffalo when you could be living someplace else?" (Grandpa wasn't a grandpa then, and he never swore, but you get the idea.)

He beat it to Los Angeles the next day. When he got there a man waiting on the station platform asked what kind of work he did. Grandpa showed the man his tools. The man pointed him to a small group of contractors looking for carpenters. Grandpa went over and was hired a few minutes later.

That was a long time ago. But most of us today still assume that life elsewhere is too good to be true. We make excuses about why we can't move. We put up with bad air, traffic, high prices, and cockroaches where we are now. But does it make sense to continue to struggle in San Francisco, Philadelphia, or Boston? If you're 40 years old, you have over half of your active adult life ahead of you. Do you really want to spend it on the Lexington Avenue Express or the Garden Grove Freeway?

Some years ago Vicki and I went to a birthday party in an Italian part of Brooklyn where it seemed everybody was related to everyone else. Talk centered around Dick and Angela's upcoming move. It would be so hard on everyone. Grandma would see the baby less. Dick would drop by less often. Angela would have her next child without her mother nearby. It was all quite sad, until I finally met Dick and asked where he was moving.

"Queens."

We all want to live near people we know and love. But family and friends tend to move around. About 25 percent of Americans move every year. Sometimes it's across the street, but many times it's across the country or even out of the country. And just because you move doesn't mean you'll never see your friends again. When you're retired you can travel for months on end. You'll have plenty of time to visit friends and relatives on *their* schedule, fitting in with *their* lives. Since Vicki and I retired we feel we've become closer to our friends. We spend huge blocks of time with them, typically several *days* rather than hours. We are often welcome as houseguests. That way we're around to chat when *they* have the time, even if it's only an hour or so between "after work" and "at the gym."

CONTROL YOUR HOUSING COSTS

You move to cut your housing costs. I'm talking about extremes here. In college calculus we found that as a curve slopes toward a line, it gets closer and closer. How close? Infinitely close. How close is infinitely close? As close as possible and always getting closer. In retirement, you want your housing costs infinitely close to zero.

Vicki and I own a small apartment in Buenos Aires. Our total monthly cost, besides a small opportunity cost in having maybe $20,000 of capital tied up, is about $40. That includes property taxes, maintenance, condo fees, utilities, and insurance.

Use your imagination to come up with a way to house yourself for less than you pay now. Start with the options most immediately open to you.

A woman from Los Angeles retires to her modest second home in the Mojave Desert. A developer in Providence retires and moves into one of his rental units. A Detroit architect moves into his sister's guest quarters over the garage. The sister doesn't need the space—the guest room in the house is more comfortable— and likes having her brother around for security. A San Francisco couple retires to the family farm in Idaho. Mom and Dad had sold the acreage but got stuck with the old house. When Mom and Dad moved to the city, the "kids" moved to the now-abandoned farmhouse. The whole family is thrilled.

These lucky people have second homes, rental units, rich sisters, and a family farm. They reduce their housing costs without shaking up their lives. But the rest of us have a more difficult time of it. The rule?

Go south

RETIRING IN THE UNITED STATES

Mount Olive, North Carolina, is an hour by car from Raleigh and has a population of maybe three thousand people. It's a charming throwback to a more leisurely era. Colonial mansions with shaded entrances and flower gardens line Main Street. The railroad cuts through the center of town, tooting a friendly salute as it passes. You can walk from one end of downtown to the other in ten minutes or so, with time to greet people and catch up on gossip.

Vicki and I went to see a realtor there. We told him we were retired and thinking of moving to Mount Olive. Did he have a house for us? Maybe three bedrooms, big front porch, lots of trees in the backyard? Someplace near town, where we could walk to buy groceries, cash a check, or eat.

He nodded. "How much do you want to spend?"

I hesitated. I had heard about $30,000 houses in North Carolina. But they couldn't be as gracious as what we'd seen. If I mentioned $30,000, he'd think I was one taco short of a full combination plate.

I gulped. "Maybe $50,000?"

He smiled. "That makes it easy, Mr. Terhorst. For $50,000 you can buy this whole town."

We laughed. He was kidding. But he did have several listings for houses between $25,000 and $30,000. "This city can only support a few houses worth more than $50,000," he said. "The demand isn't there."

We asked him to describe the $30,000 houses he had listed. "Most are here in town. You get more house for your money in town than on a couple of acres of farmland. The houses seem right for a couple like yourselves: brick, two or three bedrooms, one or two baths, and big yards. They won't impress your friends. But they're easy to maintain and easy to secure when you travel."

Rand McNally's 1987 *Retirement Places Rated*, by Richard Boyer and David Savageau, ranks over 100 retirement spots in the United States. Boyer and Savageau searched for places with good climate, low-cost housing, low cost of living, low crime rate, good health care, and things to do. They wrote the book for "normal" retirees aged 55 and above. But low-cost living, a healthy place to live, and low crime appeals to us 35-year-olds as well.

The best five places they found are Murray-Kentucky Lake, Kentucky; Clayton-Clarkesville, Georgia; Hot Springs-Lake Ouachita, Arkansas; Grand Lake-Lake Tenkiller, Oklahoma; and Fayetteville, Arkansas. The Rand McNally book also says very good things about parts of Maine, New Mexico, and Washington. But most of the best places are in southern or bordering states. You can buy houses there for $40,000 or rent them for $250 a month. You can largely forget about air conditioning in summer or heat in winter. The crime and tax rates are a fraction of what you're used to. The cost of living is as low as any place in the U.S. And the best places are a few hours by car from major urban areas like Charlotte, Louisville, and Atlanta.

Peter A. Dickinson reviews retirement areas in *Sunbelt Retirement* (Dutton, 1980). The book speaks to those who want good weather without the high cost of Boca Raton or Scottsdale. Dickinson says a retired couple can live on $10,000 a year, including $3,390 for housing, in the places he reviews.

Rather than take the word of these authors, Vicki and I decided to check out the Southeast for ourselves. In June 1986, we flew from Los Angeles to New Orleans and, on a Greyhound bus, worked our way east and north to Washington, D.C. We went to Mobile, Montgomery, and a small town on Perdido Bay in Alabama; to Pensacola and Jacksonville in Florida; to Savannah, Georgia; to Charleston and Columbia in South Carolina; and to Raleigh, North Carolina. In between we saw hundreds of small towns. We stopped to talk to realtors, merchants, bankers, and cabdrivers.

Except in the large urban and resort areas, we found a healthy, easygoing way of life. The air was clean, the sidewalks swept. We met friendly people who want to keep drugs out of their schools, bureaucrats out of their lives, and high-handedness out of their businesses. The nearby big cities, with their international airports, provide plenty of bustle. But with cable TV, home computers, telephone data bases, and a full mailbox, one feels in touch with the larger scheme of things even in very remote places.

So why isn't everyone moving down there? No jobs. Young people I talked to told me they would prefer to stay put. But those who take their careers seriously move to Washington, D.C., Atlanta, or Chicago. They intend to return, but few actually do. The result is low demand for housing back home.

When you retire at age 35 you reverse the migration. Cash out of your home up North, put the money in the bank, and head for a small town in the South that offers few jobs. Rent or buy a $20,000 to $40,000 house and you're set to start your new life.

Why not plan to visit some of these places next summer? If you don't like the South, try Vermont, Washington, or Montana. Look for places where you can:

Live where the jobs aren't

Once you move to your low-cost living space in the United States, you can think about living part of the year overseas. Think about it long enough and you may say good-bye to your U.S. housing costs altogether. You'll stick your furniture in someone's basement and head for the beaches of Yugoslavia, the cool plateaus of Mexico, or the tropical warmth of Thailand.

WHY IT'S ALWAYS CHEAP IN THE THIRD WORLD

One day after a major devaluation in Argentina, I went to buy a dozen eggs, bread, milk, and a stick of butter. Because the maid usually did the shopping, I was out of touch with prices. Even so, I was in for a surprise at the checkout stand. The total came to 85 cents.

Prices in Argentina didn't stay that low for very long. But even in 1987, during a so-called "high cost" period, two adults could live well in Buenos Aires on $900 a month, including housing. Two adults living on $50 a day could live in the upper middle class.

Argentina is one of several low-cost countries you can choose. The dollar buys paradise in parts of Greece, Spain, Mexico, and Brazil. Hungarians and Yugoslavs often earn in the United States and then go back to the "old country" to retire. With a dollar income back there you can lead an extraordinary life, providing you avoid trouble and don't play the Ugly American. In most of the Third World, $50 a day provides a fabulous standard of living and plenty of time to do what you want: travel, reflect, write, learn something new and slip into an interesting challenge, or simply come up with novel perspectives on life and work.

It's not that living is cheap in the Third World, but that *money* is cheap in the Third World. Locals often struggle to subsist. Tell them that the cost of living is low and they'll think the cheese has slipped off your cracker. But with dollars in your pocket, instead of pesos, florins, or dinars, you can live far better than in the United States. You earned and paid taxes in dollars. You did it in the richest country in the world. You were fortunate. When you retire, you can spend some of your wealth in the economies of the less fortunate.

The dollar goes a long way in the Third World regardless of whether the dollar happens to be "up" or "down" at the moment. The United States trades mainly with Canada, Japan, and Western Europe, not with Yugoslavia, Costa Rica, and Thailand. When we say the dollar is "down" we mean it buys fewer yen, pounds, or francs. But the dollar is invariably "up" in Third World countries. That's because those countries export low-cost farm produce and import high-value airplanes, machine tools, and computers. Because of that imbalance, Third World countries are starved for hard currency. To encourage exports and reduce imports, they "compete" by devaluing their money—again and again and again.

Some of this seems unfair. Libraries set aside whole sections of material on terms of trade between the rich and the poor. But Third World countries keep their currencies low precisely to attract dollars. When you move to those countries you're playing into their hands. You get a low-cost place to live and they get the dollars they need.

What's a Third World country? For our purposes it's any

country with a weak currency. With this definition, Brazil, the eighth largest economy in the world, is in the Third World. So are Spain and Greece, two of history's greatest cultures. So are socialist countries like Hungary and Yugoslavia.

Third World countries sometimes get expensive, but only for short periods. In 1979 and 1980 the world's bankers saw fit to flood Chile, Argentina, and Mexico with hard-currency loans. Billions of dollars, marks, and yen pushed pesos in those countries far beyond their true value. Things got expensive for dollar-based buyers. But the propped-up values collapsed in 1982 when the banks cut back on lending. Now most Latin American currencies are back to their former levels.

WHERE IN THE WORLD TO LIVE

The cost of living is so low, and the thrill of adventure so high, that the question is not whether you should head for the Third World, but what country you should try first. For fun, get a map of the world. Close your eyes and point to a country. Chances are your finger will hover over a place that costs a tiny fraction of what you're spending now. Of all the countries in the world, only two dozen or so are developed. The rest are waiting for you.

So how do you select a country that fits your needs? One way is to consider places you've visited. Does that week in Puerto Vallarta stick in your memory? Do you remain fascinated, after all these years, by the Malaysia you saw as a child? If nothing pops up from the past, what about places your friends or business associates have moved to? You can write them, asking their opinion.

You say your friends live in Gary, Lodi, and Pittsburgh rather than Rio, Bali, or Zagreb? Then put your imagination to work on where you might like to live. Do you think of beaches, mountains, villages, cities, rivers, lakes, deserts, jungles, or caves?

Once you have a list of two or three places you might like to try, head for the library. Tourist books tell about climate, language, altitude, food, visa requirements, and currency values. Encyclopedias cover history and politics, geography, religion, culture, and commerce. Check out nonfiction and, if you can find any, fiction by native and foreign authors who know the country. For more current information, read recent magazine and newspaper articles. If possible, get a copy of the English-language newspaper in the target country. The newspaper will cover current affairs and give you a feel for housing, things to do, and what's going on in the expatriate community.

In addition to going to the library, write or visit the country's nearest consulate. Most consulates have both tourist brochures and facts and figures for businesses.

Before you leave, ask people you know if they have friends or business associates living in the host country. Get their names and phone numbers and plan to call them when you arrive. You'll be amazed at how many of your friends know people in Tahiti and Barcelona. When Vicki and I moved to Buenos Aires, most people asked questions like, "Where *is* Argentina?" But every so often someone would have a cousin living there. By the time we were ready to move, we had over a dozen contacts.

When you arrive in the host country, whether for five weeks or five months, the rule is:

Live like a resident, not like a tourist

LIVE LIKE A RESIDENT

The best way to visit a country is to pretend you're moving there. New residents have more fun than tourists. Tourists go to museums, take pictures, eat at colorful restaurants, and do sightseeing. New residents do those things as well. But new residents go beyond the surface. They get out of hotels and into people's homes. They visit the neighborhoods, meet the locals, and learn the language.

New residents try to find short-term apartments or apart-hotels rather than tourist hotels. That gives them a chance to cook the local fish and vegetables at "home." New residents read the English-language newspaper not so much for international news but to find out what social events they might enjoy. They visit the American Club, the American library, and the University Women's Club. They travel with their hobbies. They take cooking classes or golf lessons, even for short periods. They take time to figure out the buses and trains rather than take cabs everywhere. They order what others are eating in restaurants rather than choose from a menu in English. They buy, rather than stare, in the fruit and meat markets.

New residents telephone people on the list they brought from home. In 1985 Vicki and I spent a month in Madrid. During the first week we called three of the four names on our "contacts" list. One invited us to play bridge, another to a jazz club, and a third to a bullfight. They introduced us to their friends and gave us advice on what to do and see. Some went so far as to laugh at my jokes.

WHERE WE'VE LIVED

Here, following, are short, selected comments on some of the countries Vicki and I have visited since retiring four years ago. We "lived like a resident" for at least a month in each of them. My comments show bias and personal preference based on what we found. I focus on feelings and impressions rather than on the facts you can get in a tourist guide.

Before we get started, there are three preliminaries. First, Vicki and I prefer hot weather. All the countries I discuss have warm climates during part of the year. But for those who hate to sweat, most have cooler periods as well. Mexico's Yucatán peninsula stays warm, or even hot, virtually year-round. But in Oaxaca, over five thousand feet up in the mountains, temperatures are moderate to cool. Spain heats up in July and August, but it's cold—or at least too cold for Vicki and me—the rest of the year. Before you visit a country, choose the right season for you.

Second, we try to avoid crowds. Since most tourists seem to detest the hot weather we like so much, we rarely have to fight for hotel rooms, seats on planes, or to get into restaurants. Most tourists visit Seville, Spain, for example, in the cool months of May and June. We avoid the crowds by going in August, when it's hot. Similarly, we go to the Yucatán in July, during the hot, sticky, rainy season. Humidity is good for us and good for our bodies. When we go, it seems we're the only tourists there to enjoy it.

Finally, the countries we visited have weak currencies. You'll find it hard to spend as much as $50 a day. Don't worry about it, though. You'll bring your average back up the next time you go to Oslo, Geneva, or Washington, D.C.

ARGENTINA

Buenos Aires is an urban sprawl of some 9 million people. The city's opera, ballet, music, art, and theater keep us entertained. Buses, taxis, trains, and sturdy walking shoes get us around town or across the country; a car, in our view, is a senseless bother. We enjoy high-quality meat and poultry, milk and cheese, bread and pasta, and local beer and wine. Health standards compare to the world's best.

Every year Gallup takes a worldwide poll on optimism. The question is, "Do you think next year is going to be better than the one you just had?" Only Caesar knows why Gallup or anyone else wants to know such a thing. You'd think they'd focus on important issues: whether softness or absorbency sells toilet paper; whether we want our toothpaste to fight cavities, freshen our breath, brighten our smile, polish our fillings, massage our gums, or, I suppose, protect our gold-plated toothbrush.

But Gallup really does check on optimism every year. And the polls show that Argentines are the world's most optimistic people.

Argentina has had a declining standard of living for decades. Grandparents live better than parents. Parents live better than children. Yet Argentines insist that next year will be better. After a bad year, when Gallup returns and points out that last year's optimism was unfounded, Argentines admit they made a mistake. Then they quickly insist that good times are just around the corner. And so on, year after year.

When people are that optimistic it's infectious. Nothing ever goes too wrong; something better is always on the way. The optimism translates into a wonderful, childlike enthusiasm for birthdays, outdoor barbecues with friends, or simply a sunny day. Argentines ignore life's little hardships and focus instead on a soccer game, a new dress, or a funny drawing. One learns to relax and enjoy each day instead of struggling to prepare for tomorrow.

Move to Argentina and you not only have to learn a new language, you have to adapt to some different customs. Perhaps because it's farther away, Argentina seems less influenced by the

United States than other South American countries. Better restaurants in Buenos Aires open at ten in the evening, parties can start at midnight, and jazz clubs open their doors at one in the morning. Arrive on time to a dinner party and there's a good chance the hostess will be out doing last-minute shopping. If she happens to be home, she may greet you in a bathrobe. Formal dinners can include as many as three or four desserts, one after the other, until four or five in the morning.

Argentines love to talk, but according to certain rules. All conversations start with inquiries about one's health and family. All conversations end with best wishes for one's health and family. In between, subject matter varies. But whatever is discussed, images, concepts, and metaphor are preferred to facts, figures, or anything that can be objectively proved or disproved.

Maddening shortages in Argentina can try the patience of a family therapist. In the Argentine beach town of Pinamar, I once went to buy beer, a couple of steaks, bread, and bus tickets back to Buenos Aires. The beverage store was out of beer. The owner explained that he had no empty bottles; the beer company was short on bottles and wouldn't deliver unless the store had empties to exchange. The butcher had no beef—his supplier had failed to show up that day. The bakery had a few cookies but no bread. And the bus station ticket office had run out of ticket blanks. The woman behind the counter told me she had run out of tickets several days before; she wondered why Buenos Aires was so slow in delivering new stock.

I returned home empty-handed and frustrated. But Vicki served wine instead of beer, chicken instead of steaks, and pasta instead of bread. We showed up at the bus station the following day, got on board, and paid the driver.

MEXICO

Most tourists to Mexico do a one-week package deal to Cancún for $729 plus tax, or about $1,500 for two people. Their Mexico sparkles with glass and glitter. Their Mexico brings in more hard currency than any Mexican export except oil. Their Mexico is carefully controlled by the National Tourist Board. Their Mexico pegs its prices to the U.S. dollar, makes sure everyone speaks at least some English, and has a ready excuse when the air-conditioning breaks down.

Their Mexico is as different from the Mexico Vicki and I know as Kansas City is from New York. With $1,500 Vicki and I buy our plane tickets and live in Mexico for two months rather than one week. We live in peso-based rather than dollar-based Mexico. And we feel we're closer to the Mexican people, their culture, and their traditions.

In 1982 foreign bankers began to rein in their lending to Mexico. A few years after that, oil prices fell. The one-two punch of tighter money and falling oil prices pounded the Mexican peso from 25 to the dollar to over 2,000. But you'll never find those peso bargains if you stay at the high-rise hotels in Ixtapa or Puerto Vallarta, because those places peg prices to the dollar. Their customers are worn-out executives, battered lawyers, and unappreciated civil servants who want a week on the beach without complications. But if you venture a couple of miles away from the tourist areas, you'll find cool fruit drinks for a dime, complete meals for a dollar, hotels without nonworking air-conditioners for $5 to $10 a night, and taxis that will take you on a half-day tour for $20.

Like most visitors to Mexico, Vicki and I land in international airports in Cancún, Zihuantanejo/Ixtapa, or Puerto Vallarta. But once on the ground we head for small fishing villages or larger cities rather than the concrete and glass tourist strips. We prefer the municipal beach in Zihuantanejo, for example, to the manicured sand of nearby Ixtapa. On the beach in Zihuantanejo a boy comes around every so often and asks for a nickel. That's a fee for using the beach. He'll also run to get you a beer for a quarter or a taco for a dime. In Ixtapa, a few miles up the Pacific, the Mexican tourist board has built a massive resort. A taco on the beach in Ixtapa comes with a plate of things you don't want and costs $5. The waiter who brings it to you accepts the American Express card.

Whether they stay in shiny, dollar-based resorts or in the unpackaged countryside, about half of Mexico's visitors wind up with intestinal problems. Called "Montezuma's revenge" or simply the *turistas*, the painful stomach pains and diarrhea can ruin short vacations. Avoid drinking the water, they say, and you avoid the *turistas*. But I never drink the water, and I nearly always get the *turistas*. The problem goes away after a few days and seldom comes back. One dose seems to immunize you for the rest of the trip. For those who stay in Mexico for a month or two, there's a fifty/fifty chance of avoiding the *turistas* altogether. But if you get it, it will probably appear and disappear during the first week. After that you should feel fine.

In 1985 John Howells and Don Merwin wrote a book called *Choose Mexico—Retiring on $400 a Month*.* The $400 figure comes from a poll of retired Americans living in Mexico. Howells and Merwin found that the median retired American spends $250 on housing. Many rents are in the $150 to $200 range. Food costs $150 a month, including meals in restaurants for about $3 a person. Maids cost 60 cents an hour, the government keeps gas prices low, and for $100 or less national airlines will sell you local, one-week package tours to Guadalajara, San Miguel de Allende, Taxco, or other spots you may want to visit.

The authors of *Choose Mexico* emphasize that you can live a full, active life on $400 a month. Those who seldom travel or go out to eat live on $300 or even $200 a month. The authors use $400 because that's what they spend. They thought it would be presumptuous for them to advise others on a lifestyle they have not experienced. But with very little effort you can live for less than $400.

Perhaps the best bargains Americans find in Mexico are rents. Low rents result from overbuilding during the boom years of the late 1970s and from the large number of retired Americans there who want to rent out their homes for short periods. Interested in a furnished, two-bedroom apartment in Acapulco with a view of the ocean? Figure on $200 a month. How about colonial, artistic San Miguel de Allende, with its huge American population, in the mountains just four hours from Mexico City? Rent a two-bedroom apartment beginning at $125 furnished, $100 unfurnished; or a house for $250. You prefer the Yucatán peninsula, with warm winters and blistering summers? Say $200 a month for a place close enough to the water to be cooled by sea breezes.

*Choose Mexico—Retiring on $400 a Month costs $8.95. You can get it from Gateway Books, 66 Cleary Court, Suite 1405, San Francisco, CA 94109. Phone (415) 821–3440.

VENEZUELA

If Mexico doesn't agree with you, head farther south. Tiny Costa Rica has a large American community and miles of coastline. Panama offers easy access, fabulous beaches, and perhaps the world's best seafood. And, for the first time in many years, Venezuela is finally affordable.

Decades of oil money have given Venezuela the highest per capita income in Latin America. But, like Mexico, Venezuela has been hammered by tighter money and lower oil prices. The country was forced to devalue in 1985–86, and economists believe more devaluations are on the way. As a result, Venezuela is a bargain for the first time in many years.

Stay away from Caracas, the country's smoggy capital and business center. Land at the big airport there and spend a night or two to relax after the trip. Then head for the warm-water beaches to the east. If you prefer, try the mountains or the great central plateau called the *llanos*.

As soon as oil prices go back up, Venezuela will become expensive again. Take advantage of the window now.

BRAZIL

An American friend who grew up in Brazil maintains that Brazilians are the world's most laid-back people. I don't doubt it. Anything anyone wants to do, as long as it's in good fun, seems all right with the Brazilians. Stroll into a fine restaurant wearing a string bikini, dance on a sidewalk, or play soccer on a downtown street and you may draw a crowd. But no one will ask you to leave.

Brazilians believe their mix of Portuguese and African blood gives them their sensuous, fun-loving attitude. They worship their bodies and everything they can do with them: sing, dance, play volleyball, have sex, eat, drink, and jog. A given body may be fat or thin, black or white, or male or female. It may be beautiful or marred. But that body loves to prance around Ipanema, showing itself to others in various degrees of undress.

In Rio de Janeiro, the English-language newspaper tells of furnished apartments or apart-hotels. For shorter stays, I recommend one of the smaller hotels in Ipanema. Stay a block or two from the beach and figure on $6 a night for a double room. If you want to splurge, the Hotel Praia Ipanema on the beach offers spectacular views and first-class luxury for about $30 a day. We sometimes stay there if we're only in Rio for a day or two.

Every Saturday afternoon Brazilians eat *feijoada*, a black-bean stew with sausages, pork, beef, preserved salted fish, and mysterious animal parts. When my mother-in-law first hoisted a spoonful of *feijoada*, it had a small tail on it. One accompanies *feijoada* with white rice, stir-fried collard greens, sliced oranges, and root meal.

For the less adventurous, Brazilians put meat on three-foot-long swords and roast it over an open fire. Waiters bring the skewers to your table, put the point on your plate, and slide off a chicken heart, small sausage, or piece of chicken, or slice off a bit of pork, ham, or beef. The meal is called a *churrasco*, and includes french fries, fruit, and all the skewered meat you want for about $3.

If you know any Romance language you'll be able to get by in Portuguese. But if all you ever learn to say is *tudo bem* you'll do fine. *Tudo bem* means "everything's great." Brazilians say *tudo bem* instead of "good morning," "how are you?" or even "how was your day yesterday?" Since to a Brazilian everything is always great, the presumption is that *tudo bem* covers all possibilities. Even if there's a problem to resolve, both sides start their talk with *tudo bem*.

Rio has a lot of street crime. Leave your gold jewelry and watches—or even phony gold jewelry and watches—in a safe-deposit box in the United States. Carry only a small amount of cash in your sock or money belt and you won't have any problem. While walking along the Copacabana sidewalk one evening, I was accosted by two lovely young pickpockets masquerading as whores. Instead of panicking, I relaxed and enjoyed their physical overtures. I had nothing in my pockets, so a pickpocket posed little danger.

Vicki and I sometimes sit in a Copacabana sidewalk café and watch transvestites, prostitutes, beggars, pickpockets, and any combination of the above at work. If you're uncomfortable taking in the action on the sidewalk, head for the Ouro Verde hotel. The bar there has a small outdoor area protected by plants.

You can sit behind the plants, sip a *caipirinha*, and watch the action in private.

SPAIN

Spain can best be thought of as several smaller countries united by a government that they all hate. To see Spain you need a "See Spain" pass from Iberia Airlines. The pass offers sixty days of unlimited air travel within Spain for only $200. (Chapter 8 explains how to get a "See Spain" pass or a similar pass in other countries.)

Four hundred years ago Spain controlled the high seas. Spanish settlers colonized the New World. The Spanish flag flew over most of Europe, and Spanish culture was at its highest level. Except for the Rome of a thousand years before, Spain had the greatest empire in history. Yet, the Spanish empire declined. Historians are still puzzled as to how it happened.

I think I've found the answer.

Spain lost control of its empire because Spaniards failed to agree on how to run it. The fact is that, left to their own devices, Spaniards fail to agree on anything.

The problem is that Spaniards are firmly convinced that all transactions necessarily involve both a winner and a loser. In their view, it's impossible for both parties to gain. You may be the biggest widget seller and I the biggest buyer. You may have an oversupply of widgets and be desperate to sell; I may be in short supply and desperate to buy. We may deal of our own free will, openly, with perfect information on both sides. But if we eventually do a deal, according to the Spanish view of the world, one of us is sticking it to the other.

At first blush this winner/loser view may appear harmless. I can assure you it's far from harmless. Suppose, for example, you want to sell your home, worth $50,000. I want to buy. We're both Spaniards. After considerable haggling, gamesmanship, name-calling, and good-natured bickering, we reach a deal. Surprise of surprises, the sale price is set at $50,000. Before signing the final papers, we go home to sleep on the deal.

You're the seller. You figure the house is worth the sale price, and that means you're not sticking it to me. But if you're not sticking it to me, I *must* be sticking it to you. That's the only alternative, given the winner/loser view. Similarly, I as buyer decide I'm being fair. Therefore, you *must* be sticking it to me. How can it be any other way?

The next day we meet, supposedly to sign the papers. But you've raised your price to $60,000. I've dropped my offer to $40,000. Inevitably, the deal falls apart.

Extend this example to an entire country and you'll see why, in Spain, private deals don't get done. Only direct orders from the government can ensure that trucks roll, buildings get built, and products get sold. In Spain today a bureaucracy controls bus rides and hotel rooms, medical care and interest rates, steel and rice prices, and beer and wine production. Private deals are best viewed as aberrations, flukes in the system.

The winner/loser view is most pronounced in Galicia, the tiny state in Spain's northwest corner. Gallegos, as the people who live there are called, are so hopelessly unable to deal with one another that most of them have emigrated. Those emigrants have had success, and often a great deal of success, in the United States, France, Brazil, China, and many other countries. But in Galicia, where they have to deal with one another, Gallegos can't agree. Their tiny corner of Spain remains the poorest, most backward part of the country.

Vicki and I started and ended our three-month visit in Madrid, Spain's capital and, since the demise of Barcelona, the cultural, artistic, and business center of the country. Placido Domingo, the Spanish opera star, sings in the local opera house. But music in Madrid includes everything from *zarsuela*, a sort of light opera, to some of the finest jazz in Europe.

Spain was ruled by Moslem invaders for several hundred years, and the best place to see their influence is in the south. The mosque in Cordoba, the Alhambra in Grenada, and the cathedral in Seville take you back a thousand years. Narrow footpaths, buildings with painted doors, and hidden patios add an air of mystery to your journey back in time.

Spain made great strides after kicking out the Moslems. At times, though, one gets the feeling that not all Spaniards have made it to the twentieth century. In 1985, for example, I saw a newspaper article entitled "Deodorants Can Eliminate Ugly Odors." The article featured an interview with a prominent "deodoran-tologist." (I'm translating here, but you get the point.) The deodorantologist affirmed that, although sweating is normal, one *doesn't* have to stink. I saw another article entitled "Vasectomy Is *Not* Synonymous with Castration."

Wide, sandy beaches line much of Spain's southern and eastern coasts. The beaches attract hordes of retired Europeans and a handful of retired Americans into prefab towns. Some retirees build grand villas for a fraction of what they would cost in Florida or the south of France. But the Mediterranean water in that part of Spain is filthy, and the weather and water are cool most of the year. Remember that Madrid is as far north as New York City. If you want warm days and balmy nights, for nine or ten months a year you can forget about Spain—or any other part of Europe.

Farther to the north and east, Barcelona is the capital of Catalonia. Fifty years ago Barcelona was the manufacturing, artistic, and cultural center of Spain. But Franco hated the Catalonians, and during his three decades of rule he shifted the country's power to Madrid. Upon Franco's death in 1975, the Catalonians fell into a small-minded, nationalist backlash. Franco forbade the teaching and use of Catalonian, so Catalonians now want to limit the use of Spanish and other languages. Street signs, tourist maps, museum guides, billboards, and promotional flyers are in Catalonian, leaving the tourist little access to the heart of the city. Much manufacturing moved to Madrid and other parts of Spain, so Catalonians want to require that only locally produced goods be sold there. Franco built up the museums in Madrid, so Catalonians seldom exhibit Spanish art.

Barcelona won the right to host the Olympic games in 1992. You can bet the Catalonians will publish programs, press kits, schedules, and other information exclusively in their own language. Foreign swimmers, I suppose, will have to learn to speak Catalonian to find out where the pool is. Fanatics will try to prohibit the use of foreign languages at any time. They'll insist that groups of athletes from, say, China speak to one another in Catalonian.

Many Basques in the north want independence, but rather than make their country inaccessible to tourists, they open it up. We found the Basques as friendly as anyone in Spain, eager to help and see to it that we had a good time. Advertisements, tourist material, and street signs are in both Spanish and Basque, and tourist material is in English. To force the independence issue, a tiny group of Basque terrorists have been bombing their country for years. But the terrorists target local officials rather than tourists. Your chances of getting caught in the crossfire are remote. You're safer in Basque cities like San Sebastián or Bilbao, for example, than in hotter war zones like Times Square or the Jerome Avenue line.

Before going to Spain you should read Michener's *Iberia* and Hemingway's *Death in the Afternoon*. Michener's lengthy work tells why he loves Spain and gives details of his lengthy travels there. Read it as background before you go and as a tourist guide while you're there.

Death in the Afternoon, now over fifty years old, is Hemingway's classic, nonfiction work on bullfights. Vicki and I went to bullfights most Sunday afternoons and many Friday nights. When we couldn't get to the bullring, we watched bullfights on TV. I bought bullfight magazines and spent days in the library reading up on the subject.

Bullfighting is a spectacle, not a sport or a fair fight: the bull always dies. Bullfighting owes its popularity to the Spanish fear of death. One way to confront that fear and try to overcome it is through bullfights. The bulls are wild and fierce, stronger and more savage than tigers or elephants, and seemingly without fear of death. The *torero* can come as close to death as he wants by moving closer to the bull's horns.

Madrid hosts the most serious bullfights during its festivals in May and October. If you're interested, make sure you plan your trip around those events. Tickets, especially for the good seats, are expensive and hard to get. Try to have a friend in Madrid pick them up for you in advance. If you don't know anyone in Madrid, arrive a few days early and buy them at the bullring.

YUGOSLAVIA

The Adriatic coast of Yugoslavia offers sparkling clear water, five-hundred-year-old stucco hotels, a wonderful blend of Latin and Slavic cultures, and people as friendly as anywhere in the world.

Yugoslav tourist pamphlets note that "since the break with

Stalin and the Eastern bloc in 1948, the country has followed a foreign policy of nonalignment and has developed its own brand of socialism based on worker management of industry, commerce, and public services, which are socially owned. However, most agricultural land (85 percent) belongs to individual farmers and there are numerous privately owned small businesses."

In terms of vigilance and control, Yugoslavia is as different from its communist neighbors as the University of Miami is from West Point. Yugoslavs can go to Italy, Austria, Hungary, or anyplace else, as they wish, for as long as they want. Yugoslavia has mutually abolished visas with most European countries. U.S. citizens can get a free one-year visa that permits multiple entry.

Consider renting a house or apartment in Yugoslavia year-round. Use it as an inexpensive base of operations to explore southern Europe. Yugoslavia has beaches on the Adriatic and world-class ski resorts in the mountains. You can go hiking or backpacking, water ski, relax in health spas, hunt, or fish. If you get bored, head to neighboring Austria, Italy, Greece, Bulgaria, Romania, Russia, or Hungary. You're only a few hours by train from any of them.

Spend plenty of time in Yugoslavia's tranquil cafés. Many are on sidewalks, where you can tap your feet to the rhythm of engines backfiring. Others are tucked away in white stucco rooms that were once the ground floor of Venetian-era bourgeois homes. Still others are in shady gardens, central plazas, or along the rivers. Waiters never rush; once you've finished your coffee you can stay forever. Cafés are an ideal place to observe the world around you, ponder philosophical questions, and catch up on reading.

WORKING VERSUS RETIRING IN THE THIRD WORLD

Vicki and I live in Buenos Aires, Argentina. If you've heard anything at all about Argentina it probably has to do with war and killings. Some horrible things have happened there over the past several decades, and many of them get a lot of press. Partly as a result, people tend to ignore Argentina's startling economic collapse. If Japan is a jet and the United States a turbo prop, Argentina is the Wright brothers' airplane, crashing into the North Carolina sand dunes time and again.

In 1981 *Euromoney* magazine studied how the world's economies had performed since the 1973 OPEC oil crisis. Researchers fed tons of data through an econometric model. They concluded that Argentina has the world's sickest economy. Curiously, Argentina is floating in oil. OPEC had little to do with Argentina's problems. It might be more correct to say that Argentina managed to fail *in spite of* OPEC's efforts to help out.

Economists categorize countries as developed, less developed, or developing. The idea is that a country *be* developed or *get* developed. Argentina requires a label all its own. Eighty years ago Argentina *was* developed. Argentina traded more than Canada or Australia. The standard of living compared to that of Western Europe and the United States. But Argentina managed to undevelop itself. The Argentina of today faces declining real wages, growing unemployment, hyperinflation, and huge foreign debt. Once an exporter of meat and other food, Argentina now imports or wants to import beef, chicken, and eggs from neighboring Uruguay. The Argentine peso used to trade in world markets. Now the peso's successor, the austral, trades in Uruguay alone. Argentina once had a fine phone service. Now ENTEL, the state telephone company, brags in newspaper ads that the average waiting time to get a phone has been reduced to ten years.

No one could confuse Argentina with a country that works. A couple of years ago Vicki and I happened upon a charming winery in the Andean foothills near Mendoza, a thousand miles or so from Buenos Aires. The owner, a second-generation German-Argentine, had inherited the winery from his father. His pride and joy, a full-bodied cabernet sauvignon, tasted like "poetry in a glass." I told him I liked it and asked where I could buy a couple of bottles in Buenos Aires.

He said, "I'd like to sell more in Buenos Aires. That's 90 percent of the market for quality wine in this country."

I pulled out a small notebook. "You've got a new customer. Give me the names of a couple of stores where I can buy it. Better yet, I'll call your distributor and order a couple of cases."

He shook his head. "I don't have a distributor. They want too much money. Better call me here and tell me what you want. I'll ship it to you."

Knowing the problems with telephones, I began to have doubts. But I decided to play along. "What's your phone number?"

He shook his head. "I don't have a phone. And mail doesn't always make it. Maybe you can call my son in Mendoza. He shares a phone with five other students. Sometimes I get through after only a couple of tries."

I said, "I'll take my chances on a letter. Shall I include a check with my order?"

He shook his head. "No checks. The bank won't cash a check. Besides, how would you know the price? With inflation the way it is I have to change my prices every week. A couple of weeks can go by before I get your order and ship it."

I said nothing. At this point I figured I had done my best. But I began to doubt that I would ever taste that wine again.

Finally the vintner brightened. "My brother lives in Buenos Aires. Maybe you could take the cash to him."

I said, "Maybe. But could you ship directly to my apartment? I don't have a car."

He shook his head. "I ship to the freight forwarder. He's in the Buenos Aires warehouse district."

"He'll call me when the shipment comes in?"

He shook his head. "They're not reliable. It's better to run over there every few days to check if the wine has arrived. You can try to call, but it's hard to get through by phone."

"Can't he just deliver to me?"

He shook his head. "Too expensive. He charges more to ship from his warehouse to your apartment than from Mendoza to Buenos Aires. Better go pick it up yourself. Just track down a friend with a truck. Or maybe you can rent a car with a big trunk. . . ."

Like many deals in Argentina, this one didn't get done. It's pretty hard to sell without a way to take an order, make delivery, or receive payment.

The wine story illustrates how hard it can be to get something done in Argentina. Some of the most pleasant places in the world can be hell if you have to go to an office and struggle. Routine things in the Third World almost never happen in a routine way. Even top executives spend their days tracking down cash transfers, collecting overdue accounts, and signing government forms.

But working in the Third World is one thing. Retiring is quite another. Business requires infrastructure: money wires, banking services, phones, mail delivery, and computers. When those things break down, you get frustrated. But those frustrations are only minor blips if you're retired. Retirement, as we'll see in chapter 8, requires hardly any infrastructure at all. Retirees walk over to visit friends rather than talk to them on the phone. In the afternoon they go to a café rather than to a bank. They write personal letters rather than crank masterpieces out of a word processor.

Forget what you may have heard about tough times in the Third World. You've been talking to disgruntled businessmen. You're going to retire rather than work. You retire to beaches, mountains, or ranches rather than to offices or factories. Choose a country because you like its people, climate, and way of life rather than its efficiency in getting a job done.

PRACTICAL MATTERS IN LIVING ABROAD

The rules are:

Try living abroad for three to six months
Keep calm; you can always return to the United States

Here's some practical advice to make sure you get started right.

VISAS

With an American passport you're entitled to live and work in the world's richest country. In the United States you enjoy the advantages of having freely elected statesmen, a strong military, a system of justice, and teenagers with glue in their hair. But the United States requires that all foreigners visiting the United States have visas. Most foreign countries outside of Western Europe reciprocate by requiring visas of visitors from the United States. Unfortunately, that means that with a U.S. passport you have to put up with the hassle of getting a visa for almost every country you visit.

A visa is a stamp placed by officials of a foreign country in your U.S. passport. A tourist card is similar to a visa but it's a separate piece of paper rather than a stamp in your passport. To get a country-by-country list of visa and tourist-card requirements, write the U.S. Government Printing Office, Washington, D.C. 20401. Ask them to send you a free copy of the U.S. State Department's Bureau of Consular Affairs pamphlet *Visa Requirements of Foreign Governments*. Visa requirements change, but the State Department keeps the pamphlet fairly current.

How hard is it to get a visa or tourist card for three to six months? Most countries issue them as a matter of course. Mexico's consular offices around the United States issue six-month tourist cards for the asking. Spain lets you stay for six months with only a passport. Slip over the border to Portugal, France, or Morocco, and when you return to Spain the six months starts over. Argentina grants multiple entry visas good for four years; each trip there can last up to three months. Yugoslavia, as we've said, grants free one-year visas with multiple entry.

In most countries you can keep your tourist status even if you plan a prolonged stay. In Mexico, for example, make sure to head back to the United States before the six months on your tourist card is up. When you return to Mexico, you get a new tourist card and begin a new six-month period. After a year or two you may want to apply for residential status. And after three or four years the Mexicans may refuse to give you any more tourist cards. But most countries welcome Americans who don't want to work and who can show they have a steady source of dollar income from the United States. You need to make sure, though, that the residential status you choose doesn't require you to pay local taxes on interest income earned back in the United States (see below).

HOUSING

The rule on living abroad is:

Rent, don't buy

Chapter 4 talks of the American dream to own your own home. Leave that part of the dream in America. When you go abroad, rent to remain flexible, to avoid exposing yourself to devaluation, and to keep out of legal hassle. If after a few years in a country you insist—like I did—on buying a place to live, keep your total dollar investment as low as possible, certainly below $30,000.

INCOME TAXES

You'll maintain your U.S. citizenship abroad even if you officially become an overseas resident. U.S. citizenship is your ticket back to the United States when you want to return for a few days or a few years. But the United States is the only major country in the world that taxes all of its citizens' income, regardless of where those citizens live or the source of that income. You can live forty years in the south of France without returning to the United States. You can earn in francs, invest all your money in France, and forget how to speak English. But if you happen to be a U.S. citizen, after all that time you may still have to file annual U.S. tax returns.

Other countries have a territorial concept in their tax laws. Those countries let their citizens move away and forget about paying taxes "back home." Many countries don't pretend to tax their residents on interest income earned abroad. Not so in the United States. Uncle Sam spends most of your money to prepare for war or pay for past wars. The theory is that you benefit from that effort no matter where you live. If you benefit, you ought to pay.

Certain provisions in the U.S. tax law ease the burden. For example, in 1986 overseas residents could exclude $80,000 of income earned abroad. But those rules are for people who live, work, and earn abroad. They don't apply to a 40-year-old retiree whose only income is interest on CDs back in the United States. *Your* U.S. income tax return will look the same whether you live in Monterey, California, or Monterrey, Mexico. You'll have interest income, personal exemptions, the standard deduction, and tax due.

The good news is that most foreign countries will *not* tax your U.S. interest income. Even if you become a resident of the host country, you'll have no taxable income and should never have to file a tax return there. However, tax laws vary throughout the world, so you should check with a local adviser before applying for residency. Beware of residential status that makes you subject to local taxes on U.S. interest income.

INFLATION AND MONEY CHANGING

You'll want to keep your CDs in the United States, where they're guaranteed by a U.S. government agency. But what about inflation? You've heard of 25 percent *monthly* inflation in Argentina, 15 percent in Brazil, and 5 percent in Mexico. Those numbers frighten you. Won't things get very expensive very fast?

If the local currency devalues by the same amount as inflation, the answer is no. Suppose you live in Brazil and have your money in dollar CDs back in the United States. Suppose further that prices in Brazilian cruzados go up 15 percent in a given month. As long as the cruzado devalues by 15 percent against the dollar, your spending power remains the same. Your dollars buy enough additional cruzados to pay the higher prices. Inflation can go to 150 percent a month for all you care, as long as the cruzado devalues by the same amount.

Do inflation and devaluation move at the same rate? Many times they do. But every once in a while one can move faster than the other. If devaluation is greater than inflation, you gain. If inflation is greater than devaluation, you lose. If you lose for very many years in a row you could be squeezed. But Third World countries are so cheap you can withstand a squeeze. Suppose a dozen eggs goes from 10 cents to 20 cents. That's a whopping 100 percent increase—but it's still only a dime. Only if things get very bad—eggs go to $5 a dozen—will you have to move. Even in this extreme case you can expect to return after the inevitable currency crash.

Day in, day out, you'll be more pressed by money-changing than by inflation. To avoid having too many exposed pesos, cruzados, or australs in your pocket, you'll want to change small amounts of dollars into local money several times a month. In many countries you'll have to go to an exchange dealer to get a free-market exchange rate. The free-market rate is also called the black-market or parallel rate. In many countries both the official and free-market rates are published in newspapers. To find a reputable exchange dealer, ask a hotel clerk or someone else who seems reliable in the host country.

HEALTH CARE

America's fee-for-service health care costs a bundle. The *Economist* has found that "the American taxpayer . . . is paying between four and six times as much for the health care of his poorest and sickest aged fellow-citizens as the British taxpayer does." In 1984, health care cost $1,500 a head in the United States, an outrageous amount by international standards. In West Germany it cost $900, in France $800, in Japan $500, and in healthy Singapore only $200.

Whether Americans get value for all that money is another question. Newspapers tell of malpractice experiences that make us shudder: surgeons amputate the good arm or leg rather than the bad one; nurses mix up shots and kill people with injections. Europeans have a lower infant mortality rate and less infectious disease than Americans do. Life expectancy in low-cost Singapore is longer than in the United States.

Yet, some U.S. hospitals can provide state-of-the-art treatment for rare cancers or problem pregnancies. For brain surgery you go to New York, not Prague or Belgrade. For heart disease you go to Houston rather than Mexico City.

No wonder Americans are confused about health care abroad. It's confusing enough in the United States.

First, we need to define health and health care. When Americans talk about health care what we really mean is sickness care. Fee-for-service can do that to you. But health has more to do with diet, exercise, and state of mind than with fancy hospital equipment. I've explained how I gave myself a severe stomachache shortly after I retired. Some say that as much as 30 percent or more of illness is psychosomatic and that 70 percent or more has a psychosomatic component. Have the right attitude about your body and chances are you'll stay healthy and have better health care. It matters very little whether you're in Brazil or Boston.

Shortly after our move to Argentina, Vicki tripped and broke her foot in a small beach town three hundred miles from Buenos Aires. The local clinic set the bone but it proved unstable. The clinic doctor recommended surgery to put a pin through the bone and hold it in place. It sounded complicated. Should we fly back to Buenos Aires?

The clinic doctor found an "excellent" orthopedic surgeon vacationing nearby and brought him in. Vicki "interviewed" him—he didn't speak English and we were still trying to learn Spanish—and decided to go with him. He had studied in France and had been chosen by the Argentine army to operate on soldiers wounded in the 1982 South Atlantic war with England.

The operation started at 10:00 P.M. so that the surgeon could have a full day at the beach. The operating room had cobwebs on the ceiling. Novocaine was the only anesthesia available. The X-ray equipment looked like something from *M.A.S.H.* No nurses were around, so two clinic doctors assisted. Vicki said afterward the surgical team reminded her of the Three Stooges.

All went fine. We found out later, in Buenos Aires, that the surgeon had used a fairly advanced puncture technique. Was Vicki "just lucky"? We think not. Our experience is that Americans can find high-quality medical care abroad if they use good judgment, have the right attitude, and exercise a little caution.

The surgery, operating room, medicines, and follow-up care for Vicki's operation cost $400. Medical care in the United States may be good or not so good. But one thing's for sure: the cost will be exorbitant. Medical care in the Third World may be good or not so good. But one thing's for sure: the cost will be reasonable.

Remember that you're retiring overseas at age 35, not 65. You're less likely than an older person to require specialized medical care. If you do, you may be able to get it where you live. If not, you may have to return for expensive treatment in the United States. If that happens you could be ruined. But at your age, if you live abroad, it's probably a risk you can afford to take. When you're older you may want to buy health insurance in the United States, say with a $2,000 deductible, to cover the "worst case" contingency.

LEGAL PROBLEMS ABROAD

Stephen H. Collins wrote an article on the U.S. tort system in the November 1985 *Journal of Accountancy*. It began with this:

> Pick up a newspaper and one of the first stories to hit you involves a lawsuit. The weather bureau is sued because it fails to predict a storm, a lawn mower manu-

facturer is sued because its product is too hard to start, Little League baseball officials are sued because a player is hit by a fly ball, students sue teachers for failing to teach them adequately, children sue parents for improper upbringing, a restaurant critic is sued because of an unfavorable review, ad infinitum.

Last year, there was one private civil lawsuit filed for every 15 Americans. An estimated 16.6 million private civil suits were tried in Federal courts, nearly double the amount a decade ago.

One of the pleasures of moving overseas is leaving the U.S. tort system behind. Foreigners tend to work through tough issues rather than "sue the bastard." Foreign courts rarely see the kinds of absurdities the U.S. system must process.

But there are certain legal problems abroad. In much of the Third World your civil rights will not be protected to the extent you're used to. Civil rights mean little to dictators. In many countries you're considered guilty until proven innocent.

How do you keep out of trouble? Avoid politics and politicians. Avoid talking about politics and politicians. Avoid giving anyone the impression that you even think about politics and politicians.

Respect local laws and customs. In Milwaukee greasing a cop is a serious crime; smoking marijuana is a misdemeanor. Not so abroad. In Rio you'll see to it that your neighborhood cop gets a couple of bucks every once in a while. And smoking marijuana can get you 25 years in prison.

SOME PERSONAL ADVICE

After years of travel and living abroad, Vicki and I have come up with the Three Cs:

Don't criticize, complain, or compare

Don't criticize. Remember you're a guest in a foreign country. Guests don't criticize their hosts. Rather, they point out the good things.

Don't complain. Complaining is for children and losers. Winners are too busy enjoying themselves to complain about minor irritants. They roll with the punches and see the positive in what they find.

Don't compare. Comparing is almost always debilitating. It's one thing to tell me a steak is good, bad, overcooked, salty, or tender. I know what those terms mean. It's quite another to tell me a steak is better or worse than the one you had the night before. Or last year in Texas. Or ten years ago at the same restaurant. I wasn't with you last night, in Texas, or ten years ago. Whether you're comparing steaks, sculpture, weather, or cars, comparisons take *you* out of the here and now and offer *me* no insight. Do it often enough, and *you* lose touch with living day to day while *I* get frustrated.

The Three Cs may seem obvious, but they're quite hard to follow consistently. Trying is the key.

Another rule is:

Learn the language

We first found out how silly it is to insist on speaking English when, the week we moved to Buenos Aires, we had dinner with an American couple there. "The people here are so dull," the wife told us. "They never do anything except play bridge in the American Club and drink scotch." Later on in the evening Vicki asked her how her Spanish was.

"You don't need to speak Spanish in Argentina," the wife assured us. "Except in the supermarket, the people here speak English."

Move to a foreign country, insist on speaking English, and you'll wind up at the American Club playing bridge and drinking scotch instead of living the adventure of a foreign post. I suppose if you're 60 you might find it hard to pick up a new language. Then again, you might not. But at age 35 or 40 you have no excuse.

Besides learning the local language, you should eat local food, tell local jokes, hire local help, take local trains or buses, and bet local horses. Live like Brazilians and you may wind up having as much fun as they do.

Take Berlitz or something similar before you leave home. Once you arrive, continue with one-on-one training and add group classes. Groups introduce you to other newcomers and can help ease you through the transition.

A final rule is:

Go with the flow

When you arrive in a new country, check in to your hotel and then head out for a stroll. Look in the shop windows, buy a city map, wander through the markets and bakeries. Stop for coffee at a pleasant café. Pay special attention to the mundane. Are the sidewalks in good repair or do you have to watch where you step? How do the locals negotiate their way through the streets, and who gives way to whom? Do people and cars obey traffic signals?

When you observe carefully you sort of exchange a bit of yourself for a bit of your temporary home. Within an hour or two you'll begin to connect with your strange surroundings.

Enjoy the new and different. Vicki's first attempt to make Turkish coffee in our rented Yugoslav apartment ended with boiled coffee grounds all over the stove. But after a couple of tries she had it down. Change your eating and sleeping patterns to accommodate the local rhythm. Instead of eating dinner at 7:00 or 8:00 P.M., like in the United States, eat when the locals eat—at 5:00 P.M., 10:00 P.M., or whenever. Get up at 6:00 A.M. or 10:00 A.M., depending on the local customs.

An American we know moved to Argentina and tried to keep his American habits. Within a few months he had developed dangerously high blood pressure, a mental block against learning Spanish, and an irritable personality. He lived in his lonely hell for about a year before he decided to convert to the local way of life. By the middle of his third year his health was excellent, he spoke Spanish well, and he was enjoying himself for the first time since the move.

6.

When Does Retirement
Make Sense for You?

When I was a student at Occidental College, I helped the college data center design a new information system. As part of my job I had to meet with the college administrative heads and ask about their data needs.

My most memorable meeting was with Clancy, head of the food service. In 1986 I heard that Clancy had come out of retirement to whip the Occidental kitchen back into shape. But when I was a student there in 1970 she was already a legend. She kept thousands of us fed and healthy at a cost we could afford. Most important, she served things we liked. Students are a thankless lot. But most of us at the time agreed that Clancy was "all right."

I finally went to meet this sturdy, stout, gray-haired woman. After introducing myself I said something like, "We're computerizing the college's data systems. [Even back then I had a certain facility for using nouns as verbs.] We've already done the registrar and alumni offices. Now we want to start programming the food service."

Clancy's eyes bored through me like a locomotive through a

mountain tunnel. "Just remember one thing, young man." Then she paused and, very slowly, emphasized each word. "I'm against all change."

THE TWO-YEAR TEST

Most of us lack Clancy's eloquence, but we have a tough time handling change. I confess to feeling a slight twinge now and then when I adjust my watch from daylight to standard time. But retiring is one of life's major changes. It's scary. Few changes work out exactly the way we expect them to. What if we're making a mistake?

But there's one thing you can do right now to prepare for retirement. I don't care if you're 45 and plan to retire at 65. I don't care if you're flat broke. I don't care if George Steinbrenner has just asked you to manage the Yankees. I don't care if you're newly wed, closing on a new house, or about to cash in big stock options. I don't care if you've just received urgent phone messages from Lawrence Tisch and John Gutfreund asking you to take their jobs. Wherever you are on your private career path, there's something you can do right now to design good timing into your future:

Take the two-year test

To take the two-year test, consider that the rest of your life is two years. Would you change anything? If you had only two years to live, would you continue to work where you work? Live where you live? Treat your spouse and kids the way you treat them now? See your friends as often as you do now? Travel about as much as you do now? If you answer yes to those questions, change nothing. All you have to do is retake the two-year test in six months or so.

If you answer no to any of those questions—if you'd do something differently if you knew you were to die in two years—you need to reflect a bit. What has happened in your life that makes you want to change? What alternatives do you see? How can you get started in a new direction?

A childhood mentor I'll call Mac taught me the two-year test.

Mac was the father of my high-school flame. He's a jolly, playful guy who never bothered to grow up. He'd rather take his family to a Dodgers' game than to a church service. His idea of a good time is a Manhattan on the rocks, a slow barbecue, and an evening of bridge with friends. Mac calls most of the people on his block friends as well as neighbors. But he seems to enjoy anyone's company, as long as they know how to laugh.

One day Mac asked if I'd ride with him to UCLA Medical Center to visit his sick wife. During the one-hour ride he told me his wife could be dying of "Lou Gehrig's disease." He paused for about twenty minutes, then said something I had never heard before:

"She's lived every day of her life exactly the way she wanted to. If we learn tomorrow she's only got a year or two left, we won't change a thing. We've always lived as if each day were our last. Life's too short to live any other way."

Six years after that ride to UCLA I heard something similar at Stanford Business School. At Stanford we called it "living in the here and now." Living each day as if it were our *only* day allows us to let go of past prejudices and to free ourselves from doubts about the future.

Living in the here and now can be compared to how a composer writes a score. First, a composer gets an idea for a melody. Past successes and failures come into play only insofar as they resolve into the creative birth of melody *today*. Once the composer sets the melody, he chooses a form—prelude, etude, etc. The form represents a guide, an outline for the future, and frees the composer to concentrate on writing measures. He works on the technical: sound, harmony, and texture. Sometimes he surprises himself and decides to start over with a new form, based on a new way he hears his melody. The whole of the piece comes into being only when the final form (future) and melody (present) fuse into a score.

Like the composer, we must live life's melody *today*. But every once in a while we need to get out of our here-and-now focus to examine the "form." We need to look down the road to take stock, to make sure we're on the right path. The question is how far to look. Lining things up for "the rest of our lives" or "forever" seems a little much. I never know what to say, for example, when people ask if I'm going to live in Argentina

"forever," or if I'm going to stay retired "for the rest of my life."
How in the hell should I know? That's like asking a 5-year-old
where she wants to go to college.

But most of us can stretch our imagination two years out.
That's long enough to get a sense of direction in our lives. If we
don't like what we see, with two years ahead of us we have time to
change it.

Take the two-year test every six months or so. Consider your
leisure, your family, your hobbies, and your job two years out.
Will you still look forward to going to work in the morning? (Or at
least most mornings.) Will your work life continue to be rewarding? Will you still be able to grow?

If you answer yes to those questions you're on a roll. You're
living through one of life's best phases. You're no more ready to
retire than is a 27-year-old graduate from Yale Law School. Enjoy
the good times while they last.

If you take the two-year test and decide you're uneasy with
your job, you may need a job change. Talk about your options
with a headhunter or someone else you can trust. If you can't find
a new job that appeals, consider going for a second career. You
can go back to law school, open a hardware store, or buy a car
dealership. Most of us go through life with a job change or two.
Some of us make a career change or two.

But one day, and you may be 35 or 65, you'll look out two
years and get bored with the whole idea of work. You'll feel
burned out on the job—any job. You'll want to shake free from
the whole concept of work and get on with the rest of your life.

When does burnout hit? For me it came when I was in my
mid-30s. Some men—Sam Walton may be an example—seem
never to tire of work. But research shows that most people begin
to get bored and dissatisfied with work at about age 40.

A. J. Jaffe, at the Bureau of Applied Social Research of
Columbia University, has found that the mid-40s are the water-
shed of life. At age 40 "upward occupational mobility comes
largely to a halt. And therein lies one of the main problems . . .
In our society the lack of continued progress is tantamount to
failure." Not only the 40-year-olds but their employers seem to
sense the change at this point. Jaffe found that only a tiny handful
of managers get any real pay increases or promotions after age 40.

Horatio Alger stories taught that only the slothful burn out.

Hard chargers like Horatio Alger, you, and me could look forward to a life of exciting challenges and sweet fruits of success. But Nancy Mayer, in *The Male Mid-Life Crisis*, puts it succinctly: "Horatio Alger lied."

In the old days, those who found out about Horatio's big lie kept right on working. They had to. They needed a paycheck to live. Some lucky few with the money to retire were wise enough to do so. But most people were too set on the American dream, too envious of their neighbors, and too wrapped up in their drive for recognition to admit that something might be wrong.

Today's 40-year-old is better educated, more open to change, and richer. For perhaps the first time in history, millions of American men and women can retire when they want to rather than at "normal" retirement age. Many achievers, including those you read about in this book, retire before age 55. Thousands more are likely to do so in the next few decades.

Retirement isn't the only way to skate through the 40s crisis. But any solution must involve a radical change in beliefs, goals, your view of work, and even your way of life. Otherwise some very predictable things will begin to happen. Those things make trips to the dentist look like life's pleasure peaks.

The man who ignores age-40 burnout or refuses to change, Mayer says, soon "ignores his wife and screams at his children. He complains of boredom and fatigue, insisting his life has no meaning. He becomes increasingly detached, withdrawn, and introspective . . . High blood pressure develops and so do ulcers. Psychosomatic illnesses erupt: a man is suddenly beset by chronic fatigue, acute indigestion, mysterious backaches, painful joints, and migraine headaches. Every pain is a sign of cancer, every rapid heartbeat the precursor of a coronary."

It's nothing, I suppose, that 30 mg. of Valium can't take care of. But living that way can get to be a drag.

You can avoid that kind of fate if you prepare to retire when the two-year test shows that it's time. I'm not suggesting you storm into the boss's office and quit. You still have productive work years in you. You still enjoy going to work, and the company still treats you well. But the two-year test shows that your *future* work life excites you about as much as a frontal lobotomy. That's when you should slowly, deliberately begin to move toward retirement. During the day, work hard on the job. But at night and on weekends, work on your retirement. Prepare your to-do list. Cut your living expenses to as close to $50 a day as possible. Start bailing out of tax shelters and long-term financial commitments. And, most important:

Talk to others

to begin to identify with life after work.

TALK, TALK, TALK

Talk about retirement with those you trust. Their feedback gives you a new slant and helps you reexamine your decision. Talk with your shrink, if you're in therapy. At least you'll know you're not crazy. Talk to those business associates you're certain will be discreet. You need to be very careful here. You want to be the first to announce your retirement, not the last. But with careful "what if?" questions, you can broach the subject with a close business associate or mentor.

Most important of all, talk to your spouse. I use the word *spouse* for convenience; *partner* or *companion* may be better words. More than anyone, he or she can help change your view of the world. And, more than anyone, he or she needs to accept your new life—and probably start to think about retiring with you.

Vicki worked the first several years after we married. But she always supported and nurtured me in my career. She moved us across the country while I was away on business trips. She changed her plans when I called unexpectedly to tell her a visiting client or partner was coming for dinner. She put up with my childish outbursts when I was under stress. She helped me think through the toughest decisions I had to make. Throughout the work years she enjoyed my promotions and raises. My success was her success.

So, when I said I wanted to retire, I pulled the rug out from under her. I was proposing to toss away what we had achieved together. She felt cheated and angry. Her response was to take another look at her life. If I was going to be so fickle, she was going to have to worry a bit more about number one. She decided to pay more attention to what she wanted and less to what I wanted.

We had profound, heart-to-heart talks on every aspect of retirement. We reviewed our relationship, roles, and chores. At times we seemed about as compatible as Greeks and Turks. We needed most of two years to prepare for the changes we saw coming.

It was a trying time in our marriage. She wanted to stay close to home. I wanted to travel. She was set on continuing most of her old activities. I wanted her to retire and spend more time with me. She wanted to put her needs first. I wanted her to keep giving me the attention I was used to.

We made decisions and compromises. We decided, for example, to travel half the year and live in Buenos Aires the other half. We redivided the household chores. We decided to give up golf, a game Vicki found boring. I had played golf to relax away from the job. With no job to get away from, golf seemed a waste of time.

Little by little we worked through the changes. At the time, we weren't certain I was going to retire. If we couldn't settle some of the key issues, we could postpone our plans. That gave us a sense of control.

We finally concluded that retiring would be fun for both of us. I could fill my days with new interests. Freed from having to be a corporate wife, Vicki would have more time and energy for herself. We still had some doubts as to how we were going to spend our time. As I said in chapter 3, we never came up with a typical day, month, or year of retired life. Those specifics were too hard to imagine. But we had developed a to-do list to start things off. We had discussed the basics of our new life. And we were confident we could handle problems that would arise.

HELP FROM YOUR FRIENDS?

Besides your spouse, you should explain your retirement to your circle of extended family and friends. To the extent that "you attract what you are," friends mirror your views. That makes them especially good sounding boards.

Tell friends your ideas about retiring in simple, direct language. They won't put up with garbage like, "We've decided to metamorphose into a unique living situation that provides more opportunity for personal growth and interpersonal relationships."

Talk like that and your friends will think one of your faucets is leaking. Instead, tell them in a clear, concise way what you're doing and why. Something like, "We're retiring. We can afford it and want to goof off. So why not?" A clean statement like that will elicit questions and comments. Respond as honestly and openly as you can, for your sake as well as theirs.

Most of our friends reacted to our retirement idea with knee-jerk enthusiasm. "You lucky SOB. I envy you. I'd give anything to do what you're doing—just chuck it all out and sit on my butt for a while." But when they realized we were serious, they concluded that I needed very early retirement like I needed a solid dose of jungle fever.

Americans come down hard on nonconformists. We condemn those who challenge life's normal sequence of events. We are suspicious of people who dress, act, or talk funny. But to this day I'm surprised by the strong negative reactions of those closest to us.

One woman really ripped into me. She's a brilliant, high-energy executive. She laughs easily, and she's a good friend. I told her I planned to retire, and we discussed it for half an hour. I could see her heating up, but when she finally let me have it I was bowled over. "You're a gutless weasel," she sneered. "You reach a career plateau and fall apart. You want to quit. That's the reaction of a weak-kneed, yellow-bellied, chicken-livered coward."

Hey, give me a break!

She denies she ever said those things, but that's the way I heard her in my overly sensitive state. Others were more delicate. But almost all our American friends and family advised against very early retirement. The rule is:

Don't expect a little help from your friends

Why did friends react so vehemently? Some, like my friend, seem to view winning the career game as life itself. To them, retirement isn't an exciting chance to grow but a shameful rejection of life's most sacred contest. Others think being rich matters most. They refuse to make the sacrifices involved in living with less. Others have ethical or moral objections: one works; retiring is wrong. Still others feel threatened: the idea of retiring at age 35 challenges their purpose in life, the core of their daily routine; if we're not on this earth to work, what are we here *for?* Finally, many marvelous, intuitive people simply say, "Don't do it. I'm telling you, it just doesn't *feel* right."

Regardless of their reasons for rejecting our idea, we paid careful attention to our friends' advice. My good friend's reaction made me reconsider, for the ten-billionth time, whether I was doing something I would regret. We found helpful pearls of wisdom in even the most irrational outbursts. All of us have to make up our own minds about what we want out of life and whether our jobs are helping us get there. But comments from our friends—all comments—help us think more clearly.

Vicki concluded before I did that retirement made sense for us. But she was careful to let me make up my own mind. Rather than try to influence me, she just smiled and nodded when I told her my thoughts. She was wise enough to make sure I felt it was *my* decision and *my* responsibility.

There's a wonderful end to the story of how family and friends reacted. Once we retired, most were thrilled about the possibilities of our new life. Good friends are like that. They give you honest, straight feedback when you need it. Once you reach a decision, friends care only that the decision makes sense for you. Rather than stick with old opinions, they check to see that you're happy. That you still care about them. That you still want to hear about their promotions and successes on the job. That you don't assume, just because you retired, that it's right for everybody. That you still tell jokes and laugh at life's absurdities. That you still play with their kids. That you still lead active, exciting lives rather than sit around and do drugs. That you observe and learn rather than stare at a TV.

Now, most of our friends wonder why they opposed our retirement in the first place. It was something so right for us, why didn't they see it?

TIMING THE BIG STEP

When should you walk into your boss's office, close the door, sit down, and tell him you quit?

Timing is one of life's great crap shoots. When we change our lives we tremble inside, like a gunslinger in a new town trembles no matter how many targets he's hit. But since I retired in 1984 I've talked to perhaps twenty-five people about very early retirement. Five of those people have since retired. Those five taught me three things about timing.

First, the right time to retire comes after you've started mental preparations. That's why the two-year test is so important. The test helps you focus on whether and when you might want to break your present routine. Second, the right time to retire comes before you're fully ready. The key word here is *fully*. You'll always harbor some doubt when you make such an important change. Third, the right time to retire is fairly obvious when it happens. It sort of jumps up and bites you.

Let me tell the stories of the five newly retired people I know. In each case the timing seems to follow a natural course, from mental preparation to the big break.

Harold is 39 and single. He worked in an oil company's treasury department. Harold's a quiet, careful plodder rather than a high-charged superstar. He prefers to talk about his summers in the south of France than his next career move. While at the office he used to dream about living in Cannes, Antibes, or Saint Raphael full time rather than for four weeks in July.

Harold's break came in September 1986. The oil company announced a program to encourage senior employees to retire. Although only 39, Harold had been with the company two weeks longer than the minimum to qualify under the program. He needed to save a bit more to hit his target net worth, but he decided to accept the offer anyway. He sold his condo, blue Toyota, and quarter share of a ski cabin. He stuck his furniture in a friend's garage, his private papers in his mother's closet, and his clothes in a suitcase. Harold is quiet and careful no longer. He's as excited about his new life as a car dealer with next year's models.

Harold thinks he needs another $100,000 of net worth to stay retired for good. He plans to try the south of France for three years and see how his money holds out. Later on, he can go back to work or move to cheaper Spain or Portugal.

*   *   *

Sarah is 48. One morning fifteen years ago she woke up in her Westchester home and found her husband had abandoned her and their three kids. Within a week she had two jobs—the first two jobs of her life—and took in boarders. For fifteen years she worked to put her kids through school and keep peanut butter on the table. And over those fifteen years her home equity grew to half a million dollars.

The turning point came last year when Sarah's "baby" graduated from college. Sarah decided she had reached her limit of fifteen- and twenty-hour days. She quit both jobs, cashed out of the big house, put the money in the bank, and packed up. She headed first for South America, where her son works at an archaeological dig. I hope she writes to tell me where she goes next. Vicki and I might try to meet up with her.

Perry is 54, married, and has a daughter in college and a 14-year-old son at home. He was president of the Brazil subsidiary of a New York bank. Three years ago I called his office and was told he was at home with a stomachache. I called home and was told he was in the hospital with arrhythmia. Perry was glad to see me when I showed up at the hospital, but he swore me to secrecy. Not even his secretary knew his real problem was with his heart. If anyone in the company learned the truth about his health, he could be passed over for promotion.

I told him he was 54 and should think about retiring rather than the next promotion. He looked at me the way he might look at someone who had just suggested he jump off the Golden Gate Bridge. He figured he would work eleven more years, to age 65. He had a big house, young children to support. How could he retire?

Two weeks later I went back to the hospital. Perry told me he had been reflecting a little. His father and brother had died in their 50s. One died in his office, the other on the golf course with a client. Perry said he didn't want that kind of fate. Who says you need another promotion? Who says you have to work until age 65? You could be dead by age 65.

Once back at work, Perry thought more about retiring. He added up his net worth, talked to his wife and children, and mused about what he might like to do. He discovered he really didn't need any more money. He found out his 14-year-old was desperate to move back to the United States and saw his wife weep tears of joy when she heard of the idea.

The break came when the home office decided to close Perry's Brazilian operation. Perry was offered jobs in Mexico or Argentina or an early retirement package. He went for the retirement deal the way an eagle swoops to grab its prey.

Lyle is 38, married for the second time, and has no children by either marriage. Lyle's a tough, tireless, hands-on manager. Since taking an M.B.A. from Wharton in 1972 he's changed jobs five times. Each was a calculated move dictated by his private game plan. In his most recent incarnation he was a $200,000-a-year president of a Cleveland-based auto-parts subsidiary. He traveled four days a week from office to office, customer to customer.

Shortly after taking his new job Lyle told me he was wearing himself out at work. He planned to retire as soon as he had a million dollars. I suggested that a lower amount would do, but Lyle felt he would have to sacrifice too much. And anyway, he'd have the million in three or four years.

A short time later, in 1986, he rubbed a new boss the wrong way and got fired. What to do?

In general, getting fired is probably a lousy way to retire. When you get fired you can lose your self-confidence and feel degraded or humiliated. The last thing you want to do is give up. You want to grab another job and hit back with all you've got. You want to prove that the boss was wrong.

But Lyle is a special case. He has a strong ego. He had prepared himself for retirement. He hadn't achieved his target net worth, even after adding his severance pay. But with a few minor changes in lifestyle he could retire with less.

When Lyle got fired, his wife, Elaine, was a doctor in a Cleveland hospital. She had started her job six months before. She wanted to stick with it for a few years. The original idea had been for Lyle and Elaine to retire together, say in 1990. But when Lyle got fired it ruined their plans.

They decided Lyle would retire and Elaine would keep working. That was in 1986, and so far they're thrilled with the new arrangement. Lyle plays golf, manages their investments, and sits by the pool and reads. He's begun to tackle some of the items on his to-do list. With no more business trips, for the first time in their marriage he and Elaine see each other every evening.

Lyle and Elaine believe they're in transition. Lyle may go back to work, at least part time, until Elaine feels ready to quit. Elaine may decide to quit sooner than planned. In the meantime, there's more joy in their lives than ever before.

Maggie is 42, divorced, and has two children living with her ex-husband. She's hyper and high-powered. Before she retired she ran public relations for a Chicago-based engineering company. She enjoyed it but never had time for her true love: architectural history. As a student she used to enjoy travel because it gave her a chance to see new buildings. Each business trip seemed more hurried than the one before. She hardly had time to take pictures of the buildings she loved, much less get to know them.

About a year ago several things happened at once. First, she started to get threatening phone calls. She told the security people at work about the calls but they could do nothing. The calls kept coming, and each time the voices seemed more desperate. Next, she collected a big block of company stock options. For the first time in her life, Maggie enjoyed a substantial net worth. Finally, an architectural magazine asked her to contribute some articles on nineteenth-century English country homes.

Maggie retired. The last time I saw her she had been traveling continuously for about a year, studying buildings and taking pictures. She was preparing for a Chicago trade show where she could show her work. She was still hyper but not high-powered. She confessed to me that, in her darkest self, she feels she wouldn't be alive today if she had kept her job.

Maggie is somewhat curious because she refuses to control her expenses. She retired with about $500,000, mostly in stocks. Instead of buying CDs in 1985, like I suggested, she put her money in the stock market. The stocks proceeded to double and triple in value. Maggie could be a millionaire by now, but she spends lavishly. She travels first-class. She goes to expense-account restaurants without an expense account. She has a big heart and in her first retired year probably gave away a third of her net worth.

I offered to help her prepare a budget, but she's too busy to budget. She may run out of money one day. On the other hand, with her luck in the stock market she may wind up buying a couple of those nineteenth-century English country homes she loves.

The last retirement-timing story is my own. The notion of retiring popped up in my two-year test when I was 33. Vicki and I started working through the idea and became convinced that it made sense. We were a little short of our target net worth when Peat Marwick eliminated the job I had held for four years and offered me a transfer to Los Angeles.

Vicki and I like Los Angeles. I was born there, Vicki and I met in college there, and we have family and friends there. But Los Angeles has some of the highest housing costs in the nation. The idea of buying a $500,000 home and two new cars appealed as much as a proctosigmoidoscopy.

I could have requested a move someplace else. But I had already decided to retire. Why push for a special transfer, work to know new clients and build working relationships, and then quit? Life's too short to waste my time and everyone else's. I decided to take the plunge while the timing was good but not perfect.

HANDLING CHANGE

You retire and wake up that first morning with everything and yet nothing to do. You can stay in bed or get up. You can go to a movie or paint the house. You can go to the library or to Tibet.

But therein lies a problem. When you can do what you want, you don't always know what you want. Sorting through the possibilities can cause stress and worry.

Alvin Toffler's *Future Shock* came out in 1970. *Future Shock* popularized the conclusion that change makes us sick. Change can give us migraines, aching backs, diarrhea, ulcers, heart attacks, and nervous breakdowns. The direction of the change matters very little. The change itself—any change—takes a mental and physical toll. A divorce torments only slightly more than a marriage. Death and birth go opposite ways, but both cause stress. Getting fired causes concern, but so does getting a new job.

Dr. Thomas H. Holmes of the University of Washington put together a 100-point scale of major changes in our lives. Death of a spouse is 100—life's most traumatic change. Divorce is 73. Getting married is 50, and getting back together again is 45. Getting fired is 47 and retiring is 45. And so on down the list. Score over 300 in any twelve-month period, Dr. Holmes found, and you have an 80 percent chance of winding up on your back within two years. To put it another way, when you lose control of your life, you get sick.

One way to get control of your life is to retire. After a few months your retired life settles into a rhythm, and you feel more in control than you ever thought possible.

But before you hit that rhythm you face a transition, a draining period of choosing between options. Every day brings the unknown, the untried, and the unusual. You need to commit yourself to weaving through the possibilities. You need to:

Manage the change

Toffler defines "future shock" as what we feel in the face of great change. "Future shock absorbers" help us get through it.

One future shock absorber is to view change as a normal, routine part of life rather than as the exception. We tend to view life as a sequence of periods of stability interrupted by windows of change. Toffler says we're better off to view life as a sequence of periods of change interrupted by windows of stability. With this view, change becomes the norm and is easier to handle.

Another future shock absorber is to keep something stable in our lives. Simple items like a favorite coffee cup, grandma's necklace, or a notebook can make us feel at home in a sterile hotel room. We should refuse, when practicable, to buy throwaway clothes, disposable cigarette lighters, paper plates, and the like.

Another future shock absorber is to anticipate and identify with change. The two-year test helps you do that. You look out two years, imagine yourself retired, and begin to design the type of life you want. That gets you talking to your spouse and friends and imagining the new life. When retirement day comes, you're ready.

Perhaps the best shock absorber is to keep from having to handle too much change at one time. Sometimes the timing of life's change is outside our control. We must accept the death of a loved one when it happens, for example, rather than when it might be convenient for us. We must accept a tax increase when Congress dictates, rather than when we're flush. Most of us must move when we retire, rather than wait a few years.

But we *can* control a great deal of change in our lives. The example is a coed who turns 22, gets married, moves to a new city, buys a house, and starts her first job, all in June of the year she graduates from college. With that much change it's not a question of whether she'll get sick but when. Neither the career nor the marriage has much of a chance. She would be better off to graduate and move, take the summer off, and then start the new job. The marriage and house purchase can wait until she feels settled at work.

Remember Lyle, my friend who got fired a few years before he was going to retire? I suggested that getting fired was a lousy way to retire. Dr. Holmes's point scale explains why. Getting fired is 47 points and retiring is 45. Do them both at the same time and you're up to 92. Move out of the old neighborhood, start living with less, and begin to travel, and that 92 jumps to 200 or so. Toss in some external change beyond your control—the death of a parent, for example, or a lawsuit—and you're approaching the deadly 300 number. Remember, the closer you get to 300, the more likely you are to become seriously ill.

When you retire you should work solely on retiring. If you can possibly help it, avoid adding other change to your life. Chapter 4, for example, tells how to avoid writing a big check to the IRS when you sell your home. That kind of trauma can really sock you when your life is already full of financial unknowns. You should also postpone getting a vasectomy, training for a marathon, getting married, chairing your town's United Crusade, or starting a course in the Zen of junk bonds. You should even postpone tackling the items on your to-do list. Instead, fill your days with the things you used to do after work and on weekends. Read, swim, play golf, watch TV, sleep late, go for a drive, and have barbecue parties. Take it easy on yourself for the first time in two decades. The rule is:

Fill your new days with old activities

When you follow this rule, don't worry about getting your new life under way. Dawdle. You're not lazy, you're just managing change. Dawdle for three or four or six months if you like. Fall into your new life with an easy, relaxed roll. You've got thirty or more years of active retired life ahead of you. That's plenty of time to accomplish what you have in mind. Take the first few months to relax a little. You deserve it.

7.

Retirement's First Few Years

One June, Vicki and I were at a backyard barbecue in Evanston, Illinois. One of the guests had just flown in from New York.

"What do you do in New York?" someone asked her.

She said, "I'm vice-president of marketing and merchandising at Fashion Center."

I turned to our host and raised my eyebrows.

He said, "She sells bras."

SO WHAT DO YOU DO?

America's favorite cocktail-party line is "What do you do?" How we ask and answer can reveal more than ten years with a psychotherapist.

Not so abroad. When foreigners go to a party they typically talk about the party: the music, how the food is presented, the paintings, sculpture, and decorations on the walls. To get to know you, foreigners ask about your last vacation, your children, your favorite restaurants, or where you live. They're much more likely to ask what you do on weekends than what you do on weekdays.

But in America we routinely kick off with "what do you do?"

When I was a Peat Marwick partner I often found myself in very short cocktail-party combats. They went something like this:

"Hi, I'm John. Harvard M.B.A., Citicorp, Park Avenue, Mercedes, smart shrink, pretty wife, jog, ski, read Shakespeare without cheat notes. How about you? What do you do?"

"I'm an auditor."

John would then spin on his heel and dart across the room in search of someone more fun to play with.

When people ask what I do, I say, "I'm retired." Some change the subject at that point, but few spin on their heels and walk away. For those who inquire further, I add, "I know I'm a little young to be retired. But except for my age, I'm retired in every sense of the word. I do all the things retired people do."

"What do you do?" really means "where do you work?" or "how do you make your living?" Those are tricky questions when you're retired. A 42-year-old retiree recently told me, "I don't tell people I'm retired anymore. They figure I lie around the house and eat all day. That's not my idea at all."

RETIREMENT, A FOUR-LETTER WORD?

In Buenos Aires one day I was sitting at the large lunch table at the American Club. One of the people at the table had just moved to Argentina, and a club member was telling him a little about each person there. "George Catson, to your left, is president of IBM Argentina. The next guy, Bill Fernandez, is in charge of production at Ford." And so on. But I noticed something curious when the host introduced the table's retirees. Eager not to offend, apparently, he introduced them with what I call "retired, but." As in, "Harry, there, was president of Kodak Argentina. He's retired, but he just opened an art gallery with his son-in-law. Next to him is Art, the former head of General Motors. He's retired now, but he's trying to get a parts distributorship. Bob, there, is retired from Firestone, but he's helping his son-in-law open a restaurant."

The host seemed reluctant to "admit" that anyone was retired—until he got to me. He looked my way, paused, and then said, "Paul, there, he's really retired. He travels, plays the saxophone, goes to the beach for three months at a time, writes novels, goes to parties, and generally goofs off. I mean, he's retired retired."

The new arrival turned to me and raised his eyebrows. All retirees except me were over 60 years old. Yet, I was the only one "retired retired."

Why was the host embarrassed to introduce people as "retired"? I think it's because "retired" has come to mean "nonproductive." The club member was too polite to call anybody names. But consider what Americans call productive. Make napalm, grow tobacco, distill whiskey, or sell handguns and you're productive. Sign forms for the government, hype toothpaste, collect tolls on a bridge, or play pro ball and you're productive. Retire and you pass to nonproductive status. Whether you write, sing, play golf, travel, or meditate makes no difference. You're still retired. And that seems to define your role in life.

In Spanish, people who work form society's *sector activo*, or active sector. Retired people belong to the *sector pasivo*, or passive sector.

Pretty blunt. Also pretty wrong. Retired young people I know are proud to be retired. We view retirement as a move from one active sector of society to another. When we retire we feel we do more, not less. We believe that what we are or do defines our lives rather than what we earn or how we earn it. We think 1950s beatniks, 1960s hippies, 1970s dropouts, and 1980s drug addicts are losers. We're winners. We had successful, reasonably lengthy careers and made some dough. Now we're active, vibrant people who want to do other things.

I suspect that many 60- and 70-year-old retirees feel the same way.

LIVING A PASSION

I recently met a 41-year-old retiree who keeps so busy he rarely has time to look at his to-do list. He had run a division of a waste-management company, "the world's largest garbage collector." When I met him he had been retired for just over a year.

"So what do you do?" I asked. (Some questions never change.)

He shook his head. "I'm so busy I sometimes feel I should go back to work to relax. When I had a job I prepared ninety-day plans for myself, updating them every month or so. I have to do that now to keep track of my activities."

Why is he so busy? This man's passion is postal history

related to diamonds. He's spent twenty years running around the world collecting stamps, envelopes, postmarks, and postcards related to diamonds. He claims to have the world's finest collection of that type, and I believe it. For all I know he could have the world's only collection of that type.

He retired to complete the collection, prepare it for display, get it photographed, and put it on exhibit. In the past year he's been on one continuous collecting trip. He's lived on rice and beans for weeks in small Brazilian diamond-mining towns. He's been to auctions in Frankfurt and Singapore. He's wandered through junk shops in Tahiti, Ecuador, and South Africa.

He also finds time to play the clarinet, collect South American paintings, and write short pieces about his travels. "When I first retired," he says, "I had vague ideas of what I wanted to do. The ideas didn't crystallize until I got going on them. After a while I realized I couldn't do nearly all the things I had hoped to. Now I keep huge file folders with things I want to do, just like when I worked. Maybe someday I'll get to them all."

MY FIRST TWO YEARS

People sometimes ask what I do all day, as in, "So how do you keep from going crazy?" So I tell them. Maybe it's time I told you too.

I grew up in a Los Angeles suburb where most of the other kids came from richer families than I did. I paid attention to what money could and could not do. Money couldn't buy good grades, I noticed, or a home run in the bottom of the ninth. Money couldn't keep your best friend from breaking his neck in a freak diving accident. Money couldn't keep people from complaining or yelling at you.

But money *could* rent a beach house. More than ice cream, Dodgers' games, or a shiny bicycle, when I was small I decided life's best thing would be a beach house. I figured our family came pretty close. Every August we took our house trailer to the state campgrounds at San Clemente or Doheney Beach. Besides my mother, father, grandfather, sister, and three brothers, my aunts, uncles, and cousins poured into the campground as well. The men commuted to work while the rest of us ran up and down the beach, rode the waves, fished, or played ball. At night we'd sit around a small fire and sing. The last Saturday night of the season we'd cook T-bones on an outdoor grill. Man, that was living.

As I grew up I started to dream a little. What would be better than a house trailer? A beach house. What would be better than August at the beach with those you loved the most? A whole summer at the beach with those you loved the most. What would be better than commuting to work? Staying at the beach all week long. What would be better than a steak on Saturday night? A steak anytime you wanted one.

I thought it was a good dream—I still do—and when I retired I decided the first thing to do was live it. When I retired in late 1984, Vicki and I headed for the beach in Pínamar, Argentina. (Remember, summer comes in January, February, and March in the southern hemisphere.) We rented a comfortable two-bedroom apartment a block from the water. Throughout the summer, friends came down from Buenos Aires to stay with us for three days to a week. I was retired, in my own beach house, all summer long with the person I loved most, without having to commute back to a job. I had a freezer full of Argentine beef. Man, that was living.

In March 1985, we returned to Buenos Aires. I started work on my second novel, kept up my sax lessons, and met old business associates for lunch. After lunch they returned to the office. I went to a movie, to a museum, the zoo, or home for a siesta.

In May we went to Spain and visited ten different cities in three months. We became amateur experts in Spanish history and bullfights. We learned to cook paella, beans, and fried fish. After three months in Spain we flew to the United States to visit family and friends. We started in New York and then flew to Los Angeles, San Francisco, Portland, and northern Washington State. In November 1985, after six months abroad, we returned to Argentina. We spent the summer in Punta del Este, across the river in Uruguay.

By March 1986, I was ready to sink my teeth into something more solid. I enrolled in a six-week Skills Development Program at the Berklee College of Music in Boston. The program started on July 7, 1986. Before going to Boston, we spent a month touring the southeastern United States. We soaked up southern hospitality, talked about the Civil War, saw the sights, and checked out inexpensive places to live.

The Berklee course in Boston improved my sax and opened my mind to different kinds of music. After two months there we were ready for another trip, so we flew back to Europe. We wandered through Hungary and Yugoslavia for six weeks. The idea was to see some commies up close. *Time* magazine had just done a cover story on Hungary, affirming that Hungary since 1956 has been the biggest economic success in the Soviet bloc. Budapest is a beautiful city, with well-dressed but sad people. We loved Yugoslavia, especially the clear water of the northern Adriatic. We felt welcome and were told that Americans can retire there with ease.

We returned to Buenos Aires in late 1986 to write and enjoy our third summer as retirees. Summer is vacation time for us. I said in chapter 2 that one concern about retiring was that I might never enjoy a vacation again. What do I have to vacate from? But our retired lives have settled into a rhythm. When in Buenos Aires we read, write, go to parties, talk with friends, linger over coffee, take walks, play the sax, sing in a choir, go to museums or zoos, watch TV, and go to plays. When summer comes we're ready to break that rhythm. We're ready to flop on the beach and enjoy vacations as much as ever.

In February 1987, we moved to Mexico's Yucatán peninsula for two months. Vicki and I are both interested in history and anthropology. We climbed through Mayan ruins and fantasized about living there fifteen hundred years ago. We decided to try to volunteer for an archaeological dig, probably somewhere in Mexico or Central America.

When we plan trips, Vicki and I both make sure we have our own reasons for going. Vicki's reasons may coincide with mine: watching bullfights in Spain, relaxing on the beach in Punta del Este, or crawling around ruins in the Yucatán. But she also pursues her own interests. For example, Vicki does energy-balancing massages and sound healing. While I was in Boston at Berklee, she learned new techniques in the Cambridge Healing Resource Center.

MY FRIEND SAM

My two mentors—the two who taught me most about retiring young—are Sam and Nick. Their stories help illustrate what to do and not to do during retirement's first few years.

You heard about Sam in chapter 1. He taught me the $50-a-Day Rule. He was 42 years old and chief financial officer of a Houston oil company when his work life tore him apart. He took a leave of absence, went to Europe with his family, and had a ball. Once back in Houston, he added up what he had spent and backed into the $50-a-Day Rule. He went to his old boss and resigned.

For the first few months of retirement Sam got reacquainted with old Houston friends. He played golf, relaxed by the pool in his backyard, read Kierkegaard, and painted still lifes in his small studio behind the garage. Sam followed the rule:

Fill your new days with old activities

Three months into his retirement, Sam made his first mistake. He went back to work as a consultant for his old company. Sam told me about it later.

"The chairman called me at home and insisted that I help him with a first-ever strategic plan. He was very flattering. 'I need someone independent, from the outside, but who knows the company. You've got the experience, the vision, you're uniquely qualified, blah, blah, blah.' I fell for it.

"It turned out to be a disaster. Others on the project saw me as an interloper. They were polite but ignored my ideas. I could have gone to the chairman for support, but I wasn't up for a fight. I figured it was their company, they could do what they wanted.

"It got worse and worse. I was half-working, half-retired, and unhappy in both. I could feel myself becoming tense and irritable for the first time since retiring. But I saw no graceful way out of the project before it was finished. That took six months, perhaps the worst six months of my retired life.

"At least it won't happen again," Sam concluded ruefully. "The chairman and staff over there hate me now."

Sam's experience is worth a rule:

Make a clean break

During the first few months of retirement you'll likely receive job offers. That's when your business associates hear about your new life and have your name fresh in their minds. They'll invariably come up with something you can do. In my case I got an inquiry from Washington, D.C., within a week of resigning from Peat Marwick. The job was a lower-level presidential appointment in the Treasury Department. A week after that an American firm called to see if I wanted to represent their products in Argentina. I was tempted to follow up. But I believe it would have been a mistake. Part of retiring is breaking the old work habit. That takes time. You'll never know what a good thing you've got going if you give it up after a month and go back to work.

My friend Sam recovered from his consulting disaster and decided to learn something about political campaigns. He drove to a campaign headquarters in a small town south of Houston, met the candidate, and signed up. His first job was doing phone solicitations, but after two weeks Sam began to take over day-to-day operations. He checked that prepaid ads ran as scheduled, called people to get them to donate restaurants and clubs for rallies, arranged coffee meetings in people's homes on Sunday mornings, and got posters printed.

Sam thoroughly enjoyed himself, but the candidate lost, and Sam went knocking around for something else to do. That's when he made his second mistake. He bought retail space in a shopping center in northern Houston and leased it to others.

"Looking back on it, I think I wanted an anchor in my life," Sam told me. "The anchor used to be my job. I identified with being chief financial officer of an oil company. When I retired I needed something to replace that anchor. Real estate is tangible, physical, something I could relate to. Besides that retail space, I considered buying other real estate: a new house, farmland, and a mansion in West Texas. I managed to keep from doing so. But in total I probably lost $60,000 on the retail space. Stupid."

The rule is:

Avoid making major purchases for two years

Sam feels so strongly about this rule that he told me to write it out and sign it when I retired. "I, Paul Terhorst, won't make major purchases for two years." I decided to go even farther. I turned control of our assets over to Vicki. She has more common sense than I do.

Sam's prediction came true. Shortly after retiring I came up with "great deals" everywhere I looked: a farm in Paraguay, a larger apartment in Buenos Aires, a home in Punta del Este. Vicki had the good sense to smile and, if I persisted, laugh at my ideas.

Sam believes you need only $300,000 to retire comfortably. "Put it in the bank and live off the interest. Don't worry about inflation. If the interest runs out, live off the principal. You'll never exhaust the principal before you die—as long as you stay away from hard assets."

The last time I saw Sam he was back in politics. On his most recent campaign he had assumed a policy role for the first time. He and his wife had had another baby, something they had been trying to do for nineteen years without success. And Sam was back at work full time, putting in eighteen-hour days, working harder than ever. Why?

Sam says one reason is the baby. He thinks he should fulfill the role of a working father while the baby's young. A second and, I suspect, more important reason is the job itself. Sam consults to a Houston newspaper about their marketing and ad sales. He helps the paper grow. He works with the directors and is getting to know Houston's movers and shakers. He accompanies writers when they interview important people. "I'm totally wrapped up in it," he told me. "I have no idea how long it will last, or where it will take me. I can't keep up the pace forever. But right now I'm having a ball."

The rule is:

Go back to work if you feel like it

Retirement is breaking the work habit and arranging your affairs to live off unearned income. As long as you *feel* retired and can live off unearned income, you're retired. I think you should settle in during a transition period and then concentrate on your to-do list for a minimum of two years. That way you'll develop a comfortable rhythm in your new life. But you can go back to work whenever you feel like it, full or part time, in two years or two decades.

MY FRIEND NICK

My second mentor, Nick, just turned 50. He was born in Albany, prepped at Groton, majored in history at Dartmouth, and spent two years in the army. During breaks he relaxed at the family estate in upstate, New York, or wandered through Latin America with Colombian friends from Groton.

Once his stint in the army was over he moved to Latin America for good. He tried Spain, Italy, and Yugoslavia before settling in the Costa del Sol. He now lives in a five-bedroom, view apartment in Marbella with his French wife, 16-year-old son, 10-year-old daughter, two maids, two dogs, three toucans, and anyone else who happens to be in town. That last category includes writers, artists, producers, actors, dancers, sculptors, museum curators, art dealers, and politicians. Anyone, it seems, except businessmen. Nick has few friends in business, perhaps because he's never been in business himself. To the outside observer, Nick's never worked at all.

"That's not true," he said when I asked him about it. "You just think I don't work because I don't spend much time working. But I buy things and sell things. I own a bookstore. At one time or other I've owned a restaurant, art gallery, hotel, and real estate company. It's just that I never run the businesses myself. I don't want them to interfere with my life."

Nick's a trader, a twentieth-century *marchand*. He buys in one market and sells in another. He has simple ideas on how to make money, like "buy low, sell high."

"If I'm in New York and see an undervalued painting, I'll buy it. It may sell better in Paris than in New York. The next time I go to Paris I'll take the paintings and sell them. I may go to Paris in six months or in six years. So I need pretty good margins when I sell."

Does he make enough money to live?

"My apartment is paid for," he told me. "To buy it I sold a Picasso painting I had picked up in Paris when I was a kid. My car is a piece of junk. My only expenses are food, the maids, clothing, school supplies for the kids, and incidentals. I figure I spend $1,800 a month, a little over $20,000 a year. I can make that much by selling just one painting."

Is Nick retired? Since he never set out to work in an organized way, the idea of breaking the work habit never came up. He has no office, secretary, stationery, or any of the trappings of the modern businessman. Whether he does a deal in a given week, month, or year means nothing. With his low expenses— just over $50 a day—he feels little pressure to make deals happen.

Nick's father inherited the family business and sold it at age 34. Dad lived on the income for the rest of his life. Perhaps it's Dad's influence, but Nick thinks not working is more natural than working. "I can't understand why so-called liberated women want to bash their way into the executive suite. Working at the office all day is the most unliberating thing anyone can do. To lead a rich, fulfilling life you need to free yourself from the job, not enslave yourself to it."

When he's at home in Marbella, Nick gets up at about 11:00 A.M. to answer the phone. The caller is likely to get invited to lunch or dinner. Nick then pulls on a pair of swimming trunks and heads to the beach, writes a letter to a friend from college, works up an article on a current art exhibit for an English-language newspaper, or runs personal errands. At about 2:00 P.M. he returns home for lunch, a leisurely, two-hour affair with guests from Mexico City, New York, New Delhi, or wherever. In the afternoon Nick may take photographs of pollution around Marbella, research a word processor he wants to buy, plan the family's next overseas trip, play tennis, watch his son's soccer game, visit a friend in an old folks' home, or arrange for an art gallery to invite an American sculptor to visit. Dinner is a repeat of lunch, with different guests and hours of leisurely talk. After dinner Nick reads a book, watches TV, or relaxes with his family.

SO YOU WANT TO BE RICH?

If you're a bare-bones retiree (chapter 11), you'll most likely do some part-time work after you retire. You'll need the money. But for the rest of you, whether you earn any money after retiring is purely a matter of choice. I think it's perfectly noble and valid to retire young and never earn another dime the rest of your life. When I retired that was my idea, and I still think it's a good one. On the other hand, some of your retirement activities may earn you some dough. It seems silly to reject an activity just because you might make some money at it.

Your first two years of retirement should be a clean break from your old life. After that you can be more objective in evaluating offers and options. You may decide to go out and look for part-time work in your old profession. But, assuming you choose to work, you're probably more likely to want to try something new. Turn a hobby into a business, start a software company, or make movies. Build a small lab in your garage and invent a new building material. Speculate in commodity futures. Start a plumbing business with your children. Any number of things can make you money. Some may even make you rich.

My friend Chambers Tate taught me how one becomes very rich. Chambers, now 42, spent ten years starting businesses that failed. At various times he's had a chain of bookstores, a suburban produce market, an engineering consulting firm, and a mail-order catalog. He drove them all into the ground. He finally stopped creating companies and started showing others how to avoid the mistakes he made. He now works with entrepreneurs, helping them with "anything they're bad at." He seems to have found a niche. He works two weeks a month and hauls in close to half a million dollars a year. His stock options alone are enough to make a Silicon Valley junkie green with envy.

Chambers lives in Southern California with his wife, four sons, and enough off-road vehicles to keep a Boy Scout troop amused for decades. During his off weeks each month, he and his sons race around the grounds of their Laguna Hills mansion in clouds of fumes and dust.

Chambers can rattle off ideas for exciting new ventures as easily as most of us tell time. He may be playing pool in his billiard room, flying his antique Piper Cub, or polishing his

Honda 1000 when an idea hits him. One day he was staining a table in his basement when he told me, "The next generation will be digital X-ray machines. Digital images are sharp and precise, far better than the dull, fuzzy, shadowy X-ray photos we're used to. Imagine what a surgeon could learn from a clear, detailed picture of a brain tumor and its surrounding tissue. The machines would be cheaper and safer than anything on the market today. Doctors would have small ones in their offices. Hospitals would have fancy ones for more complicated shots." Once Chambers has the germ of an idea, he moves to the details: how to get the best technology; how to test a prototype; why doctors would go nuts over the thing.

By the time he's finished, I'm clutching my checkbook, desperate to go out and try it.

One day I asked Chambers if he ever worries about someone stealing his ideas. He shook his head. "To turn a good idea into a business you need two things: capital and time. Anyone can come up with some capital. But almost no one has the time. I know I don't. We're hustling to make a buck selling cars, making soap, or suing people. We're riveted on the next promotion, transfer, or raise. We work to pay off a new sailboat rather than to pile up enough dough to carry us through a start-up. At the end of the day we're worn out, exhausted by constant pressure. Our minds aren't likely to spark with the creativity one needs to start a potential billion-dollar business."

Chambers has hit on a paradox. For most of us, working keeps us from becoming rich. When we work we spend time and energy on defined tasks. For that effort we can make $50,000 or $200,000 or more each year. But to become very rich one needs to work not on defined tasks but on new concepts. H. Ross Perot, Sam Walton, Carl Icahn, and Peter Ueberroth made their fortunes by looking at products and markets in new, creative ways. They became very rich by observing and imagining.

It takes luck as well as creativity and imagination to make a billion dollars. But to get yourself into a position to make "big" money, you probably need to stop chasing after "little" money.

Perhaps the best example of what I'm talking about is Joseph P. Kennedy, Sr., the president's father. In the 1920s Kennedy amassed a tidy sum running a Boston bank, mixing in show business, and playing the stock market. In 1929 he had the foresight, or luck, to sell out before the Depression wiped out paper gains. In 1934 he became the first chairman of the SEC and, later, ambassador to the Court of St. James.

At the end of World War II, Mr. Kennedy was out of both business and politics. He retired to mansions in New York, Cape Cod, and Palm Beach. According to *The Founding Father*, by Richard J. Whalen, Kennedy's "life in Florida was pleasant and well ordered. On a typical day, he awoke about seven, ate breakfast in his room, and read his mail and several newspapers before going downstairs around nine-thirty. From mid-morning until noon, he basked in the sun beside the pool, conducting his far-flung businesses by long-distance telephone. Lunch included a special dessert to appease his sweet tooth. Afterward he usually took a half-hour nap, then played a round of golf."

So what happened to Kennedy during this semiretired life? He became super-rich. "I really began to make money," he once told a friend at poolside, "when I came down here to sit on my butt and think." He invested primarily in real estate and oil. And he made more money than during all his work years combined.

Son-in-law Stephen Smith still manages the family fortune the way Kennedy did in his later years. Said to be one of America's shrewdest investors and asset swappers, Smith never runs businesses himself. He refuses to clutter his mind with day-to-day operations. Rather, he moves hundreds of millions of dollars based on ideas and concepts.

You don't have the Kennedys' millions. But you do have enough money to retire. When you retire, you free yourself from demanding schedules, unhappy clients, and drops in sales. Like Joseph Kennedy, you can ponder the business world at your leisure, choosing your investments carefully.

If you're like me, you'll decide to let others worry about becoming millionaires or billionaires. You'll decide that putting extra money in the bank improves your life so slightly it's not worth the bother.

On the other hand, as you ponder the current state of affairs you may come up with an idea you want to try. Buy and sell paintings and sculpture like my friend Nick. Consult part time like my friend Chambers. Invent and market a new rat poison, instant wine, or a microwave oven that doubles as a garbage incinerator. Whatever you do, you'll do it with a clear mind, unhurried by the demands of the career game. You can focus your full creative powers on ideas rather than on bureaucratic snarls.

Our world is full of people who started making really big money or became truly important in the second half of their lives—after letting go of what they did in the first half. Ronald Reagan didn't leave acting to turn to political life. He left acting to retire and relax. Only after settling down for a time did he become interested in being governor of California. Even J. Paul Getty, as we've seen, retired to goof off after he made his first million. His very early retirement set the stage for his later success.

The third basic rule of retirement, from chapter 1, is:

Do what you want

After a few years of retired life you may decide to return to work. If you do, you may decide to try out a new idea. If you try the idea, you may make it or not. If you make it, you're a zillionaire. If you don't, you go back to being retired.

But if you stay working where you are right now, you may never even get the chance to think about it.

8.

Life on $50 a Day

In the Dominican Republic they tell of a man who used to toss his fishing line into the deep waters of a splendid Caribbean cove. One day a tourist came by and asked what he was doing.

The fisherman, a descendant of sugar-plantation slaves, looked up. "I'm trying to catch a fish for my family's dinner."

"Why don't you fish a little longer, maybe catch two fish?" the tourist asked. "Eat one and sell one. In a short time you'd save enough money to buy a pole."

"What would I do with a pole?" the fisherman asked.

"Why, with a pole you can throw your line farther out. Just a few feet off shore you'd catch more fish. Sell the extra fish and pretty soon you'd save enough money to buy a boat."

The fisherman began to perk up. "What would I do with a boat?"

"You could row out into the cove," the tourist said, raising his voice a little. "Out there you'd catch even more fish. Pretty soon you'd save enough money to buy a second pole."

The fisherman's eyes sparkled. "With a second pole my son could fish with me."

"Exactly!" the tourist said. "You and your son would catch many more fish. After a while you could buy a second boat and hire fishermen to work it for you. Then you'd buy another boat and then another and another."

The tourist started to speak more rapidly, perspiration covering his face. "Pretty soon you'd have enough money to buy a modern, oceangoing fishing boat. Then you could buy a fleet of boats and a shop to repair them. Eventually you'll set up an air-conditioned office in town and run your business from a comfortable chair, with a secretary and batteries of accountants to help you. One day you'll be able to hire people to run the business for you."

The tourist was gasping for breath. "Don't you see?" he screamed. "In no time at all you'd have so much money you'd never have to work again."

"What would I do then?" the fisherman asked.

"Why, you could do anything you want! You could forget your troubles, head for a beautiful cove, and just go fishing. You could sit and relax and fish all afternoon!"

The fisherman shrugged. "That's what I do already," he said. He turned back to his line and continued fishing.

SIMPLIFY, SIMPLIFY

Bare-bones retirees spend somewhat less than $50 a day. Wealthier very early retirees, if they have children, spend more than $50 a day (you'll find out how much more in chapter 9). But the $50-a-Day Rule is the basis for all very early retirement, and the basis of the $50-a-Day Rule is to simplify your life. Your infrastructure should serve rather than complicate. If what you want to do is relax and fish, all you need is a fishing line. A large fishing fleet takes you away from your goal, not toward it. The idea is to fish, not race through the day in a frenzied struggle to keep the fleet in the water. The rule is:

Cut down your infrastructure

My friend Ray first showed me how silly it is to complicate our lives with more infrastructure than we need. Ray seemed to prefer sitting in the quad and watching people go by than studying to get ahead. He went to every party he heard about and drank beer in industrial quantities. He chose graduate school in electronics not to prepare for a fast-track career but because it intrigued him. His first job was in electronics in Phoenix. Soon he was earning good money, and he and his wife decided to buy a house.

"Before we went to see the realtor," Ray told me at the time, "we wrote down what we wanted. We agreed on a formal living room, separate dining room. That meant we needed a family room for informal parties and TV football games. And it's nice to have a separate den with a desk, away from the TV. We planned to wait several years before having kids, but for resale value we decided on three or four bedrooms. We wanted a large master bedroom suite to have a comfortable, private place to sit and read. We had a puppy, so of course we needed a big yard. And so on."

Ray laughed and shook his head. "It was crazy. We didn't need *any* of that stuff. The next day we went out and bought a two-bedroom, 950-square-foot house a few miles from the office."

Ray's good judgment prevailed when he was 23. But by the time he was 35 he had moved to a house the size of the Grand Canyon. He had a maid, three refrigerators, two freezers, six phones, two VCRs, and five TVs. What happened to Ray's good judgment?

A couple of kids changed things a bit. A larger family requires more space. But even without kids, as we get older I think we tend to buy more freely, get used to household machines, and convince ourselves that luxuries are necessities. We're not always sure we like or need the more complicated life. Maybe that's why camping—living with next to nothing—is so much fun for many of us. But we naturally take on more infrastructure as we move along in our lives and careers.

If you're like Ray and his wife, for example, you and your spouse both work full-time jobs. As soon as you can afford it, you hire someone to clean the house, mow the grass, and wash the cars. If you've got small children, a daily baby-sitter makes life easier. You begin to work late and the older kids stay after school. That's when an extra refrigerator full of frozen, cooked food comes in handy. Trips to buy groceries become harder to squeeze in. An extra freezer means you can stock up without worrying if there's room to stash everything.

You and your spouse travel on business, so you each own several pieces of versatile luggage. You keep extra toothbrushes, deodorant sticks, and hairbrushes to make sure you can pack in a hurry. You never know when you'll get to the cleaners, so you have more suits and shirts, more dresses and blouses, than you'd otherwise need. You carry extra money, credit cards, and traveler's checks to be prepared when your plans change.

When you reach your 40s or 50s you buy a duplicate set of golf clubs. That way you can leave one at the country club and another in the trunk of your car. You buy a Mercedes but keep the Honda for emergencies. Maybe you put a tennis court in your backyard because you're too busy to arrange games at the tennis club. But you keep your club membership because you may want to play tournaments.

After a while the infrastructure seems to cause more hassle than the hassle it was designed to eliminate. Rather than relax on Saturday mornings, you get up early to get the cars washed, sweep the tennis court, wipe off the patio furniture, move the refrigerators around, straighten up the work shop, add pool chemicals, interview a new gardener, and go shopping. You feel out of control of your life because you're out of control of the infrastructure you set up to help you.

This state of affairs changes when you retire. When you retire you live without the demands of a prestigious job, business travel, or exclusive neighborhood. Without two washing machines, three computers, and five vehicles. Chapters 4 and 5 suggest you sell the big house and move to cheaper living space. Over time your simple cottage in the North Carolina woods will seem quaint or rustic rather than old. Your eight-hundred-square-foot apartment near the beach in Rio will seem cozy rather than small, eclectic rather than overcrowded. And you'll be able to relax and read every day rather than work to support your assets five days a week and maintain them the other two.

But cutting down on infrastructure means more than selling the house. It also means selling the car.

VEHICLES

If you thought I was missing a few spark plugs when I advised you to sell your home, you must think my engine has frozen up now. You could no sooner live without a car than you could live without food, water, or touch-tone telephone.

But as incredible as it may seem, it *is* possible to live in the 1980s without owning a car. I know. Vicki and I haven't owned a car since 1974.

The last time I drove my own car was in San Francisco on January 1, 1974. I had to work that day because a client was taking inventory. Young auditors prefer that clients count their wares on January 2, 3, or 4, but if clients want to count on New Year's Day their auditors oblige. The warehouse was forty-five minutes south of our apartment in San Francisco. I figured I could drive down, observe the count, and be home by noon to celebrate New Year's with my brother. He was driving from Los Angeles to Seattle that day, and I had persuaded him to detour to San Francisco to visit for a few hours.

A huge rainstorm and the resulting traffic snarl ruined my plans. The Bayshore freeway flooded and I was stuck in traffic for four hours. Instead of watching football games and laughing with my brother, I was sitting in a steamy car surrounded by fumes, noise, and irate drivers.

By the time I got home my brother had come and gone. I took three aspirin and went to bed. The next day Vicki and I decided to see if we could live without a car. We stuck the car in the garage and told ourselves we would drive it only if desperate.

We began to use buses, taxis, trains, and our feet to get around San Francisco. For longer trips we rode with others or, once or twice a year, rented a car. About that time the first OPEC crisis began to show at the pump. We watched people wait for hours to buy gas. We never waited in lines because we never needed gas. We began to feel a bit smug.

Six months later we still hadn't needed any gas. That's when we got a big insurance bill. Rather than pay it, we sold the car. And in over ten years we've never been tempted to buy another one.

Think about cars in your life. If you're like me, both parents had cars when you grew up. As far back as you can remember, you spent interminable hours riding and waiting in a car. As each member of the family turned 16, he got a license and then a car. Conversation around the dinner table soon centered on fender benders, gas prices, repairs, and buying and selling.

By the time you were 25 or so you had crashed and traded up a couple of times. In your short driving career you had spent a small fortune on gas, tires, insurance, repairs, tickets, parking, and fines. That was bad enough. But then things got really expensive. Gas prices per gallon went from 30 cents to over a dollar. A few years later Detroit managed to get Congress to limit imports. That gave GM, Ford, and Chrysler a free hand to jack up prices.

According to Hertz there are 42 million trucks and 129 million cars in America today. It costs 33 cents a mile to own and operate a car. At an average eight thousand miles per car per year, that totals $2,640. At 1.8 cars per household, that's a total car expense of $4,752. Add the cost of household pickups, motor homes, motorcycles, and other toys, and over a lifetime what you spend on vehicles alone could pay for your retirement.

Don't be fooled by lower gas prices in the late 1980s. Hertz says those savings are outweighed by higher depreciation, license costs, fees, insurance, repairs, and maintenance.

Divide your life into two parts. One part is cars: buying, selling, insuring, crashing, repairing, maintaining, lubricating, driving, washing, parking, and putting gas in them. The other part is everything else. Which do you prefer? If you're like me, you're fed up with devoting half your life to your vehicles.

When you retire at age 35 you need neither the expense nor the headache cars can bring. Ride with others or use bicycles, taxis, buses, or airplanes. At first it will seem an inconvenience. You'll have to learn to call cabs, arrange to meet others, and read bus schedules. You'll have to allow extra time to walk. But you can adjust if you work on it. The rule is:

Sell your vehicles

In some parts of the country living without a car may be next to impossible. Most of the cheap places listed in chapter 4 are small towns without much public transport. You may have to use bicycles to get around town and have a local cabbie take you shopping. If you absolutely must have a car, buy an $800 "station car." A station car is the clunker someone who lives in Cold Spring Harbor, Long Island, might leave at the train station—

exposed to vandals, thieves, and the elements—while he commutes to New York City. Insure your station car for the minimum required by law. Use it for trips around town that are too far for a bike. For longer trips, ride with others, take Amtrak or Greyhound, or fly.

THE $50-A-DAY BUDGET

Thoreau wrote, "Our life is frittered away by detail . . . I went to the woods because I wished to live deliberately, to front only the essential facts of life, and see if I could not learn what it had to teach, and not, when I came to die, discover that I had not lived."

Cutting down to the "essential facts of life" may be a little much. Even Thoreau got bored and returned to civilization after two years. But when you retire you need only a modest infrastructure in your life. You can certainly get by with less house. And if you're willing to try, you can almost as certainly get by with less car—or no car.

The simplifying rules from chapters 4 and 5 are:

Convert home equity to cash
Convert other assets to cash
Move

Additional rules from this chapter are:

Cut down your infrastructure
Sell your vehicles

Follow the rules and you'll have plenty of money for what you used to think was expensive. Vicki and I live in beach houses for a couple of months each summer, spend six weeks to three months in Europe, attend special programs at Berklee College of Music and Cambridge's Healing Resource Center, and wander through Mayan ruins in Mexico. We go to ballet, symphony, theater, and movies far more than when I worked. It's all possible if you follow the rule:

Spend on yourself, not on your assets

In 1982–83 higher-income Americans spent a median $2,552 per month after taxes, savings, and retirement contributions, as shown in column 1 below. If your personal expenses after taxes, savings, IRAs, life insurance, and the like are higher or lower, you may want to substitute your own figures for those in column 1.

Column 2 is a $50-a-day budget for a hypothetical 40-year-old American couple who retire according to the rules in this book.

	PRERETIREMENT COLUMN 1		POSTRETIREMENT COLUMN 2	
Housing	$ 849	33%	$ 200	13%
Transportation	579	23	50	3
Food and drink	442	17	300	20
Apparel	171	7	100	7
Entertainment	154	6	500	33
Health care	90	4	150	10
Other	267	10	200	14
Total	$2,552	100%	$1,500	100%

Remember that total expenses of $2,552 in column 1 come from government statistics for the top 20 percent of American households. The *average* household lives on only $1,440 per month. When you retire on $50 a day and spend $1,500 a month, you outspend half of the families in the United States.

Column 1 shows you're spending to support your assets. Your house and car take up 56 percent of your budget. Food, apparel, and other costs are high because of that inflated infrastructure we talked about. Those costs will plummet once you retire, move, and bring a more relaxed pace to your life.

Column 2 shows your expenses when you're retired on $50 a day. You spend over half of your budget, 53 percent, on food and entertainment. That's a huge increase in spending on *you*. Entertainment of $500 a month includes airfare, hotels, and eating out when you travel. We'll talk later about managing those costs. But remember that entertainment is an average throughout the year.

When you travel you'll spend more than $500 on entertainment; when you're at home you'll spend less. If you choose not to travel, you'll spend that money on your hobbies: collecting Civil War memorabilia, taking postgraduate courses, playing golf, fishing, or whatever.

The $50-a-day budget allows you only $250 a month for housing and transportation costs. To live on $250, you have to move to Tennessee or Georgia or one of the other places in chapter 4. You also have to live with only a cheap station car. Don't worry, though. You'll be so busy traveling abroad, enjoying your hobbies, or taking it easy you'll pay little heed to your smaller, simpler living space and old Betsy.

Column 2 shows reduced expenditures on the infrastructure costs: food, apparel, and other items. And because you pay for your own health insurance when you retire, column 2 shows an increase from $90 to $150 a month for health care.

IS EVERYTHING INCLUDED IN $50 A DAY?

When people hear that Vicki and I live on $50 a day, their first question is usually, "Does that include rent and everything?"

The people most likely to ask that question rent two-bedroom apartments in New York City or have mortgagitis. They can't imagine getting control of their housing costs. But in truth our $50-a-day budget *doesn't* include "rent and everything." We allocate $4,000 a year in a separate category for airfares.

Round trip from Buenos Aires to almost anywhere costs a lot. We want to feel free to get up and go when we please, and the budget for airfare helps us do that. Airfare is our only "special" expense that falls outside the $50-a-Day Rule. Our total budget, then, is $22,000 a year: $18,000 for living expenses and $4,000 for airfares. With the high real interest rates we talked about in chapter 4, we can afford it.

Airfares in the United States are so low it's hardly necessary to budget them separately. As of this writing one can fly coast to coast for $99 and to Europe for $149. But you may want to budget separately for an expensive hobby. If you retire to the coast of Maine, for example, you may want to set up a separate budget for a boat. A camera buff might want a separate budget for equipment, film, and development.

The rule is:

Spend more than $50 a day if you must

Especially if you have $500,000 of net worth, with high real rates you can safely spend more than $18,000 a year and still keep capital intact. But follow this rule with caution. You don't want to get so carried away with special expenses that you lose sight of the $50-a-Day Rule.

Throughout this book I've referred to $50 a day without adjusting for inflation. I've done that to keep things simple, even though I recognize that, over time, the $50 a day will creep up a little. But since you keep your capital growing with inflation, you'll be able to afford the increase. And in the several years since we've been retired, Vicki and I have found we spend less each year. That's because our infrastructure costs continue to fall as we get more set in our retirement pace. We tend to walk rather than bother with taxis. We seldom feel like eating in expensive restaurants. When we do, we're likely to do it in cheaper cities: Buenos Aires rather than New York, Madrid rather than Vienna. And as we'll see right now, when we travel we're more savvy about finding cheaper airfares, hotels, and things to do.

HOTELS: DON'T PAY FOR AN ELEVATOR

If you're like most young retirees, travel will be a big part of retired life. You'll do it at a more leisurely pace. Instead of racing through Europe in twenty days you'll spend a week or two in a fishing village on the Adriatic. Instead of hitting five Viennese museums a day, you'll spend afternoons writing letters in a café. Instead of going on quickie bus tours the day you arrive, you'll take two or three days to walk around and get the feel of a new city.

The change of pace means your travel needs change. When you dash through Europe on a one-week business trip, you spend only two days in Madrid. You head straight for a $150-a-night international hotel. The cabdriver knows right where it is. The desk clerk speaks English. Tours of the city start and end there, and you buy the *International Herald Tribune* in the lobby. You've got a phone and color TV in your room.

But when you retire you need less infrastructure—both at home and when you travel. A two-star, $15-a-night hotel that offers a clean room with bath will do fine. The desk clerk speaks English poorly? Try your Spanish. You're trying to learn it anyway. You need to make an occasional phone call? Ask the clerk to dial the number and talk in the lobby. Or walk over to the phone company's local office and call overseas for a fraction of what you'd pay in a hotel. You'd like to catch a bullfight on TV? Watch it in a bar around the corner.

In 1983 Vicki accompanied me to Rome on a business trip. The first two nights, before the meeting started, we were on our own money. We stayed at the Hotel Piazza di Spagna near the Spanish Steps. The owners run the hotel and chatted happily in broken English while we checked in. We got a room on the third floor with a new, king-size bed. The room had a private bath and cost $30 a night, including breakfast.

After two pleasant days in the Hotel Piazza di Spagna, on Sunday evening we moved to the "luxury" hotel where the meeting was to be held. We waited in line to check in. When we finally got to the desk, the clerk snarled at us and insisted we leave our passports with him for "processing." I told him it made me nervous to leave my passport on the counter in a high-traffic area, and he basically told me to shove it. I asked for a double bed and he told me two singles would have to do.

The creaky elevator took as long to get to the fourth floor as the Chinese took to build the Great Wall. The bellboy showed us to a garish, tawdry little room in the back. The single mattresses were so worn and soft that when I sat on the bed I slid to the floor. I told the bellboy I wanted to change rooms. Rather than try to explain the problem, he took me to the room next door. The mattresses there were just as bad. When I insisted he do *something*, he pulled two plywood boards from the room across the hall and shoved them under our mattresses. The price for all this "luxury": $225 a night.

Make the comparison yourself. Go to Rome or Paris and spend a night in the Hyatt, Intercontinental, or Georges V. Then go to an ordinary hotel, where European tourists might stay, near the Spanish Steps in Rome or the Sorbonne in Paris. Ask yourself if the difference is worth $150 a day, over $1,000 a week.

Most luxury hotels have beautiful lobbies. To enjoy them,

check in at a simple hotel around the corner and go to the beautiful lobby for drinks. You'll pay two or three times more for your martini than at a local bar. But the total tab will be only a couple of bucks, not an extra $150 a night. The main luxury hotel in Montevideo, Uruguay, is the Victoria Plaza. When in Montevideo, Vicki and I go to the piano bar there. We meet people in the lobby there. We buy international papers and read them in the lounge there. But we *stay* in an $8-a-night hotel three blocks down the street.

The rule is:

Choose hotels that offer what you need and nothing more

Don't pay for elevators, phones, TV, air-conditioning, newsstands, restaurants, and other things you'll rarely use. Choose basic hotels in the center of town. Look for a clean room, private bath, and other features you feel you need. In Rio, Mexico City, Buenos Aires, and most other cities in Latin America, you can get a double room with bath for $5 to $10 a night. In parts of Europe you'll pay more. Last time we were in Vienna we paid $40; in Paris we paid $35. But in Budapest we got a two-bedroom apartment, with kitchen, for $9. In Yugoslavia we stayed in private homes for $6. We've found that, on most trips to Europe, our *average* hotel bill is less than $20 a night.

In the United States, $20-a-night hotels are hard to come by, especially in urban areas in the Northeast. Try to stay with friends when you visit Boston, New York, and Washington, D.C. If you don't have friends in those cities, stay in a hotel, cut your visit short, and cram everything in. There's always time to relax later in cheaper, quieter Vermont, New Hampshire, or Virginia.

Whether traveling in the United States or abroad, never make hotel reservations. Hotels that accept reservations have telex machines, computers, and extra reservation clerks. You pay for that infrastructure in the price of your room. Instead, plan to arrive in town at about the noon checkout hour. You'll be able to set up in an inexpensive hotel that doesn't bother with reservations.

I learned this trick on our second visit to Spain. Before leaving home I asked my travel agent to reserve rooms in some of the hotels we had enjoyed on our first trip. To my dismay, none of the hotels accepted our reservation. I assumed they were fully booked. But when we got to Spain we found that those hotels had plenty of rooms. They had denied our reservations because they prefer not to go through the bother and expense of making them.

Since we retired in 1984 Vicki and I have stayed in literally hundreds of hotels around the world. We've never made reservations. And we've never had a problem finding a room.

Savvy travelers suggest that if you arrive without reservations and can't find a room, you head for a local café. Explain your plight to the owner and he'll find *something* for a night, even if it's an unused maid's room in back. In most countries we've visited, I've sensed that this technique would work. But, as I said, we've never had to try it.

A growing racket in the hotel business is the so-called guaranteed reservation. Give the hotel your credit card number and you get a "guaranteed" room. The hotel charges you for the room whether you show up or not. But a friend was recently on a delayed flight to New York. He got to his hotel at 4:00 A.M. to claim his guaranteed room. The desk clerk apologized and said that no rooms were available. It seems some guarantees are more guaranteed than others. Since my friend showed up to claim his guaranteed-room-that-wasn't, he didn't have to pay for it. If he had *failed* to show up to claim his guaranteed-room-that-wasn't, he would have been charged $250 on his American Express card.

Avoid being ripped off by unscrupulous innkeepers. Travel without reservations and stay in hotels that keep their rooms for walk-in customers.

AIRFARE: TAKE A TRAVEL AGENT TO LUNCH

For retired travelers, deregulation of the airline industry was like manna from heaven. Most airlines now give deep discounts to travelers who can live with "restrictions." Buy your ticket thirty days in advance, stay over a Saturday night, and fly midweek, and you can save 50 percent or more. Those conditions may restrict some people. But retired travelers almost always plan in advance, stay for more than a week, and choose to travel midweek, when airports are less crowded.

Ask whether your travel agent offers big discounts. If he

doesn't, choose one of the "bucket shop" operators that advertise in *The Village Voice* or publications that cater to students. "Bucket shops" do high volumes and receive special discounts from the airlines; they pass those discounts along to you. Once you find a travel agent you like, take him or her to lunch. Explain that you're retired, want cheap airfares, and that restrictions don't bother you. Explain too that two-week package deals appeal to the tourist in a hurry. When *you* travel you stay longer and move slower.

My travel agent in Buenos Aires has standing orders to call me when *any* discount fare comes across his screen. Once he came up with a way for Vicki and me to fly to Europe and actually get paid for doing it. For a brief period in Argentina, a traveler with a plane ticket to Europe or the United States had the right to buy U.S. $2,000 at the official exchange rate of, say, 2 million pesos. On the free market one could convert that U.S. $2,000 into 5 million pesos. Those 5 million pesos covered both the 2 million to buy the dollars and the 2.5-million-peso plane ticket. You were left with a free plane ticket and money in your pocket.

When traveling within the United States, use a travel agent in your departure city. For example, if you live in Dallas and want to fly from Chicago to New York, you're better off using a travel agent in Chicago than one in Dallas. In 1986 my Los Angeles agent flew us from L.A. to New Orleans for only $89. After touring the Southeast we wanted to fly from Washington, D.C., to Boston. The best my L.A. agent could do on that leg was $149. It seemed high, so I called a friend in Washington, D.C. He checked with his agent there and came up with a $39 promotional fare.

When traveling overseas, from country to country, it's usually cheaper to buy the entire trip from your U.S. agent before you go. He can get a triangle fare to Europe, for example, with a stopover in the Caribbean at no extra charge. And plane tickets in Western Europe cost a pile if you buy them there. A short hop Paris–London–Paris ticket purchased in Paris, for example, can cost more than the much longer New York–London–Paris–New York ticket purchased in New York.

On the other hand, local, within-the-same-country airfare is best purchased once you arrive at your first stop. For example, you should buy your tickets from Mexico City to Acapulco once you arrive in Mexico City. You'll get lower fares and pay for them with cheap, free-market pesos.

The exception to the "buy locally" rule is when you can get a special, travel-all-you-want deal. Several large countries—Spain, Brazil, Argentina—offer special fares to tourists from abroad. For example, fly on Iberia with an L.A.–Madrid–L.A. ticket, and for only $200 extra Iberia will give you a sixty-day "See Spain" ticket. Like a Eurorail pass for airplanes, the ticket lets you fly all over Spain without additional charges. The deals change all the time, but many countries offer them—including the United States for those retirees who establish residency abroad. You have to buy these deals before you go, and travel agents know little about them. After all, how many customers do travel agents have who want sixty or ninety days to wander around Brazil? So give your agent a day or two to find out if the country you want to visit has a travel-all-you-want program.

One final point: fly coach. You're on a plane trip, not an ego trip.

LUGGAGE

Travel only with carry-on luggage. It will force you to pack more carefully and think more clearly about what's important to you. With carry-on you never give airlines a chance to lose your luggage. When flights are canceled you'll be able to change flights or carriers at the last minute. You'll be able to check in at the Pan Am Clipper Club or TWA Ambassador Club, if you're flying those airlines and are members of those clubs, rather than waiting in line in the lobby. Perhaps best of all, you'll never be tempted to buy souvenirs or other trinkets—they won't fit into your bags.

Vicki packs her bags with her things and I pack mine with mine. Pack your own and you avoid arguments about what to leave behind.

SIGHTSEEING

Do your own sightseeing at your own pace, using local buses, trains, and taxis. Let cabdrivers rip you off for a dollar or two. It's better than spending $20 each to wait in line for a two-hour city tour.

Avoid renting a car in a foreign country. Foreigners design their cities for people rather than cars. Rent a car and you incur expense and waste time doing paperwork. Better to take a plane, train, or bus from city to city. Once you arrive at your destination, walk or take cabs or local buses. You'll have a more pleasant trip. Rental cars are for Americans who don't know any better.

CHECK-IN

Checking in at airports, train stations, bus stations, and hotels can test the patience of the most unhurried traveler. The Bible's Job himself might have lost his cool trying to get in and out of O'Hare in a snowstorm. Give yourself a break by assigning check-in tasks to one spouse or the other.

When Vicki and I arrive at an airport or bus station, I put her and the bags in the coffeeshop. I check in and inquire about departure gates and the like. She never questions the seats I choose or other details I decide on. When we arrive at our next destination, it's Vicki's turn. She deposits me and the bags in a park, bar, or café. She then heads off and chooses a hotel. I never second-guess her choice.

The system means that, if there's a line, only one of us has to wait in it. We avoid silly disputes over inconsequential details. And after doing this on several trips we began to notice a side benefit. We started getting better prices on hotel rooms. Remember that room prices are negotiable in many parts of the world, and all hotels have some rooms that are cheaper than others. We believe we get better rates because the front-desk clerks see Vicki walk in without bags. They figure she's searching the neighborhood for a good price on a room, and they're right. So they offer their best deal right up front. Vicki rarely has to haggle. On the other hand, if we both show up laden with luggage, the clerks figure we're desperate for a room. They'll quote a higher price or try to put us in a suite.

LESS IS MORE

Perhaps more than anything else, retiring on $50 a day requires a new state of mind. Simplify your life by having only the things you need or want. Consume less to enjoy life more. Living with this new state of mind works because of what economists call the Law of Diminishing Marginal Utility. I call it the Coin Toss Law.

I offer to toss a fair coin. If it comes up tails, I pay you a dollar. If it comes up heads, you pay me a dollar. Sure, you say. Why not? We play a couple of times. Then I ask if you want to play for $10. Of course. We continue to play. Then I offer to play for, say, $500,000, your entire net worth. You laugh. It's ridiculous. Yet, the game hasn't changed at all. The coin is still fair and the odds are the same. What's happened?

What's happened is that you've moved down your "utility" curve. Lose the $500,000 coin toss and you're wiped out. You're without a house, car, furniture, savings, everything. If you're retired, you'll have to go back to work. If you have one job, you'll have to work at two. You're in worse shape than a chow mein joint without a reliable noodle supply. You'll probably have a nervous breakdown. It's a disaster.

Winning half a million dollars, on the other hand, wouldn't do that much for you. You could buy a shiny car and a house a couple of blocks farther up the hill. You could stick the kids into a more expensive private school. You'd like to have an extra half-million dollars. But your day-to-day life would change hardly at all. To the extent that you become a victim of upscale marketing, your life could even deteriorate. Status cars upset us when something scratches them. Home computers that do our banking and lock our house can make us feel helpless and frustrated when something goes wrong. Fine furniture and paintings demand that our fire insurance become a part of our life rather than an annual bill. Modern insurance ads show smiling, wealthy couples surrounded by their possessions. In the next sequence we see the possessions destroyed by fire, flood, or theft. At best the couple recuperates, but only after hours of paperwork, phone calls, and tense talks.

Result: winning the toss offers little or nothing. Losing is a mess. You don't want to play the game.

The Coin Toss Law means that the upside, past a certain point, isn't all that great. If you already have forty pairs of shoes, adding ten more isn't a big deal. If you already have a Mercedes with a small engine, getting one with a bigger engine is a cheap thrill that costs a fortune. Buying a new car makes you feel good, but it doesn't excite like that first clunker when you were sixteen. A bigger house can be pleasant, but it brings bigger problems as well. Compact discs are cute but you have to strain to hear the improved sound.

Millions of Americans in their 30s and 40s already have much of the American dream along with some fun little extras. You're a candidate for retirement at this point if you feel you want more out of life than a new car. You're a candidate for retirement if you suspect that time isn't money—it's better than money. If you live in a four-thousand-square-foot house with two extra rooms, would adding on make you that much happier? How many fur coats are enough? If you already have $40,000 dollars' worth of jewelry you never wear, would a new necklace make a big difference?

It's ironic, but the only way to change this state of affairs is to have less, not more. If it's been four years since you bought a new tie, choosing a tie might be fun. If you've lived ten years in a small apartment, having a place with a yard might be very pleasant. In every case the marginal whoopee is greater, the less you have to begin with.

Remember the Coin Toss Law: Less is more

9.

Retiring with Kids

Twenty-five years ago half the households in America contained children under age 18. You grew up in one of them. Dad drove a Chevy to work and Mom was a housewife. You lived in Peoria with your 2.2 brothers or sisters. You watched Walter Cronkite on TV, went to Marilyn Monroe movies, ate at the new McDonald's across town, and feared that Khrushchev would bury you. You and everyone in your family could read, write, and speak English.

Now only a third of America's households contain children. Those households bear little resemblance to the one you grew up in. Nearly half of all mothers return to work within one year of their child's birth. Moms labor at the office, factory, or store rather than wait with milk and cookies when Johnny comes home from school. Over half of America's kids live with one parent or the other, but not both. Half-brothers and half-sisters may be scattered across the country or around the world. Instead of Peoria, today's family is more likely to live in fast-lane Los Angeles, Dallas, or Miami. Dad drives a Honda or Volkswagen rather than a Chevy. Mom and Dad, if they speak English at all, seldom read or write it. Many kids never read it or write it for the simple reason that they don't know how.

But this chapter isn't for the average family with kids,

whatever "average" means in the 1980s. This chapter is for *your* American family with kids. Vicki and I have no children, but we know something about your family. Your family's dad, mom, or both want to retire young. Your family has quite a bit more net worth than average, perhaps $400,000 or more. The Census Bureau reports that in 1984 "married-couple households had a median net worth of . . . about four times that of female-maintained households and five times that of male-maintained households." So your family's dad and mom are probably married to each other. The Census Bureau also reports that "householders with a college education had nearly twice the net worth of those who graduated from high school but did not attend college." So your family's head most likely graduated from college. You want your kids to have the same chance of getting a good education as you had.

The hypothetical Doe family from Pasadena may be something like yours. Dad Doe, an account executive in J. Walter Thompson's Los Angeles office, pries his eyes open at 6:30 A.M., turns down the jazz music on his clock-radio, pulls on his swimming trunks, and heads for the heated swimming pool. After ten laps he drips his way through the kitchen, pours himself a cup of coffee, and turns on the TV. The sounds of *Good Morning America* mingle with the heavy metal blaring from 17-year-old Alex's clock-radio. Dad dresses, gulps a second cup of coffee, and eats a pop-up tart in one smooth, well-rehearsed motion. His Mazda RX-7 is roaring down the Pasadena freeway, slicing through traffic, before he realizes his day has begun.

Mom rolls out of bed and makes her way to the bathroom medicine cabinet. With heavy eyelids, she debates whether two aspirin will get her through the morning. She takes three, claws into the wreckage of Alex's room, and shuts off his radio. The silence wakes him up. She pounds on 14-year-old Monica's door and yells at her to hurry in the bathroom.

Alex chugs a Coke for breakfast and screams at Monica that he's ready to leave. Driving Monica to school was the string attached to the new Honda Dad and Mom gave Alex for his 17th birthday. Monica dashes through the kitchen, grabs a granola bar, and says good-bye to the cat. They're off.

Mom takes a quick massage shower and then enjoys a moment to herself, with a cup of coffee and a bowl of tasteless breakfast cereal. She remembers hearing, many years before, that the cardboard box her cereal comes in contains more nutrients than the product inside. She used to feed the kids a real breakfast every morning. She no longer feels guilty about leaving them on their own.

Mom dresses and then punches up her to-do list on the computer: buy groceries, call the therapist to arrange a makeup appointment, call Alex's high-school counselor to arrange to talk about his absenteeism and bad grades, call the car dealer and arrange a ten-thousand-mile checkup, call Mary Witherspoon to arrange lunch at the club, call . . . Mom sells life insurance in her "spare time." Most of the rest of the calls are to set up appointments with prospective clients.

Mom starts in on the telephone. A client puts her on hold and Mom asks the computer to balance her checkbook. She finds she's bumping against her overdraft limit. She decides to call the bank to arrange more credit. At the same time, she wonders if she could sell the branch manager a life-insurance policy.

Still on the phone, she touches up her fingernails and has the computer print out her shopping list. She straightens up the kitchen, feeds the cat, activates the burglar alarm, and heads off to the club.

After Mom's luncheon meeting and two sales calls, she does the grocery shopping. As always, she packs the frozen food and a bag of ice in the cooler she hauls around in the trunk of her car. She picks up Monica from school and drives her to her violin lesson in Hollywood. During Monica's lesson, Mom stays in the car and makes sales calls on her cellular car phone. The lesson over, Mom drives Monica to the Glendale mall. Monica plans to meet a friend there and shop for a black dress for her upcoming violin recital.

Mom arrives home and puts away the groceries. She notes that the refrigerator has been cleaned out of edibles, a sure sign that Alex and maybe a few of his friends have passed through the kitchen. She calls Alex at the Superscoop to tell him about the appointment with his high-school counselor. Alex says fine, he'll be there, but please don't bother him about such triviality while he's working.

Mom updates the shopping list on the computer, makes more phone calls, and heads off to call on a young professional couple. Most of her clients, it seems, are young professionals who can see her only between 7:00 and 10:00 P.M.

Dad gets home as Mom backs out of the garage. They honk greetings at each other. Dad fixes himself a scotch, tunes in Dan Rather on TV, and peeks in the freezer. The freezer has more gourmet dinners than the menu at Chasen's. He chooses beef Stroganoff with rice and a spinach soufflé, and sticks both in the microwave. He used to like to cook. Now he wonders how he ever managed to prepare something to eat before they had a microwave.

He leaves the Stroganoff and spinach-soufflé box tops in a basket by the computer so Mom can update the grocery list. Mom's inventory system, he figures, has better controls than most Pasadena retail outlets.

Dad wolfs down his gourmet dinner in front of the TV. Even so, he arrives late to his school-board meeting. He volunteers to chair the fund-raising committee this year.

Mom gets home at 9:30 P.M., excited with her success. She sold $300,000 of life insurance. To celebrate, she makes herself a weak wine spritzer. She zaps a diet-delight frozen dinner and goes to the TV room to be near Dad while she eats. Dad is watching a well-worn video copy of *Caddyshack* and trying to catch up on business reading during straight lines. He punches the pause button to tell Mom they have to miss Monica's violin recital because an important client invited them to Opening Day at Dodger Stadium. Mom asks him to talk to Alex about the dangers of driving under the influence. While he's at it, he should also say something to Alex about his bad grades. Mom tells him about her appointment with Alex's counselor.

At 10:00 P.M. Mom leaves to pick up Monica at a friend's house. Mom and Monica drop by the Superscoop to see Alex and remind him that he has to take Monica to ballet class the following afternoon. Alex had forgotten about it. Mom and Monica buy a half-gallon of ice cream and return home. Monica kisses her father, scoops a huge bowl of ice cream, and goes up to her room to practice. She forgets to model her new black dress for her parents.

Mom and Dad eat ice cream and go over their weekend to-do list. They finalize the invitation list for their annual spring barbecue party. They coordinate their calendars.

Alex arrives home after everyone is asleep. He punches the night sequence in the burglar alarm and wakes Mom up to tell her he's home.

Does the Doe family sound anything like yours? Mom, Dad, Alex, and Monica rush from one activity to another. They have a car for every driver. When they see one another they coordinate schedules rather than spend "quality time" together. They have a large home with modern conveniences. Two incomes go into paying for it. Yet, the four of them rarely have time to enjoy the house together.

In retirement this family can shed some of that weighty infrastructure. Dad, Mom, Alex, and Monica will live at a slower pace, have more time together, and do without expensive gadgetry. They'll make some sacrifices. But they'll be out of the pressure cooker that destroys so many American families.

YOUR KIDS NEED YOU NOW

Adults thrive on attention. We bring sales in over plan to get the boss's attention. We drive a long luxury car to get the club members' attention. We plan a charity raffle to get the neighbors' attention. We fill our lives with games to get the others to notice and admire us. If our games fail, we can even *ask* our spouse or close friends for attention and feel fairly certain we'll get it.

Not so with kids. They thrive on attention too, especially from their parents. But their games are often too naïve, their behavior too transparent, to get them much rich attention. They may paint their faces, for example, or try to embarrass you by roller skating in the nude through an intimate dinner party, rather than come out and tell Mom or Dad that they want some of their time. Sometimes kids who need their parents' attention do get the message across. But even then, parents can seldom devote the huge amounts of time their youngsters seem to require. By the time he's a teenager, Alex may get into fights, rob cars, drop out of school, or do drugs in a desperate, unconscious effort to get attention.

Some parents try to give their kids quality time, a relatively new idea that means they spend less but more-focused time with the kids. Unfortunately, in too many cases parents who say they spend quality time give their kids little or no time at all. And when they try to spend quality time, they face a tough task. According to Alison Clarke-Stewart of the University of Chicago, during quality time, dads are especially "warm, loving, nonrejecting, . . . stimulating and enriching." That's a pretty tall order, not only for Dad but for Alex and Monica as well. And too much so-called quality time can overload. Kids probably need quiet time with Mom and Dad as much as they need quality time.

But with today's pressures, most parents have little time for their kids—quality or otherwise. Last summer in San Francisco a friend invited Vicki and me to watch his 7-year-old son's first-ever baseball game. It turned out to be quite an inaugural. Organized by the local Jewish Community Center, sixty boys and girls divided into four teams and played two games. For every batted ball, six or seven players tried to scoop up grounders in the infield and another six or seven ran to shag fly balls in the outfield. Teenage coaches pitched to each of the fifteen children on a team until he or she hit the ball. Innings ended after all kids had batted, regardless of the number of outs. The umpires made up rules based on each player's skill. For example, a little girl who hit and ran toward third instead of first was awarded another time at bat.

Our friend, Vicki, and I sat in the stands behind third base and watched the game. We cheered a little, and soon the kids started to make plays to third, in front of us, rather than to first. Our friend's son changed positions, from right field to third base, so we could see him in action. Base runners smiled and waved as they rounded third. This went on for a couple of innings until we realized why we were getting so much attention. We were the only adults there.

As we neared the end of the game a few parents came to pick up their kids. We could tell whose parent had arrived by watching whose face lit up. Once he had Dad's attention, Johnny started to cheer, hustle, and run after balls. We noticed that Dad, too, seemed to change from a sweaty, beaten executive into a smiling, proud father after watching a few minutes of play. And then it was over. The rest of the parents drove up, honked, packed up their kids, and headed off.

The game was played in a park about three miles from the San Francisco financial district. It started at 5:30 P.M. on a Tuesday, and I assumed several parents would make it. After all, it was their child's first-ever baseball game. Yet, not a single one of them did. The demands of the business day kept them glued to the office until 6:00 or 7:00 P.M.

A friend of mine has a 38-year-old son. Father and son are uncommonly close. One day the son told me why:

"When I was growing up my father was self-employed. Whenever I went to a spelling bee, gave a speech, or acted in a school play, he'd leave the office and come watch. Many times he was the only father there."

Now Dave's son and his wife have their own law office in San Francisco. They like to brag a bit about how well their kids swim, dive, play baseball, and do other activities.

"I guess you enjoy watching them every chance you get," I told their father. "You're self-employed and can take the time off."

Dad shook his head. "We never go watch our kids perform. The law practice doesn't give us a chance to leave. We arrange for the maid to drive them where they have to go and pick them up. At night, after we get home, we try to ask them about what they did during the day. But often we get home late, and the kids are already in bed."

I reminded this father how much it had meant to him when *his* father took time out to attend his activities. He shook his head and gave a helpless shrug. "What am I going to do? I'm too busy."

Think about your childhood. If you're like me, you remember every time your dad came to your Little League game, heard your choral group sing, or took you hunting. Yet, how often do you watch your youngsters perform? How often do you and Alex— just the two of you—go fishing? If you're like most parents, you're simply too busy at work.

I don't pretend to tell others how to raise their kids. But in this chapter I assume you have to devote time to your family to have a happy family life. Similarly, I assume moms and dads who spend time with each other have a better chance of staying in love than moms and dads who don't. I assume moms and dads who spend time with their kids have a better chance of being good parents than moms and dads who don't.

Giving your kids money for a new trumpet, ballet class, exercise room, Toyota, and a college education is great. But more than money, your kids need *you*. The great advantage of very early retirement is that you can give yourself—your time and attention—to your kids *now*. Rather than wearing yourself out on the job, you can play with your children. Rather than racing around the country to attend meetings, you can spend whole summers traveling with your family. Rather than staying late at the office, you can watch your kids take swimming lessons, act in a play, or do gymnastics. When you retire you free up eight, ten, or twelve hours a day, five days a week. You can spend all the time you want with your kids. And remember that kids need time *without* you. Kids want to play alone, be with their friends, or go places with their brothers or sisters. You'll still have plenty of time left over for your to-do list.

You'll recall that the three-part formula for very early retirement is:

Do your arithmetic
Do some soul-searching
Do what you want

Let's take a look at how to apply that formula when you retire with kids.

DO YOUR ARITHMETIC

The first part of the three-part formula is financial. We've seen that two people need $400,000 or $500,000 to retire. How much more do you need if you have kids?

As a minimum, I believe you need $11 a day, or $4,000 a year, for each child.

Business Week surveys how much money it takes to support a family of four. So do *Time*, *Newsweek*, and other publications. Their surveys come up with remarkably similar numbers. Raising a child in America today, assuming he or she goes to public schools, costs about $5,000 a year.

Now, I know people who spend $5,000 on their 6-year-old's birthday party. And who knows how many ponies the $5,000 includes? How many surfboards? How many Gummy Bears and how much of that sugar powder that looks and tastes like Ajax? And I wonder if that $5,000 is net of earnings from lemonade stands, Christmas card sales, and car washes—if kids are into those things these days.

But $5,000 is an average. In 1986, *Newsweek*, for example, studied the average cost of raising one child to the age of 18 in constant 1986 dollars for a two-parent, two-child household with the child attending public school in a suburban area. The total was $95,000, or about $5,000 a year, as follows:

Food	$1,200
Transportation	1,100
Shelter	500
Household goods	500
Recreation	500
Clothing	400
Health Care	300
Personal care	300
Fuel and utilities	200
Total	$5,000

These costs assume that one or both parents work and that the family has a typical suburban infrastructure. For example, the amounts shown for shelter and transportation assume that the family lives in a standard house and drives one or two family cars. In the figures above, a portion of those costs is allocated to the children. But we've seen that when you retire you reduce your infrastructure. Instead of bloated costs for housing, transportation, clothing, and the like, you spend money on *you*.

The same principle holds for your kids. Before you retire, the family lives in a ranch house where each child has a room of his own. *You* never had a room of your own when you were small. But you figure you can afford it now. You drive the kids to the movies in a new car, maintain a motor home for vacations, buy uniforms for school, put color TVs in each bedroom, and stuff the freezer with prepared foods.

When you retire, you reduce your infrastructure. You move to a simple house in Kentucky. You make do with a modest station car or no car at all. As we saw in chapter 8, your health-care costs go up in retirement because you pay your own medical insurance. With kids, those insurance costs go even higher. But the rest of your living costs drop. Even after paying for health care, the allocated cost of raising kids should be less than $5,000.

I assume $4,000 per child per year, rather than $5,000, to reflect the lower costs of a more modest infrastructure. If you have a 10-year-old and figure on supporting him or her to age 22, you have twelve years to go. Set aside twelve years times $4,000 a year, or $48,000, in addition to your own $400,000 or $500,000 nest egg. If you have both a 14- and a 16-year-old and figure on supporting them to age 18, you have to plan for four plus two, or six child-years. At $4,000 a year, you need to set aside six years times $4,000, or $24,000.

I ignore interest in figuring what you need for kids. In the first case above, for example, when you retire you set aside $48,000 for your child. But since you'll spend that money over twelve years, you'll earn interest along the way. Part of that interest protects your money against inflation. The rest of the interest is a cushion.

As a practical matter, when you retire I suggest you set up a separate, one-year CD for child rearing. In the second example above, you'll support a 14- and a 16-year-old to age 18. When you retire, put $24,000 into their CD. At the beginning of the year, take $4,000 per child out of the CD and put it in the account you use for day-to-day living expenses. At the beginning of the second year, take out $4,000 per child plus one year of inflation. For the third year, take out the prior year's amount plus the intervening inflation. Repeat the process each year for as long as you support your children. With interest rates higher than inflation, the initial CD you set aside for your children covers their needs.

Note that unless you have several very young children, the additional amount you need to retire with kids is quite small in relation to your total nest egg. In the examples above you need an extra $48,000 or $24,000, depending on how many kids you have, how old they are, and how long you plan to support them. These amounts—$48,000 and $24,000—are small change compared to the $400,000 or $500,000 you need for you. That's because your $400,000 or $500,000 has to support you and your spouse for the rest of your life. What you set aside for your kids, in contrast, has to last only until they reach age 18 or 22 or whatever. That means you can safely spend your kids' principal as you go along, without worrying about running out of money later.

PAYING FOR SCHOOL

The minimum is $4,000 a year. Once Johnny reaches age 18 or 22, you'll have exhausted the money set aside to raise him. If he wants to buy a house, travel for a year before working, or start his own business, he's on his own. Perhaps most important, there's no money for private college. A scholar friend says "the education you get is the life you lead." You want to do everything possible to see to it that Johnny gets the education that's right for him. Yet, with only $4,000 per child per year, you can hardly pay for expensive schooling.

How much more than $4,000 a year is required to cover private schools? You can easily spend $10,000 a year on a boarding school. The College Board figures that four years at a private college costs $40,000. If your child goes to Johns Hopkins, Vassar, or Williams, you can pay twice that. Your total cost per child can run to $100,000, $150,000, or more. How are you going to get that kind of money?

You can keep working until you save it. Unfortunately, for most of you that means you can forget about very early retirement. The idea is to retire now, with your kids at home, so you can enjoy them while they're young. By the time you have an extra $100,000 to $150,000 per child your kids may be well on their way to starting families of their own.

You can have a heart-to-heart talk with Johnny's grandparents. They may be willing to pay for Johnny's education. The rule in chapter 6 is, "Don't expect a little help from your friends." Friends include family, and it's a safe bet that Johnny's grandpa and grandma would rather see you keep working. But that just means you'll have to work harder to convince them. After all, you want to retire to dedicate more time to your family while the kids are young. Grandpa and Grandma can hardly object to that. And they may already have decided to help Johnny with his education. You're simply asking them to commit the money a bit sooner.

But most of you can't count on your parents to pay for your children's education. Once you retire you'll move to North Caro-

lina or another low-cost state. As a practical matter, you'll send
your kids to public schools. When they reach college age they'll
go to a public university. How can you make sure they get the
best education public money can buy?

PRIMARY AND SECONDARY SCHOOLS

Chapter 4 suggests you spend your next vacation looking for
retirement spots in North Carolina, Georgia, Tennessee, or Kentucky. If you prefer, try Texas, Arkansas, New Mexico, and
Washington. Check for the right climate, low-cost housing, and
things to do. But with kids you need to do more. Once you find a
place that strikes your fancy, you need to evaluate the local
public schools.

SOCIAL CLIMATE

What are you looking for? For one thing, you want a good
social climate. Primary education is partly a process of learning
to deal with peers. You want Johnny to grow up with kids who
behave well, respect private property, and share. Those kids
should have a sense of responsibility and persistence. They should
enjoy life and be decent people. You'd like Johnny to avoid
growing up with youngsters who settle schoolyard disputes by
hauling out hand-held rocket launchers.

Perhaps the biggest advantage of a small-town public school
in the South is that Johnny can spend his early years in a relaxed,
easygoing social climate. He'll live without the stress, competition, and fear that can terrify a child in Chicago or Seattle—not to
mention New York City.

"There's a nervous tension you have to live with," teacher
Barbara Statlow told *The New York Times* in a 1980 interview.
"It's exhausting." Mrs. Statlow teaches at Thomas Jefferson High
in the Brownsville section of Brooklyn. When she says there's
nervous tension, she's not talking about discipline problems.
She's talking about crime. According to the article, "Crime against
New York City's public school teachers has become so common
that, for many of them, its existence no longer shocks." Officials
talk about security at Jefferson High the way a warden might talk
about a federal penitentiary. Double- and triple-locked steel doors

protect classrooms. Guards patrol the halls, bathrooms, and gyms. Yet, teachers and students alike worry about being robbed, slapped around, beaten, knifed, raped, or murdered.

Fortunately, you can largely forget about serious crime in small towns in Kentucky or Georgia. But beyond crime, how can you make sure your children are exposed to the right social climate at school? One way is to talk to other parents. Ask them why Billy likes math, Sally the playground, Tommy his fifth-grade teacher. Ask local merchants, bankers, librarians, and travel agents what they think of the local schools. They'll introduce you to others who can give you more input.

Another way to evaluate a school's social climate is to visit the school while classes are in progress. Focus on details. Are the halls swept, the walls freshly painted? Do the drinking fountains work? Notice the children's faces. How do they react when a teacher passes? Do the teachers smile at the kids or just hurry down the hall? Go out to the playground. Have the coaches done their job in organizing games? Or do the children sit quietly and polish their switchblades? In the administrative office, find out the number of kids, number of teachers, and the length of the school day and school year.

Arrange to see the principal, even if you get only a few moments of his time. If he's not there, make an appointment for the following day and keep it. Ask what he enjoys most about the school. Ask him to explain his biggest problems. Perhaps most important, ask him about the school's budget. If he had more money, what would he spend it on? Southern states spend less per student than California, Illinois, and Massachusetts. But statewide averages can mislead. School districts within a given state spend more or less than others. And some school districts spend it more wisely than others.

Even if your kids go to primary school, make sure you visit the high school as well. As likely as not, once you retire you'll stay put until Johnny finishes high school. When you visit the high school, talk to the kids. More than anyone else, frank teenagers can give you a feel for the school. Do the kids use drugs? Get into fights? Support the football team? Besides listening to what the teenagers say, size up the kids themselves. Would you be comfortable having Johnny bring them home as friends?

Chapter 5 suggests you move to the Third World to live a

better life. In my opinion, retired parents living abroad should send their kids to an international private school. An international private school is *not* an overseas American school at $600 per month per child. Rather, the international school you want has a local English or American headmaster and offers at least half a day of instruction in English. In Rio, for example, a good private school costs about $200 a month. With your lower living costs overseas you can easily afford $200 a month. Johnny will go to class with the children of wealthy Brazilians, diplomats, and expatriates. He'll learn a foreign language or two, play soccer instead of baseball, and eat *feijoada* instead of hot dogs.

International schools overseas make sense while your kids are small. Once Johnny's in high school, however, you'll probably want to move back to the United States. That's because Johnny will most likely be going to a public college or university. To get free or low-cost resident tuition, you have to have your principal residence in the state where Johnny goes to college. It's hard to demonstrate residency in, say, North Carolina when you live in Brazil.

Some states offer resident tuition to anyone who lives in the state, even if they've been there only a short time. Others offer resident tuition only after a certain number of years of residency. And states differ in how they determine who's a resident. In general, if you look like a resident, act like a resident, and pay taxes like a resident, you're a resident. But you can strengthen your case if, besides paying taxes, you register your station car, get a driver's license, and have a bank account in the state of residency.

To make dead sure Johnny meets a given state's requirements for free or low-cost resident tuition, get a copy of the catalog and application for the public university of choice. You'll find copies in state libraries and the counselor's office at the local high school. Better yet, write the university and ask them to send you a copy. The catalog will define a resident and tell how many years of residency you need before Johnny qualifies.

Is Johnny likely to have any problems going to school down South? Remember, he's not only an outsider, he's a Yankee. And within a few weeks the whole town will learn that Johnny's mom and dad are retired. Rather than going to work every day like good, honest, decent, Christian folk, you sit in the park and read books. If you're not careful, the townsfolk will become suspicious? Are you a communist or what?

You can handle the pressure, but what about Johnny? For his sake if not yours, you should try to make sure your family is accepted in the new town. Perhaps the quickest way to obtain acceptance is to spread money around. Give $50 each to the local church, Boy Scout troop, United Crusade, and hospital. Your gifts say you may be wealthy, but you're sensitive to human needs. You should also volunteer your time. Remember, you're one of the few people with time to spare. Organize a school picnic, raise money for a new police car, serve as a volunteer fireman, play a part in the community theater's next project, and sell Christmas trees to help send kids to camp. You want to be visible and, most important, open about yourself. People suspect what they don't understand. Disarm them by unraveling the mystery of very early retirement. Tell them what you did before, why you retired, and why you moved to town. You and your way of life may become a topic of conversation. But by opening yourself to inspection, you'll make it easier for others to accept your decision—and for Johnny to get along in school.

SPECIFIC KNOWLEDGE

You'd like Johnny to get more out of school than the ability to get along with others. You want him to learn specific subjects as well: reading, writing, math, science, history, geography, civics. How do you check whether a school does a good job of imparting specific knowledge?

In my opinion, you can't. You're better off assuming that the local school does a *lousy* job of imparting specific knowledge.

I don't mean to dump on public schools in the South. A 15-year-old girl we know comes from a wealthy San Francisco family and goes to what I'm told is one of the best private high schools in the United States. She's an "average" student, according to her parents. She gets Bs and Cs in a tough school. I asked her some simple questions to see what she knew in math, history, and science. For math, I asked if she knew the square root of nine. For history, I asked if she could name any of the countries that fought in World War II. For science, I asked if she knew at what temperature water freezes.

The girl laughed at me. "I can't answer *those* questions. Can't you give me something easy?"

After several more questions I learned she had heard of Adolf Hitler.

"What do you know about him?" I asked.

"Not very much."

"Let's start with the basics. Overall, was he a good guy or a bad guy?"

She shook her head. "I really couldn't tell you that."

What a child learns in school has more to do with his or her attitude than the school curriculum. More to do with parental reinforcement than class size. More to do with whether their parents can read and write than with the school's textbooks. And let's face it: the specific knowledge Johnny learns in the tenth grade hardly prepares him for life's work. We'd like Johnny to learn something before he graduates from high school. We'd like him to be as prepared as possible before he gets to college. But even in the best of circumstances he retains only a tiny fraction of what he's taught. And what he misses during the early years he can make up later.

A friend of mine teaches at one of Southern California's most respected private liberal-arts colleges. The college draws from the top 10 percent of high-school graduates nationwide. Those admitted typically score in the 90th percentile on the SAT. I asked the professor to compare entering students today with those of twenty years ago.

"Students are just as bright today, maybe brighter," he told me. "But they arrive with virtually no preparation. Twenty years ago we could assume that the brightest students from the best high schools knew *something*. We can't assume that anymore. We test all entering students, regardless of where they went to high school or how well they did, for basic reading and math skills. Based on the test results, we revise our curriculum to meet the needs of the less-advanced students. Happily, the kids are so bright and eager to learn that they can pick up what they need very quickly."

COLLEGE

My scholar friend who says "the education you get is the life you lead" also says, with respect to higher education, "It's not where you start, it's where you end up that counts." Small southern towns may provide a relaxed way of life that children love. An international school in Brazil may give a child memories he'll cherish all his life. But what about college? How does Johnny get into Cornell with a high-school diploma from rural Georgia rather than Grosse Pointe? How does Suzie get into Cal Tech when her high school in Kentucky doesn't even offer calculus?

Let's look a little closer at your children's college career. First, start with the premise that there's no such thing as a good college. "Good for what?" is the question. Colleges come in all sizes, in all parts of the country, and with all kinds of standards. You may want Suzie to go to Yale and later become a lawyer. But Suzie may want to go to Arizona State and party, thank you. You may want Johnny to major in biology and be a doctor. But Johnny may want to major in economics, take an extra year to study chemistry, and then go to medical school. Doing it that way will take a year longer, and Johnny may have a harder time getting into medical school. But if that's the way Johnny wants to do it, you're probably foolish to try to talk him out of it.

Second, recognize that Johnny will most likely go to a public university. On a budget of $4,000 a year you won't have money to pay for private college. And with $400,000 or $500,000 on your Parent's Confidential Statement, Johnny will have a tough time getting financial aid.

But two-thirds of four-year-college students attend public institutions. Some of those institutions are among the finest in the country. Both Stanford and the University of California at Berkeley, for example, rank among the top ten universities in the country. Their San Francisco Bay Area campuses are about fifty miles apart, date from about the same era, and are about the same size. Both schools have excellent libraries, medical schools, historians, and football teams. A degree from either Stanford or Berkeley opens doors from New Mexico to New Guinea. The schools seem similar in every way except one. Stanford is private and costs up to $20,000 a year. U.C. Berkeley is financed by the state of California. According to the College Board, a commuting student there paid less than $1,500 in academic 1986–87. That amounts to only $5,880 over four years, about average for public four-year colleges.

The Association of Research Libraries ranks universities

based on their research potential. Listed according to the quantity of books, tapes, microfiche, and other material, the top ten are:

Harvard	Private
Yale	Private
U. of Illinois	Public
U. of California (Berkeley)	Public
U. of Michigan	Public
Columbia	Private
U. of Texas	Public
Stanford	Private
U. of California (Los Angeles)	Public
U. of Chicago	Private

Of the top thirty research institutions in the country, the association found that seventeen are public and thirteen private.

Peterson's Guide to *Competitive Colleges* covers the most competitive schools. Their tougher-than-tough list—those colleges that accept fewer than half of their applicants—includes Amherst, Bowdoin, Cal Tech, Haverford, Swarthmore, and Tufts. But their tougher-than-tough list also includes seventeen public institutions. Among them are the University of Virginia (Charlottesville), the College of William and Mary (Williamsburg), Cal Poly (San Luis Obispo), the University of Florida (Gainesville), and the University of North Carolina (Chapel Hill).

Some private colleges excel and some don't. Some public colleges excel and some don't. But one thing is certain: public colleges cost less, usually a lot less. In a public college or university, students can earn enough to cover tuition, fees, books, and living costs in just three months of summer work.

The College Board figure of $1,500 a year applies to commuting students. That's why it's so important to establish residency where Johnny is to go to college. Let working parents worry about saving money for Johnny's college education. As retired parents you do something almost as important. You *move* judiciously. You make sure you live in a state that runs a public university that's right for Johnny. If you can't decide what public university is right for Johnny, move to North Carolina or Texas. Both of those states offer low-cost living. Yet both states are renowned for their extensive, high-quality public university systems. Both the University of North Carolina (Chapel Hill) and the University of Texas (Austin) appear in Peterson's Guide to *Competitive Colleges*. Those top-notch universities are backed up by scores of other state universities, colleges, junior colleges, and technical schools. Johnny's bound to find a place that's right for him.

What if Johnny's a truly gifted youngster who thrives in a strong academic environment, or has wanted to go to MIT since he built a mainframe computer at age 6 and a first, cute little nuclear device at age 12? It could be a crime to take Johnny out of Beverly Hills High and put him in a small school in Georgia. Johnny may wind up bored and unhappy. And by putting him on a slower track you may ruin his chances of getting into the most competitive colleges.

If your child is very bright and academically minded, you may need to give his schooling extra attention. You may decide, for example, to postpone your retirement for a year or two until Johnny finishes high school. That way you can set him up in a U.S. college while you're still flush. If you retire and move to the South, you may have to play more of a role in Johnny's education. Many U.S. colleges offer correspondence courses. For those subjects not available in the local high school, you can arrange for Johnny to take courses by mail. You can also supervise Johnny's reading, making sure he reads English classics, for example. You can arrange for a tutor in a foreign language, calculus, or physics.

Even after doing your best, MIT may reject Johnny's application. But that's when Johnny gets a second chance. He can apply to MIT as a sophomore. All schools know that a certain number of freshmen drop out during the first year. Schools look to transfer students to round out the sophomore class. Provided Johnny attends a good college and does well as a freshman, he should have a good shot at transferring to MIT for his sophomore year.

I'm an example of a transfer student. As a freshman I went to a small college in Michigan. Before my second year I applied at Occidental College. Occidental has very high standards, and my SAT scores were such that I doubt I'd have been accepted as a freshman. But, as my friend says, it's not where you start but where you end up that counts. Occidental accepted my transfer application and gave me full credit for my freshman year at the other school. I wound up in one of the best colleges in the country without the competitive struggle that bright high-school seniors can lose sleep over.

Once your child is in MIT, someone has to pay the bills. Assuming he transfers as a sophomore, you'll pay for only three years instead of four. That helps. But MIT can cost $20,000 a year. To help defray that cost, Johnny will have to work after school and during summer vacation. Thankfully, he's so smart he'll be able to work after school without hurting his grades. And he can borrow money, perhaps under low-rate programs. Once he graduates and starts his high-tech career, he'll be able to pay off even large loans without undue strain.

Finally, you can dig into your retirement stash. If you retired with $500,000 rather than $400,000, you can spend your $100,000 cushion on Johnny's education. And don't forget that your primary responsibility is to move judiciously. Find out which public university Johnny has selected for graduate school and check out its residency requirements. Johnny may be eligible for free or low-cost resident tuition when he works toward his Ph.D.

DO SOME SOUL-SEARCHING

The second part of the three-part formula for very early retirement is, "Do some soul-searching." If you choose to retire young, you give up the American dream of a big house, two cars, and life in the fast lane. You replace the American dream with a life of time and energy to do what you most want to do.

But what about the kids? You're willing to give up the American dream for yourself? Fine. But when you retire young you may be giving it up for your kids as well. They'll go to small-town southern schools rather than Choate, to the University of Texas rather than Radcliffe. They'll enter adult life without much financial support from Mom and Dad. That may hold them back if they want to start a business, for example, or go to graduate school.

If you have kids, very early retirement involves a tradeoff. Retire at age 35 or 40 and you spend more time with your kids when they need you most. You take charge of their education instead of leaving it to others. You know you'll never wake up crying because your daughter is 18 and you were busy working or away on business trips during the wonderful years of her youth.

On the other hand, when you retire young you limit the amount of money you can give your kids. They'll have to go to public schools whether they like it or not. I went to Occidental College and Stanford University, two of the finest private institutions in the country. Because my family lived in California and qualified for financial aid, California State scholarships and fellowships covered most of the cost. To cover the rest, during college and business school I worked at night and in the summer. But my mother went back to work and my father worked overtime to earn money to help me out. My parents gave me and my brothers and sister the gift of unconditional love. They taught us to laugh, take responsibility for our actions, and get things done. When I think back, those are the things I remember most. But they also worked to come up with a few bucks when I needed them. I remember that too.

In Providence last summer Vicki and I met Frank and Emily Winter and their three sons, ages 10, 8, and 6. Frank's a self-taught carpenter; Emily's a therapist. They were working full-time to keep their children in one of Providence's experimental private schools. They were pleased with the school. But they felt their children were growing up without them. Frank and Emily wanted to be a part of their boys' daily discoveries, not just to hear about them for a few minutes before bedtime. They wanted to be there when the boys came home from school, not just to call them on the phone to see how they were doing.

After many late-night discussions, Frank and Emily opted for bare-bones retirement (see chapter 11). They moved to a farm in a remote corner of Vermont. Now the children attend a two-room school rather than the modern experimental center that seemed to work so well in Providence. Frank and Emily walk the boys to school each morning. After school the family plays ball, hikes, or works in the garden. At night Frank and Emily help with the boys' homework rather than tell them to go to their room and do it on their own.

Frank does odd jobs around the county and Emily sees one or two patients in her home. Their lives have none of the hurry and stress that wore them down in Providence. They've recovered their sense of family. Frank and Emily believe they did the right thing—for themselves as well as the kids.

To help decide how to make the tradeoff between retiring and stashing money away for your kids, you may want to ask your kids themselves. After a barbecue one day Vicki and I were drinking coffee with our hosts and their 11-year-old daughter. Dad is a high-powered executive with an airline. Mom stays at home and raises three children. We were talking about retirement when their 11-year-old put down her book and started to listen. She's bright, vivacious, studious, and quick on the uptake. We had been beating up on her father a little, and Vicki wanted to turn the tide. She asked the daughter to name the three things she liked most about her dad.

She thought a bit, then said, "He's a great sport. He's always ready to play catch with me, or go sailing or swimming."

"Anything else?"

"He helps me with my homework. And third, he's always there when I need him. He'll come get me at a party, for example, if I'm uncomfortable and want to come home early."

I thought her answers were tender and poignant, but to my surprise her father got upset. "You little jerk," he said. "You didn't even mention how hard I work to be able to afford a big house, a room of your own, piano lessons, new clothes. Not to mention your college education."

She recovered quickly. "That's important too, Dad."

TOWARD A QUALITY FAMILY LIFE

In 1969 the North Pole Santa Claus Company hired me as a department-store Santa Claus. Kids on Santa's lap yank, grab, cry, spit, and steal candy canes. So, before sending the new recruits to the front, the North Pole Santa Claus Company gave us a short training session.

We learned that Santa should get little Junior on his lap, find out what he wants for Christmas, and get him off his lap. Santa must avoid at all costs anything that interferes with that neat, speedy process. We learned, for example, never to ask a kid's name. Kids want to tell Santa the presents they want, not their names. Santa can waste valuable time cajoling a name out of a child who has other things on his mind. It's better to call all boys Junior and all girls Sister.

We learned that Santa should end each lap visit the same way: "Your old buddy Santa can't promise anything. But if you behave, and obey your folks, Santa will do the best he can."

The key word here is *folks*. One of the most dangerous things Santa can do is tell a child to obey "mommy and daddy." In 1969 a third of the children likely to wind up on Santa's lap were living with a mommy or a daddy but not both. If Santa says "obey mommy and daddy," a good number of those kids will well up with tears and stammer, "I don't have a daddy." Once a kid starts to cry, others follow. The chain reaction results in the kind of pandemonium Santa wants to avoid.

I remember being shocked, in 1969, that so many children lived with only one parent. Now we take it as the norm. We know that children do better living with both parents, or at least with two married adults. Yet, Americans continue to destroy family units in record numbers. Foreigners look to the United States as a wealthy, progressive country. But if you ask them to trade their family life for what we have in the United States, they'd say, "No, thanks."

Retirement doesn't guarantee a happy family life. But retirement does allow mom and dad more time together and more time with the kids. For those who feel their job is keeping them from enjoying their family, retirement makes sense.

Some tireless parents seem to divide their attention between the office and home. Chambers Tate, the consultant from chapter 8, works every other week. That way he can spend his off-week with his kids. Another friend has an infant son. Three days a week she works at home, writing magazine articles, while a baby-sitter takes care of the baby in another part of the house. Another friend runs his own business but refuses to expand and take on employees. He believes people problems exhaust one's energy. He'd rather have time and energy for himself and his family than the prestige, power, and money an expanded business would bring.

But who can afford to work half-time, write three days a week, or refuse to expand? As we rise through the ranks, most of us have to devote more time to our jobs, not less. But does that make sense? If you can afford to retire, wouldn't your family be better off with a full-time mom and dad?

DO WHAT YOU WANT

The third part of the three-part formula for very early retirement is, "Do what you want." Like the first two parts, what you do
in retirement changes when you have kids. Those of us without
kids travel off-season rather than during summer vacation. We
take tours of France's wine country without having to worry about
boring the kids. We wander around Mayan ruins in Mexico's
Yucatán peninsula without having to worry about the children
contracting a rare disease.

But when you have kids, your to-do list changes. Instead of
only the things you want to do, your to-do list includes the things
your kids might want to do as well. After all, you retired to spend
more time with your kids and have a richer family life. That
means your kids deserve a say in what the family does.

A retired friend from Southern California is the father of
three boys, ages 14, 11, and 7. He assigns one weekend a month
to each of them. He reserves that weekend for father and son to
do anything the son wants to do. Anything? Dad is pretty flexible.
In the past few years he and one or another of his boys have gone
hang gliding, hired horses for a ride into the back country, flown
to Las Vegas in a rented plane, gone to drag races, and torn up
the San Bernardino Mountains with rented dirt bikes.

Other dads or moms, and sons or daughters, may have
different ideas about how to spend their time. But retired parents
can find out what their kids want to do and follow through. In
most cases you'll find you have time for the kids and plenty of
time for yourself as well.

Retired parents with kids travel less. Wanderlust is fine
when it's just you and your spouse. But travel takes more out of
kids than adults. Kids thrive on having a schedule, a certain
amount of predictability in their lives. Travel exposes them to
constant pressure to adapt. We saw in chapter 6 how hard we
have to work to handle change. But because of their limited
experience, children have to work even harder than adults do. It's
cruel to disrupt their school, sleeping schedules, Girl Scout
meetings, and Little League games just because you feel like
sailing in the Caribbean.

Even so, your family can still travel. If the kids are in school
you can travel for three months every summer and maybe a

couple of weeks during Christmas vacation. And you can safely pull them out of school at other times if circumstances warrant.

Remember Nick and his family from chapter 7? Nick is a trader, one of those who seems never to work but always has enough money to get by. He and his French wife have a 16-year-old son and a 10-year-old daughter. A couple of years ago his son, then 14, seemed immature compared to the rest of the kids at school, partly because he didn't share the other boys' interest in girls. Nick's daughter, then 8, hated school so much she refused to go. Every morning she fought, screaming and crying, as her parents pushed her toward the school-bus door. What to do?

Nick and his wife decided to take both kids out of school and travel around the world. The kids soaked up the sun in Bali, saw India's worst poverty, rode camels in Pakistan, and cried tears of joy when they finally reached Germany's clean sheets and McDonald's hamburgers.

When they returned to the Costa del Sol a year later, both kids went back to school where they had left off. They were a year older than the rest of the kids and had an easier time adjusting. They seemed more dispassionate, more ready to accept the bad with the good. The son started to take girls to parties on weekends. The daughter began to go to school without much fuss.

In chatting about very early retirement over the years, I've found that many people find the idea scary at first. It *is* hard to grasp. But when people without children hear the idea, they tend to react differently than parents. Those without children tend to focus on *why* very early retirement threatens them. They think through the implications of quitting work, selling the house, and moving to the South. They wonder if they have enough net worth. They imagine what life might be like if they didn't have to go to the office. I'm generalizing here. But whether the idea appeals to them or not, people without children tend to go to the *substance* of the idea of very early retirement.

A parent, on the other hand, tends to react to the idea by asking if I have kids. When I say no, I invariably see and hear a sigh of relief. "Ah," says the parent, with a knowing look around the room, eyes pleading for confirmation from other parents. "You don't have kids, Paul. It's impossible to retire with kids."

I like parents. I've got parents of my own. Some of my best friends are parents. And not all parents react the same way; many get past the knee-jerk reaction. But I sense that, in many cases, parents use their kids as an excuse not to retire. I suppose if one wants an excuse, kids are as good a one as any. But this chapter has shown that it's entirely possible to retire with kids. Sam and Nick, the mentors you met in chapter 7, both retired with kids. And, more to the point, kids could very likely get as much out of retirement as Mom and Dad. After Mom and Dad retire, the kids get time with Mom and Dad when they need it most rather than when the time happens to be available. Perhaps for the first time ever, the kids have a mom and dad who can help them with their homework, take them to ball games, and watch them perform. In short, kids have a mom and dad full-time.

In the end, the question comes down to why you have kids in the first place. To provide them with the best money can buy? To play with them, to grow with them, to share their lives? If you work until you're 60, you may be able to send your kids to private college. If you retire young, you probably won't. But what means more to your kids: private college at age 20, or Mom and Dad's time and energy at age 10?

Working parents point to their kids and say, "I keep working to pay for them." Retired parents point to *their* kids and say, "I retired to be with them."

10.

Building Your Net Worth

My friend Nancy is 42 years old and divorced. Her life revolves around her job, a string of men friends, and two teenage daughters. Nancy is bright, perky, energetic, sexy, charming, and quick to laugh.

Nancy is vice president of marketing at a small San Francisco leasing company. She makes $75,000 a year, which is double what she made three years ago, and half of what she's likely to make three years from now. She's on a fast track, and with a little luck she'll climb her career ladder for several more years.

Nancy has other income besides her salary. She gets child support from her ex-husband. Her parents pay for private schools for her two children. But whether Nancy's income is $35,000 or $135,000 makes little difference to her net worth. She spends everything she has no matter what she has. Eight years ago, when she got divorced and started her career, she had zero net worth. Except for a new car, she has zero net worth now. And unless she changes her ways, she'll have zero net worth in five, ten, or twenty years.

Nancy gets raises every six months or so, but the raises never help. She spends her year-end bonus and tax refunds before she receives them. She has three MasterCards and four VISA cards, all charged to the limit. When she gets the bills she pays the minimum due, without bothering to check the charges. Every month or two she requests an increase in one of her credit lines. Nancy's idea of a sustained, long-term savings program is to get a good interest rate on a bill-consolidation loan. When you ask about her household budget, she gets a blank look on her face and asks you to repeat the question.

Nancy pays high rent on her San Francisco apartment. She skis in Tahoe most winter weekends, and pampers herself with extravagant summer vacations. She buys stylish clothes for herself and her daughters. Every few years she gets a new car.

So Nancy has high expenses. But everyone has high expenses. The question is why some people who earn as much as Nancy seem to manage to live a good life and save something to boot. Nancy has several friends who can retire now. But unless she robs a bank, Nancy has as much chance of retiring young as does a $20,000-a-year office clerk with seven small children.

Millions of young Americans have $400,000 or so of net worth and can retire with class. But what about the rest of you, the millions of Nancys with good incomes but with little net worth and little hope of increasing it? If you're someone who views $400,000 as an impossible dream, this chapter and the next are for you.

This chapter gives four rules for building your net worth. Follow the rules and you'll be on your way to the $400,000 plateau. If you decide not to follow the rules, or if you decide you *can't* follow the rules, read about bare-bones retirement in the next chapter. Bare-bones retirement requires some sacrifice. But you can do bare-bones retirement with as little as $100,000 of total net worth.

BUILDING YOUR RETIREMENT STASH

You're like Nancy in that you have a reasonable income but no savings program. You might have more net worth than Nancy does. You might have some equity in your home, for example, or a small IRA. But to start building your retirement stash you need to make changes in your life.

I'm fresh out of clever advice on how to make others pick up dinner checks. How to buy wholesale from a cousin in New Jersey. How to get professional services free of charge. And I'm not going to suggest you live like a pauper, forgo vacations, or wear old clothes. But I am going to give you four rules. In most cases I think you'll find that the rules disrupt your life very little. With the right attitude, you may find that your new retirement-track life beats the one you lead right now.

Here are the rules:

Manage your career
Control your spending
Set up a savings routine
Start a high-risk/low-risk investment program

I've listed the four rules in order of importance. That is, the best way to build your net worth is to manage your career. When you're making $200,000 a year, it's a whole lot easier to save than when you're making $30,000. The second-best way to build your net worth is to control your spending. You've read about the $50-a-Day Rule for retirees. You need to adapt the $50-a-Day Rule while you're still on the job.

If you follow only the career and spending rules you can probably reach your target net worth. But to reach it more quickly, you should set up a savings routine and start a high-risk/low-risk investment program. This chapter gives details on how to do both.

MANAGE YOUR CAREER

The first rule is to manage your career. Making more money in your present job or switching to a new one can make the difference between retiring at age 40 or at age 70.

When people hear that I retired at 35 they often get a shrewd look on their faces. "Real estate, huh?" I shake my head. "Oil wells?" I shake my head. "Stock market?" Again I shake my head. They get desperate. "What the hell did you do? Rob a bank?"

All I did was become a partner in a big accounting firm. It's no secret that partners in the big accounting firms enjoy substantial incomes. And it's no secret that it's easier to build your net worth with a substantial income than with two-dollar tips.

I'm being a little cavalier when I tell you to go out and make more money. If it were so easy to get a high-paying job you'd probably have one already. And you may enjoy being a poorly paid teacher, nurse, letter carrier, journalist, or librarian, thank you. If a job you enjoy pays $20,000 a year, well, that's what it pays. Life's too short to give up willy-nilly a fun, rewarding job just to make a few bucks.

But you may not have to change jobs to make more money. In a July 1986 *Boston Globe* article on career changing, Sarah Snyder reports that "if there is a consensus among career counselors . . . it is that people tend to overlook ways to make a current job more fulfilling." More fulfilling, in most cases, means more money as well. Cynthia Scott, co-author with Dennis Jaffe of *From Burnout to Balance* (McGraw-Hill, 1984), says that before changing careers, you should push your present job to the limits of its challenge—and remuneration.

If you're a computer programmer you can become a systems analyst and then a computer salesman. If you're a legal assistant you can go to night school and become a lawyer. If you're a doctor you can become head of a hospital. If you're a store assistant you can become a store manager and then a store owner.

My friend Chuck is a senior architect in a fifty-person firm in Saint Louis. The firm's two partners each make upward of $100,000, while Chuck struggles along at $35,000. What are the chances of Chuck's becoming a partner and breaking into the big time?

"Until about six months ago the chances were pretty good," Chuck told me. "I was spending three hours a day on staffing and office work. The partners were thinking of admitting me to the firm as administrative partner. But I hate office work. After two years of it I insisted on going back to the creative side full-time. I don't think I'll ever make partner on the creative side, but I'm happier now. I drive home after work feeling good about myself rather than tired and mad."

I respect Chuck's decision. Chuck is a jovial, easygoing guy who leaves the office promptly at six each day. He has an adorable wife and three small children who mean more to him than anything he could possibly do at the office. He's 30 years old and wants to enjoy these next few years—on the job *and* at home.

But what makes good sense for Chuck at age 30 may leave him feeling stale and useless at age 35. His children will be older and will want more time of their own. Family life will go more smoothly, leaving Chuck more energy for other things. And, most important, Chuck may change his views about what type of work he enjoys. In five years the *creative* side may leave him sapped. Chuck may want to take on a new office project. Chuck loves to work with computers, for example. If the office continues to grow, Chuck may be just the man to program a computer to do staffing, scheduling, and related tasks.

When was the last time you reevaluated career decisions you made ten, five, or even three years ago? You hated sales, but are you sure you'd hate sales now? You panicked at the thought of running your own business, but would you panic now? You stewed over people problems, but you're more mature now. Perhaps what used to be people problems are now ways to help others.

To get more out of your career you have to stretch a little. A man I know used to teach private English lessons in Madrid. He saw about ten people a week and charged $15 an hour. But he got fed up with the constant promotional push to attract new students. "I'm an English teacher, not a hustler," he griped. He finally got rid of his private students and took a $3-an-hour job in a language institute.

This man is now working forty hours a week instead of ten. He's earning $120 a week instead of $150. True, he doesn't do any promotional work. But seeing students forty hours a week leaves him feeling beat up and exhausted.

This man now thinks he made a mistake. "With word of mouth alone I could have maintained an average of five or six students," he told me. "And I could have hired a kid one day a week to make phone calls, place ads, and do the other stuff I hated."

When did you last stretch in your job? Agree to take on a slightly unpleasant task to get ahead? Take the initiative to learn more about jobs in your area or another area? Ask for a transfer to a new department with a more exciting future? And don't forget the basics: when was the last time you asked for a raise or promotion?

I'm not suggesting you "sell out," give up what you most

enjoy, or take on duties that make you sick. But I am suggesting that you stretch. With a bit of willpower you can handle a bigger job. Make the right moves at the office and you could find yourself making bigger bucks and enjoying work more than ever.

A friend recently left her personnel job and went into sales. For the first time in her life, she's making cold telephone calls. To handle the stress she keeps a sign on her desk that says "I'm stretching." Whenever she makes a cold call—or does anything else she's never done before—she holds the "I'm stretching" sign for her assistant to see. Invariably she begins to feel better and enjoy the task more.

In spite of your best efforts, though, you may be unable or unwilling to stretch in your current situation. Or you may be stretching like a rubber band and still not getting anywhere. Perhaps the time has come to change careers.

The *Globe* article by Sarah Snyder concludes that "the number of professionals who from frustration, boredom, or simple lust for more money abandon their careers for new ones in their early 30's are increasing." Richard Grossman, author of *Choosing and Changing* (Dutton, 1978), says "it's a legacy of the 60's. It is as legitimate to question career commitments as everything else."

The *Globe* article tells of a nurse who became an investment banker, a college professor who became a vice president of Kidder, Peabody, and a newspaper reporter who became a lawyer. These people were motivated to change careers when they asked themselves, "What am I going to be doing ten years from now?" In every case they decided their old jobs offered little hope for the future. In every case they enjoy their new career at least as much as the old. And in every case they're making more money— generally a lot more money—in their new jobs.

My friend Suzanne is a research psychologist. Her field is personality testing. Ten years ago she became a full professor at the University of Southern California. A few years after that she wrote a college textbook, then a book on research technique. She became chairman of the psychology department. But two years ago she decided she was tired of applying for grants, writing textbooks, and teaching sophomores. She was reluctant to give up what she had worked so hard to achieve. But when she got an offer to work for an executive search firm as a consultant, she took the job.

Suzanne now studies potential top executives, and she loves it. She never has to apply for grants; if she wants to do a project, the money's there. The money's there for Suzanne, too. She's earning about three times what she made in the academic world.

Changing jobs and careers is a major step, and you should move with caution. But if you act with a clear head, and are honest about your motives, you're bound to be a success. You'll get a kick out of your work, learn new skills, and make more money.

And you'll be on the road to very early retirement.

CONTROL YOUR SPENDING

Pushing your job to its limit, changing jobs, or changing careers may put you on a faster track. But Nancy is already on a fast track. She makes good money. Yet Nancy can't save a dime.

The problem is that Nancy spends recklessly. Money flies out of Nancy's purse the way newspapers fly out of a high-speed press. Nancy's attitude is: why walk two blocks when you can take a cab? Why drink $30-a-bottle champagne when you can afford to drink bubbly for $100? Why pay $200 for a dress at Macy's when you can pay $300 for the same thing at Neiman-Marcus? Why be a member of a health club you never use when you can be a member of two health clubs you never use?

To control spending you need to adopt a spending plan that fits your personality. You like to do things first-class? Then a spending plan that compels you to buy cheap theater seats, eat in greasy dives, and drink in local taverns is bound to fail. Instead, plan to go out first-class but to do it a little less often. If you're too impatient to check prices at the supermarket, try to get a spouse or child to take over that task. If certain stores tempt you to buy, avoid the stores. Better yet, shop by mail.

Still, when you save on household expenses you save nickels and dimes. Nickels and dimes can add up, and you *should* try to control household expenses. But to save big money—thousands of dollars, rather than hundreds—you've got to control the big killers. And whether you're working or retired, the big killers are the same: the huge house and the fancy car.

In a January 4, 1987, article in *The New York Times Magazine*, Richard B. Elsberry talks about what he calls his "preretirement" at age 53. Elsberry's piece is a personal, moving account of a retired life that makes sense for him. But in commenting on his new spending patterns, he says: "I've found that double coupons can cut the grocery bill 25 percent. I haunt tag sales and factory outlets for bargains. . . . And we subscribe to half as many magazines these days."

Like Mr. Elsberry, you can clip coupons, shop in factory outlets, and cancel magazines. If doing those things appeals to you, by all means do them. But in the scheme of things, saving $50 on a magazine subscription doesn't help much when you're living in a $3,000-a-month rental apartment. Saving $100 in a factory outlet is a drop in the bucket when you're spending $5,000 a month on mortgages and property taxes. You can scrimp and save for ten years in the supermarket, clipping coupons and stocking up on sale items. But if every year you spend $20,000 on your vehicles, I can almost guarantee you'll never save much money.

Saving on housing and car costs is easy when you're retired. Chapter 5, for example, lists great places where you can live cheaply. Unfortunately, Nancy can't very well work in high-cost San Francisco and live in, say, a $200-a-month rental in North Carolina. Similarly, retired people can get by with a cheap station car. If the cheap car refuses to run in the rain, retired people avoid driving in the rain. But Nancy needs her car to call on customers. She relies on her car, and a car that breaks down in the rain just won't do.

So Nancy will have a tougher time than retirees do in controlling housing and car costs. Still, Nancy *can* do a great deal to reduce those two killer costs.

Nancy lives in a $2,500-a-month rental apartment on top of Nob Hill. By moving a block or two down the hill she can save $500 a month. By giving up her view she can save another $500. By getting a slightly smaller, slightly older place she can save another $500. If she does all three, she saves $1,500 a month. That's a huge savings, enough to build a nest egg very quickly. She may miss the view and the extra sitting room. But by moving she saves big money now, without changing her day-to-day life-style one bit.

If you rent your home, can you move a few blocks away and save a pile? Can you move to the suburbs and commute by bus or train for a while? Can you move to a smaller place, or one without amenities you never use? I'm not suggesting you live in the type of burned-out, bombed-out neighborhoods that flash across the screen at the beginning of Eddie Murphy movies. But if you're like most young people who rent, you can save big money by giving up luxuries you don't appreciate, common-area facilities you don't use, and neighborhoods that are frankly out of your price range.

If you own rather than rent your home, you should consider selling. Chapter 4 explains my view that home ownership can be a lousy investment. I won't repeat my arguments here. But in trying to build your retirement stash, you should ask yourself if your home is likely to go up in value. Forget about whether it went up in the past. Ask yourself what's likely to happen in the future, with changing tax laws, real interest rates, and demographics.

If you decide your home's value is likely to go up sharply, sit tight. You're building your net worth by increasing your equity. But if you decide that further appreciation is unlikely, you may want to sell. As we saw in chapter 4, owning a home in the absence of rapid increases in housing values makes little financial sense. You're better off to sell, put your equity to work in other investments, and rent cheaper quarters.

You'll have to pay some taxes if you don't plow the gain on sale into a new home within two years. But you're going to retire young, and when you do you'll have to sell your home and pay taxes anyway. Doing it now frees up your equity that much sooner. And by moving to a low-cost rental, your housing costs will plummet.

After you sell you'll need to muster up some discipline to keep from squandering your newly liquid stash. You'll also need discipline to save the money you would otherwise spend on house payments. This chapter's last two rules help you maintain that discipline. But if you lack the discipline to manage your finances—if you're tempted to spend every cent you have—you're better off owning a home. That way, every time you make a mortgage payment you're forced to save.

In summary, if you rent you should look for a cheaper rental. If you own, you should consider pulling your equity out now rather than later. Either way, you'll be without the "fuzzy blanket" of home ownership. For most of us, that fuzzy blanket is important. What to do?

My suggestion is to buy a vacation home, but a vacation home with two important characteristics. First, your vacation home should cost no more than $40,000 or so. Second, your vacation home should be a place you'd like to live in once you retire.

Why do I like vacation homes? First, a vacation home serves just as well as the all-important fuzzy blanket. But it's a fuzzy blanket that costs only $40,000, far less than what you'd pay for a first home. Forty thousand dollars won't buy a decent back porch on Manhattan's East Side; for that matter, it won't buy a vacation home on Long Island or the Jersey shore, either. You'll have to buy quite a ways out—Maine, perhaps, or New Hampshire. So your vacation home will be too far away to use on short weekends. Still, you'll have a home of your own.

Second, by buying a vacation home you'll save money on vacations. Remember, you'll be retiring in a few years. After you retire you'll have plenty of time to see the world. For now, save vacation dollars by spending part of each summer in your second home. You'll relax, enjoy fixing up the place, and dream about living there full-time.

Third, by having a vacation home that will become your residence when you retire, you ease the transition to retired life. One of the most stressful parts of very early retirement—or any other retirement—is moving. By setting up your retirement home now, you avoid that stress later on.

Fourth, if real estate *does* take off again, you'll have a piece of the action. I think the action in lower-cost vacation homes may be particularly good. Baby boomers have already driven up prices on first homes; prices on vacation homes could go up next. We've already seen price rises in "close in" vacation areas: Cape Cod, near Boston; eastern Long Island, near New York; Lake Tahoe, near San Francisco. For younger baby boomers, prices in those areas are already out of range. Younger baby boomers will have to buy lower-cost vacation homes, farther away from urban centers. The increased demand could drive up prices in those areas.

If my theory about a coming boom in lower-cost vacation homes is correct, when you're ready to retire you may find your vacation home is worth, say, $200,000 or more. That'll be a pleasant surprise. But that's far too much money to have tied up in your retirement home. You already know what to do: sell, put your equity in the bank, and head to one of the low-cost areas mentioned in chapter 5. At least some of those areas are bound to be unaffected by housing booms elsewhere.

The second killer under the control-your-spending rule is car expense. Can you get by without a second car? Without recreational vehicles? With a modest station car as your second car? Remember that, although you need a way to get around, you can live without a car that's a pricey yuppie status symbol. If you need to entertain someone or want to make a scene, rent a limousine with a driver for the evening. You'll have fun. And you'll pay far less than the $40,000 you'd have to spend to own the luxury car.

SET UP A SAVINGS ROUTINE

In building your net worth, the first two rules are the most important:

Manage your career
Control your spending

Push your after-tax income from $40,000 to $75,000. Cut your housing costs from $20,000 to $12,000. Cut your car costs from $10,000 to $5,000. If you do those things and nothing more, you're saving big money.

The question now is: how should you invest it?

Chapter 4 tells retirees to invest in bank CDs. If that advice is good enough when you're retired, you could figure it's good enough when you're working. You *could* figure that way, but you'd be wrong.

Workers have more options than retirees. Workers can get into employee stock ownership plans, 401(k) plans, and incentive plans. And workers, with an income stream from their jobs, can accept more risk than retirees.

Rather than buy CDs, I recommend that workers pursue a high-risk/low-risk investment strategy. We'll talk about that strategy in a minute. But first, we need a rule on saving.

In this context "saving" refers not to cutting down on expenditures but to getting money out of your spending stream. We've already seen how to get your income up and your spending down. But unless you get that extra money *out* of your spending stream and *into* wise investments, you may wind up spending foolishly. The rule is:

Set up a savings routine

Your savings routine should have two parts. First, you should enroll in most, if not all, of your company's optional benefit programs. If you're self-employed, you should set up tax-deferred programs like IRAs and Keoghs. Second, you should write yourself a check each pay period.

Your company's benefit programs are great ways to save. The programs involve a payroll deduction. Payroll deductions snatch money out of your spending stream before you ever get your hands on it. You're never tempted to spend what you don't have.

Beyond the discipline of payroll deductions, however, company benefit programs can be great deals. For example, 401(k) plans defer tax on earnings put into the plans. Those tax savings are a terrific benefit. Other programs may not be tax-oriented, but they can provide good returns. Most stock ownership plans, for example, give you free shares of stock every time you buy shares with your own money. Also, under most stock plans, your employer pays the commissions when you sell the stock.

You'll want to evaluate company programs before signing up. If you have any questions, ask your personnel department for help. But my experience is that most company plans are good deals. Sign up for the maximum permitted.

If you're self-employed, set up IRAs, Keoghs, and other plans that give self-employed workers some of the tax benefits employees enjoy.

Under the rules for IRAs and other tax-deferred schemes, if you withdraw your funds before "normal" retirement you have to pay tax and, sometimes, a penalty. To postpone the tax and avoid penalty, simply leave the funds intact, at the bottom of your investment pyramid, until you're old enough to withdraw them without penalty.

The second part of your savings routine is to write yourself a check each month. The need to write yourself a check arises because, in most cases, your entire paycheck goes into your checking account. Money in checking accounts represents spendable funds. You need to get that money out of your checking account and into a separate savings account. To reinforce the importance of pulling money from your spendable income stream, the transfer from checking to savings should be the first check you write each month.

How much should you transfer? The best answer is: as much as you can. Ideally, you'll have a household spending plan. Transfer the excess of your pay over the amount in your spending plan. If you don't have a household spending plan, transfer a fixed amount each month. Determine the right amount by watching your checking account balance. You want your checking account to be out of money just before you receive your next paycheck.

If you're self-employed, writing yourself a check each month is even more important than for employees. If you're like most self-employed people I know, you tend to leave excess funds in your business. When you need money for personal use, you withdraw the required amount. But that system gives you the sensation that there's money for whatever you want to do. You're better off to withdraw all excess funds. Put what you need for daily expenses in your checking account. Stash the rest in a personal savings account.

START A HIGH-RISK/LOW-RISK INVESTMENT PROGRAM

If you've followed the rules so far you've got your salary up and your spending down. You've enrolled in benefit programs where you work. If you're self-employed you've got an IRA, trust fund, or whatever. You're writing yourself a check each month to get money into your savings account.

You're ready for the final step:

Start a high-risk/low-risk investment program

In the two-year M.B.A. program at Stanford, we took courses on how to invest. We learned to reduce alpha risk, to choose the right beta risk, and to calculate returns. We learned when and how to trade commodities, foreign exchange, gold, and options. We came up with overall strategies. We managed portfolios. We played computer games to see how our ideas would have worked in the real world.

It was great fun for those who like that sort of thing. I don't happen to. As I recall, I spent more time playing foosball in a Menlo Park pub than sorting through stock tapes. Instead of figuring how to manage billions, I tried to figure how to manage thousands. *My* thousands. I finally came up with a personal investment program that worked for me. I call it a high-risk/low-risk program.

In a high-risk/low-risk program, you put most of your funds in low-risk IRAs, incentive and savings plans, employee stock plans, bank CDs, money-market accounts, savings deposits, and the like. Equity in your home, if you own a home, is also a low-risk investment. With the rest of your money, you take flyers: very high-risk investments that can produce extraordinary returns.

When I say high-risk or low-risk, I assume that low reward goes with low risk and that high reward can come with high risk. Things don't always work out that way. If you know of a low-risk, high-reward investment, by all means go for it. But here I assume the more normal case of risk and reward moving together.

As for your *low-risk* portfolio, make sure it's truly low-risk. Avoid "medium-risk" investments. Medium-risk investments offer only slightly higher returns ("medium" returns) but involve an unknown ("medium") amount of risk. Although that unknown risk is usually considered "slight" at the time of investment, medium-risk investments can go sour.

My friend Harry once bought a medium-risk investment. Harry owned a small liquor store and three bars. In 1976 he sold the businesses, stuck his money into bank CDs, and retired. But on a trip to Mexico in the late 1970s, Harry noticed that Mexican banks were offering 9 percent on dollar CDs. Harry was getting only 7 percent in the United States. He decided to stick $100,000 into dollar CDs in Mexican banks.

Those Mexican CDs seemed like a good, medium-risk investment. Harry knew he was giving up the FDIC guarantee he enjoyed back home. But he chose solid Mexican banks. And Harry was investing in dollars, not pesos. That protected him against devaluation.

Unfortunately for Harry and others, in 1982 the Mexican government confiscated roughly half of Mexico's dollar deposits. Harry, who had built his CDs up to $140,000 by rolling interest and principal, lost nearly $70,000.

Some Mexicans object to the word *confiscate*. What the government did was impose exchange controls. Banks were ordered to convert dollar CDs to pesos at the official exchange rate. When Harry withdrew the pesos and went to buy dollars in the open market, he found a market exchange rate nearly double the official rate. With the pesos he got from his CDs, he could buy only U.S. $70,000. His money may not have been "confiscated," but you'll never convince Harry of that. Harry thinks he got ripped off.

Some people haven't learned from the experience of Harry and others. As of this writing, Mexico has lifted most of its exchange controls. Thousands of U.S. investors are pouring millions of dollars into Mexican banks. Many of those investors are retired, living in Mexico all or part of the year. I feel sorry for them. It's only a matter of time until Mexico reinstates some sort of exchange control. When that happens, those investors are going to lose.

CDs in foreign banks are the kind of no-nos I call medium-risk investments. So are municipal bonds issued by poor or bankrupt cities, CDs without guarantees by a U.S. government agency, many mutual funds, second mortgages, and personal loans. In most cases those investments offer only slightly higher returns but unknown risk. Avoid them. The small extra return—usually no more than 2 or 3 percentage points—can't justify the risk, however small that risk appears to be.

High-risk investments contrast with medium-risk investments in that high-risk investments can throw off high returns. High-risk investments are flyers. Buy or short-sell volatile stocks. Play the commodities, foreign exchange, or options markets. Trade gold and silver. Invest in a friend's startup business for half of the profits. Buy an apartment building. Do an oil and gas exploration deal, or buy oil and gas reserves.

Your local bookstore is full of books on how to make a million in real estate, gold, foreign currency, or whatever. My advice is to buy one of the books, take $10,000 or so out of your savings, and get cracking.

How should you choose your high-risk investments? First, choose something that interests you. That way you'll have fun while you play around. Second, invest in areas you know at least something about. If you've lived overseas, for example, you probably know foreign currencies better than U.S. real estate. Third, make sure you control your downside risk. You can afford to lose the $10,000 you put into a high-risk deal. But you don't want to be on the hook for any more than that.

How can you control your downside? If you buy an apartment building, make sure the mortgage loans are nonrecourse to you. California real estate loans, for example, are generally considered nonrecourse; Texas real estate loans are not. If you're playing the stock market, place stop orders to cash you out before you lose too much. If you're doing oil and gas deals, refuse to sign letters of credit that put you at risk for more than your preset limit. If you finance a friend's new business, refuse to cosign the bank loan.

The final point about choosing high-risk deals is to make sure you put yourself in a position to hit a home run. Don't do high-risk deals that offer only mediocre returns. For example, make certain that if your wildcat drilling deal strikes oil, you'll get your fair share. Avoid deals that leave the big money for the drillers rather than the investors. If you help a friend start a business, make certain you get your money back and a lot more if the business takes off. You don't want to be a hog. But you're a venture capitalist. Venture capitalists take sizable shares of the businesses they help finance. If you do a risky real estate deal, make sure you stand to make out if the buildings go up in value. I've seen high-risk real estate deals that reserve the upside, beyond a certain point, for a select group. Make sure you're one of the select group or don't do the deal.

How should you divide your investments between low-risk

and high-risk? The answer depends on your attitude toward risk. Assuming you want to build your net worth to $400,000 or $500,000, I recommend you buy small amounts of high-risk investments once your net worth hits $100,000. By small amounts I mean $5,000 to $10,000, certainly less than $20,000. By net worth I mean total net worth, including your IRAs, employee benefit programs, equity in your home, and cash on hand. Later, as your net worth increases, you may want to put up to 30 percent in high-risk investments.

11.

Bare-bones Retirement

In September 1986, Vicki and I lived for a week with a couple in Pula, Yugoslavia. Aldo, 58, and his wife, Dozanka, 57, speak a fractured mixture of Spanish, French, and Italian. Vicki and I understood only a part of what they said. But they let it be known that we should plan to be at the kitchen table every afternoon at five. At that hour Aldo would break out the white lightning, Dozanka would brew Turkish coffee, and the day's discussion would begin.

Aldo retired after 41 years in the merchant marine. He loves to talk about the countries he visited and people he met. He respects the intelligence of the Nazis who occupied Yugoslavia during World War II. He reveres Tito, Yugoslavia's great national hero, and compares him to George Washington. He takes pride in Yugoslavia's modern brand of capitalistic socialism. Aldo even thinks he understands the French, although he avoids saying too many kind things about them.

Aldo's two favorite countries are the Soviet Union and the United States. Both are big, rich, and high-tech. According to Aldo, Russia makes better cars. He's driven his Russian-built model for over twenty years, and it still runs perfectly. But Aldo prefers American TV programs, music, and sense of style. Aldo says Russians tend to be dimwits. He talks about Russians the way small children might talk about a 10-year-old who can't get the hang of hopscotch.

Aldo insisted on finding out what I did for a living. I told him I was retired, but that just wouldn't do. Aldo and his Yugoslav friends had never managed to save a dinar. Only Aldo's $110 monthly pension keeps him and Dozanka from starving. He could relate to my retiring at age 35 as much as a fourteenth-century Yugoslav peasant might relate to Einstein's special theory of relativity.

I finally explained that I had been a public accountant, worked hard, got lucky, and made some money. I told him I had retired at age 35 and lived off the interest on my savings, and that Vicki and I were in Yugoslavia doing research for a book on how others can do the same.

Aldo furrowed his brow. "So the book is a fantasy story?"

I said, "Not at all. In America you can quit work at any age if you have enough money."

Aldo said, "Capitalism. It's unfair for anyone to have so much money."

"But you're missing the point," I said. "The book talks to those who value time more than money. I propose a life centered on family, friends, and simple pleasures rather than on owning and consuming. Happiness comes from living the way you want to live, not from spending a lot of money."

This talk took place after several adult portions of white lightning had disappeared. The language barrier meant that neither of us could know how much the other was picking up. But Aldo convinced me that he had the idea when he told me the following Yugoslav folk tale:

Once upon a time a king and his entourage were passing through a valley when they heard a man singing. The full, joyous sound caught the king's attention. He ordered his servants to take him to the singer. They detoured and came upon a humble blacksmith. He was singing merrily as he worked over his glowing fire pit.

"Why are you so happy?" the king demanded. "What do you have to sing about?"

The blacksmith smiled. "It's a bright, sunny day. I'm healthy, working at my trade. I have my wife, my children. Life offers beautiful things. I sing."

"Do you have a home?" the king asked. "Food on the table? A sturdy horse?" (One might say the king was materialistic.)

The smith smiled and shook his head. "My family and I sleep on the ground, close to the earth, in a room connected to the stables. We have gruel to eat. It is enough."

The king was so overwhelmed that he gave the man a bag of gold.

A few days later, the king passed by that way again but heard no singing. He went to see what had happened. He found a haggard blacksmith staring with wide, troubled eyes into a cold fire pit.

"I lie awake nights deciding what to buy," the smith told the king. "I worry about where to hide my gold so no one will rob me. My wife and children fight about who will get to spend the money." Desperation on his face, the smith pleaded with the king. "Won't you please take back your gift?"

The king took the bag of gold. As he rode away he could hear the man singing, the happy sound once again echoing through the valley. The king was happy too. With the extra gold he could buy a few more countries or another dozen wives.

Aldo paused at the end of the story. "Does your book suggest we live more like the blacksmith?" he asked.

"Exactly."

Aldo squinted a little. "But the blacksmith works."

I said, "The blacksmith finds pleasure in the beauty around him. Sudden wealth took him away from those pleasures, not toward them. The blacksmith lives simply, but he's in control of his life, doing exactly what he wants to do. Isn't that the point of the story?"

Aldo nodded, pleased that I understood. "I love America," he said. "In Yugoslavia a man works at what the state gives him to do. No one has the freedom to do what you've done. No one."

The United States is short on kings, blacksmiths, and gruel these days, at least outside of Boston. Modern living requires more infrastructure, and that costs money. We've seen that 4 million young Americans have or are approaching $400,000 or $500,000 of net worth. With that much money you can retire now, converting your assets to cash and investing in one-year

CDs. You'll be able to pay taxes, set aside for inflation, and live well.

But how about the rest of you, those with less than $400,000 or $500,000, who want to retire anyway? My first advice is to hold your horses. Keep working, if at all possible, until you get to $400,000. Follow the advice in chapter 10 and you'll get there fast.

In some cases, though, $400,000 of net worth may be an impossible dream. Your chosen vocation may pay peanuts. You may get fired before you reach $400,000 and have trouble finding a new job. Or you may want to retire *now*. You may be fed up with the system and desperate to get out. You may want more time with your kids while they're young, not when you happen to reach $400,000 of net worth. Like the blacksmith, you may choose to do exactly what you want with your life.

With a few special rules, it's possible to retire with as little as $100,000 in net worth. That's total net worth, including home equity. Retiring with $100,000 is what I call bare-bones retirement, and the formula is:

Do your arithmetic
Do some soul-searching
Do what you want

It's the same formula as for the guy with a bigger stash. Most of the rules that support the formula apply whether you have $500,000, $100,000, or something in between. But bare-bones retirees must learn to spend less than "normal" very early retirees. Instead of living on $50 a day, with $100,000 or so of net worth you'll have to live on half that amount. You'll have a tougher time protecting your capital against inflation. Your sense of financial security will have to come from faith in yourself rather than big bank balances. You'll have to count on Social Security when you reach age 62.

But you *can* retire right now. This chapter tells you how.

RETIRING ON $743 A MONTH

In 1983 the average Social Security payment to a retired worker and spouse was $743. At 8 percent annual interest—the figure I've used throughout this book—you need to invest just over $110,000 to generate $743 of monthly income.

How many Americans have $100,000 or $110,000? The Census Bureau, in a study published in 1986, found that two-thirds of America's families own their homes. Their median home equity in 1984 was $40,597. Add the value of cars, savings, IRAs, Pet Rocks, phony Cartier watches, and shoe polish, and $100,000 or so becomes a very achievable net worth for huge numbers of Americans, perhaps a majority.

Picture an elderly couple living on $743-a-month Social Security. If you're like me, you see a hollow-eyed man and stooped woman huddled around a radiator in a drafty, cold-water flat in Baltimore. Paint peels from the walls, threadbare rugs cover creaky floors, and a depressing, worn sofa looks as inviting as barbed wire. Low-watt bulbs cast just enough light to give you a headache. The TV blares constantly. The daily meal looks like what some people might feed their dog. Conversation centers around pain, doctors, nurses, Medicare, medicine, and death.

You'd do anything—even keep working at a job you hate—to avoid a fate like that. But let's look a little closer at that Social Security couple. The elderly have some special expenses you don't share. They spend much of their $743 a month on medicine, therapy, and special diets. They face huge hospital bills, even with Medicare. They have to take cabs every place they go. They refuse to move to a warmer climate, with lower heating costs, because they're terrified of the unknown. They fall prey to mail-order swindlers, stingy landlords, and quack healers.

Your retired life on $743 a month will be totally different. You and your spouse or partner are young, vital, and healthy. You'll gladly walk up three flights of stairs to save $100 or $200 a month in rent. Medical care will be a once-in-a-while expense rather than a monthly routine. You'll enjoy saving money by shopping for fresh fish, meat, fruit, and vegetables at the farmers' market. You'll need to plan for your white-haired years. You must avoid the life of the wretched Social Security couple in Baltimore. But while you're young, you'll be having so much fun you'll endure life's little hardships without really noticing.

In your $743-a-month retirement, you can collect 1890s memorabilia, travel through South America, write songs for your jazz band, play tennis, start a foundation to help disadvantaged kids, take photos, study Scandinavian history, take up farming in Idaho, chop wood in Vermont, study philosophy, restore an old Lasalle, or simply sleep a little later each morning. You may feel like reading poetry for the first time since college, and you may even try your hand at writing some. Instead of talking to your friends and family by long-distance telephone, you'll go visit them for a week or two, or write long letters. You'll not only forget about your job, you'll wonder why you put up with it for so long.

Still, $743 a month puts you below the poverty level for a two-person household in America. Uncle Sam doesn't even make you pay taxes. That's why I believe you should consider bare-bones retirement only if "normal" retirement at age 35 or 40—with $400,000 or more in the bank—is out of the question. But if you want to retire on $743 a month, you need only three special rules:

Live overseas or live in the United States like a student
Search out moneymaking sidelines
Focus on spending priorities

LIVE OVERSEAS OR LIVE IN THE UNITED STATES LIKE A STUDENT

Chapter 5 says that when you retire you should rent or buy living space in North Carolina, Kentucky, Tennessee, or Georgia. Once you're set up in one of those places, you can spend part of the year overseas. With $400,000 or $500,000 you can afford both to maintain a place in the Southeast and to cover travel costs abroad. On $743 a month, you can't.

OVERSEAS LIVING

For bare-bones retirement, your best bet is to sell your home, stick the proceeds in bank CDs, stuff your household goods in someone's garage, and beat it to Guadalajara, Rio de Janeiro, or Madrid. Forget about maintaining a residence in the Southeast. Instead, close up shop in the United States as completely as you can. When you leave, take only your clothes, hobbies, and those personal effects that serve as future shock absorbers, like a coffee cup, set of dominoes, and favorite silk tie.

Why Guadalajara, Rio de Janeiro, or Madrid? I think most retired Americans would find it fairly easy to adjust in those three cities. All three have large American communities that welcome newcomers. All three have an American Club, English-language newspapers, and American bookstores. And all three are wonderful, upbeat places to live. Heading overseas with a one-way ticket is bound to seem scary. Give yourself a break and head for those places that are most likely to welcome you.

Guadalajara, Rio de Janeiro, and Madrid also have practical advantages. You can fly to any of them on cheap charters or discount fares. You can enter as a tourist and stay for up to six months before having to renew your visa or tourist card. In Guadalajara or Madrid you'll learn Spanish; in Brazil you'll learn Portuguese. Both those languages come from familiar Latin roots, and you can learn them easier than, say, Chinese or Swahili.

Most important, with $743 a month in those three cities you'll live like the upper middle class and have money left over. As one Guadalajara retiree told *Money* magazine in 1985, "My Social Security check is $1,100. My rent is $60. I drink, but I can't drink that much." *Choose Mexico—Retire on $400 a Month* describes how thousands of Americans live in Mexico on $400 a month or less. Thousands more live in Rio de Janeiro on $400 a month. Madrid costs a little more, say $700 or so, but still falls within your bare-bones budget.

Guadalajara, Mexico, rests high up in Mexico's Central Plateau. Locals claim they live in the best climate in the world, and they may be right. Year-round temperatures stay in the 60s and 70s. Residents build homes without heating and air-conditioning, and rarely take more than a sweater to go out. For warmer weather, they head down the hill to the beach resorts of Manzanillo, San Blas, and Puerto Vallarta, all just a few hours away by bus.

Most Americans in the area—an estimated 30,000 of them—retire on nearby Lake Chapala. But Guadalajara itself is Mexico's second-largest city. With 2.5 million people it offers what we expect of a major metropolitan area: entertainment, museums, good restaurants, excellent medical care and other services, daily newspapers, and good public transportation.

The first time I went to Guadalajara, many years ago, I kept slipping back in time. I pictured a more peaceful world, with Spaniards in control of most of it. If you've ever dreamed of living in old Los Angeles, Monterey, or San Francisco when those "pueblos" were part of Mexico and the Spanish empire, you'll fall in love with Guadalajara. The city center has five major plazas, each with an impressive church and spacious gardens. Colonial buildings grace the older streets, and bright cotton materials splash the stores and sidewalks with color.

Choose Mexico reports that Guadalajara is cheaper than almost any other part of Mexico. Because of the large number of retired Americans there, you can readily find a house to take care of while the owners are visiting the kids back "home" in New Jersey. You have to be willing to move every so often. But by house-sitting you can live rent-free in country villas, lakeside estates, or large city houses or apartments.

Guadalajara beats Rio or Madrid in its proximity to the United States. Visitors from Los Angeles or Houston can drive. Others can fly in a couple of hours, often on direct flights.

A city of 5 million people, Rio de Janeiro used to be Brazil's capital and most important city. That changed about twenty years ago, when the government moved the capital to Brasília. São Paulo has taken over as the country's manufacturing and business center. Rio has been relegated to a new status as Brazil's third city. But its residents seem to be making up for the change by having more fun than anybody else. In chapter 5 I talked about Brazil's fun-loving, sensuous people, and Rio is the center of the action.

What hits the first-time visitor to Rio is its breathtaking natural beauty. Stark mountains, sandy beaches, tropical islands, and the Atlantic Ocean combine in a spectacular setting. In my experience the three most beautiful cities in the world are San Francisco, Hong Kong, and Rio. But of the three, Rio is the only one with long, sunny beaches in the heart of the city. For $100 a month you can get a decent, one-bedroom apartment within two blocks of any of them: Copacabana, Ipanema/Leblon, or São Conrado. With the $643 a month left over you can eat at the best restaurants, go to the wildest nightclubs, rent sailboats, or go hang gliding. When you're tired of spending money you can flop on the beach for an hour or two.

It took Vicki and me about two seconds to adjust to Rio. But even fussier Americans seem to have a fairly easy time settling in. Brazilians are extremely patient with foreigners, especially those who try to speak Portuguese. And Brazilians hardly seem to notice when "silly" Americans choose to eat lunch at noon rather than two or three hours later—like "normal" people.

One way to make a little money in Rio is to sublet your apartment for $500 during *Carnaval*, Brazil's one-week bash in late February and early March. Take the opportunity to fly up north, to Bahia or Recife, to get away from the crowds. By subletting your apartment you'll pay for your trip and have a few hundred dollars left over.

The history of the modern world is the history of Europe. Anyone interested in art, music, language, communications, science, and engineering starts his studies with Europe. In good times and bad, war and peace, most of what's important in our culture dates from somewhere in Europe. And Madrid is one of Europe's great capitals.

When you go to Madrid, think about those who went before you. Five hundred years ago, for example, the expatriate Christopher Columbus went to Madrid to lean on King Ferdinand and Queen Isabella. He wanted some dough for an overseas voyage, quite a risky venture in those days. The king and queen had finally driven the Moors out of Spain, and they were acquisition-minded. Think of them as the Carl Icahn and Saul Steinberg of the fifteenth century. So Columbus had an easy time getting the money, and he proceeded to discover America. (Actually, America was already inhabited by a couple of million people who had "discovered" it centuries before. Columbus didn't discover America any more than Ed Koch discovered Manhattan. But who am I to argue with what I learned in the fifth grade?)

With $743 a month you can't afford Paris, Vienna, or Geneva. But you can afford Madrid. And if you're willing to travel off-season and wait for special deals, you can arrange a low-cost trip from Madrid to the rest of Europe. When Vicki and I were in Spain in 1985, for example, we were offered round-trip airfare to London for $50 each. For a few dollars more the tour people would throw in a hotel and breakfast for seven days. With deals like that, your biggest London expense is likely to be the jam you buy at Fortnum and Mason.

Spain is Velázquez and Goya, Cervantes and Hemingway, Franco and King Juan Carlos. Madrid is bullfights, music in the streets, doughnuts at 4:00 A.M., and open-air markets. Madrid is also seafood paella, fine red wine, and Fundador sherry brandy. Stockholm, Zurich, and Rome offer a great deal. But you could have so much fun in Madrid and the rest of Spain and Portugal that you'll forget about Europe's other great capitals.

Guadalajara, Rio de Janeiro, or Madrid. Bare-bones retirement is as easy as choosing among them. Before you take off, reread the rules in chapter 5 on how to move and the rules in chapter 8 on how to travel. After that, all you need is a spirit of adventure. In 1983 Peter A. Dickenson wrote a book called *Travel and Retirement Edens Abroad* (Dutton). He dedicates the book "to those who believe the social swim is fluid and that friendships are based on what a person *is*, not what he or she was . . . that everyone has a story to tell and you learn by listening." Bare-bones retirees are the kind of people Dickenson is talking about.

LIVING IN THE UNITED STATES LIKE A STUDENT

Overseas living makes so much sense, why would you ever want to stay in the United States? For one thing, you could have an ailing parent or friend who needs your attention. Or interests could keep you in the United States. You could want to study the history of the American Civil War, for example, or follow a college football team around the country. But I suspect most who choose to stay in the United States do so because they're reluctant to give up the American way of life. As a friend puts it, "When you leave the United States, you're camping out."

But even if you insist on staying in the United States, you can retire on a bare-bones $743 a month. That amount of money buys less in high-cost America than in the Third World. Retire on $743 in the United States and you have to make sacrifices. But if you're willing to share a house with others—I call it living in the United States like a student—you can probably swing it.

Most of us have fond memories of early adult life. We owned nothing and had few responsibilities. We lived cheaply in college dorms or small apartments. We built bookcases out of bricks and boards. We decorated with posters and cascading spider plants. We built huge desks by putting a door blank on sawhorses. We sat in the last row of theaters, visited museums on the free nights, and bought bleacher seats at baseball games. We did some of the things we now laugh at in *Animal House, Porky's,* and *Police Academy*.

Somewhere along the way we outgrew the student life. We got married or moved in with a partner, bought a home of our own, and started driving newer cars. We had children, dressed more carefully, and bought life insurance. But with each of these steps toward a better life we gave up something. Falling in love and getting married is great, but it usually means fewer friends will hang around. A home of our own serves as a fuzzy blanket and helps us grow up. But it also forces us to sand and paint walls, pull weeds, and sweep driveways. Newer cars mean that when we wreck them we make the repairs rather than simply junk the car. Children bring joy, but they bring headaches as well.

One way to live on $743 a month is to rediscover how you lived as a student. Students avoid expensive restaurants. They ride to parties together and take turns driving. They save money on food by clipping coupons, buying in discount supermarkets, and using meat tenderizer. They travel on charter flights, stay in hotel rooms with bathrooms down the hall, and use buses and their feet rather than taxis and rental cars. They wear cotton denims and simple shirts. Most of their clothing budget goes to buy one or two pairs of comfortable walking shoes.

Most important, students—and bare-bones retirees—share living space with others. Sharing living space again after all these years will be a sacrifice. You value your privacy. But sacrifice is a part of bare-bones retirement in the United States. And if you use your imagination, you should be able to come up with a creative, low-cost way to share living space that fits your needs.

Last July and August, when I took my sax lessons at the Berklee College of Music in Boston, Vicki and I rented a furnished, two-bedroom apartment in Boston for $400 a month. That's a reasonable amount when you're living on $50 a day. But when you're on a bare-bones budget you've got to find something cheaper. One of the Berklee faculty members I met had found it. He shared a five-bedroom house with four other people.

I asked him how he liked it.

"I'm a big guy," he said. "I need large, airy spaces and I like our big living room. My housemates are musicians. The house sits on a big lot, so we can practice our instruments without bothering the neighbors. I like having someone to share the housework. Yet I have privacy—my own room and furniture and my own telephone. The neighborhood's coming up and the house is in good shape. I could never handle the $500-a-month rent on my own. But split five ways, it's cheap."

Another example? We know two couples who bought an $11,000 house a few blocks from the water in Pensacola, Florida. It's a fixer-upper. But the four of them plan to work on it together. They'll live in the house while they make the repairs. That will save money. And they'll take their time, doing most of the work themselves and getting the best prices on materials.

If you already rent a large place, could you take in boarders? Better yet, do you know someone with a big house who might want *you* as a boarder? Could you form a group of people who might rent a place together? Could you live in a friend's mountain cabin under a special arrangement?

SEARCH OUT MONEYMAKING SIDELINES

When you retire with the full $500,000, you'll never have to work another day in your life. You may *choose* to do something that earns money. Chapter 7 points out that you may even do something that makes you a lot of money. That's because you'll have your mind clear to think about opportunities.

Not so for bare-bones retirees. Your total monthly income amounts to only $743. You'll probably spend it all, leaving nothing in the bank to cover inflation. You'll receive $743 a month—more or less, depending on how interest rates move—as long as you live. But each year that $743 will be worth less. At age 62 you'll be eligible for Social Security. If you're vested in a company pension plan, you'll start to collect at age 55 or so. If your aunt Sally dies she may leave you something in her will. But with only $100,000 in the bank, chances are you'll need extra money before you reach age 55 or Aunt Sally dies. And remember the horrible life of the $743-a-month Social Security couple. You need a nest egg to make sure you don't wind up old and poor.

You need to supplement your income by doing a little part-time work.

In my view, you're retired when you break out of your former work habit and arrange your financial affairs to live on unearned income. When you opt for bare-bones retirement you fit this definition. You get off the career track and put your entire net worth—or at least most of it—in the bank. That gives you $743 a month, enough to cover your expenses. But you're exposed to the ravages of inflation. That means that one of these days you'll have to earn a couple of extra bucks. You won't come out of retirement. Rather, you'll keep your eyes open for occasional earning opportunities.

Vicki and I met a 42-year-old retiree in Charleston, South Carolina. He had owned a restaurant, but over time had come to hate the long hours and sour, hungry customers every night. He sold out and put his money in the bank. If he had followed the $50-a-Day Rule he could have lived off the interest. But he proceeded to spend most of his stash on an extravagant lifestyle. He bought a yacht, stayed in deluxe hotels, and regularly invited twelve people to dinner at top restaurants. Within a few years he had seriously depleted his capital. What to do?

Wood carving had always been a hobby, so this man decided to carve birds and duck decoys for others. He entered competitions and won prizes. People began to write him, asking to buy his works and if he could repair their antique carvings. Within three years he had turned his hobby into a nifty little business. Now he repairs decoys and carves birds in a friend's garage during Charleston's winter tourist season. He makes about $20,000. That money, plus interest income, supports him and his wife in Key West during the rest of the year. He feels retired, and I think he meets the above definition. But the $20,000 protects him against inflation and lets him lead a slightly better life.

An Argentine friend manages five apartment buildings near his home. It takes him eight to ten hours a month and pays him $300. In New England we met a young couple who retired and restored an old house in Maine. They run it as an inn during the summer and live in the Caribbean the rest of the year. Similarly, we met a woman who runs a catering business in Cape Cod during the summer season. She makes enough to live in Boston the rest of the year. Other young retirees we know lead tourist groups once or twice a year. For those who speak a second language, leading tourist groups pays well and includes a free trip abroad.

Perhaps the quickest way to make money is to do temp work. In 1986 *Time* reported that the professional temp business is booming. "In growing numbers, lawyers, doctors, engineers, computer experts, and college professors willing to punch in and out for up to $150 an hour are being snapped up by firms and institutions eager for their services but only for a while. Professionals now account for an estimated 11 percent of the 800,000 Americans who work each day in temporary positions." Tax specialists help out during tax season. Lawyers do discovery work to help prepare major cases. Doctors cover emergency rooms during holidays and weekends. Computer programmers hire out on a per-project basis.

Retired young teachers can work summers or do substitute teaching. Retired young writers can do three or four magazine pieces a year. Retired secretaries can fill in for regulars who have babies. And anyone, it seems, can garden, paint houses, or teach English to foreigners.

Another part-time task you should consider is making your money work harder. One-year CDs minimize risk and require little attention. I recommend them. But if you're willing to live with some risk and spend time on your investments, you can adopt the high-risk/low-risk investment program in chapter 10.

Remember that to make your stash earn higher returns, you almost always risk more and work harder. A friend of mine puts 20 percent of his retirement funds into limited partnerships that buy oil reserves. The risk? The price of oil may fall. The work? My friend spends several hours a week poring over prospectuses, talking to brokers on the phone, and doing projections. Another friend moves part of his retirement stash in and out of foreign currencies. The risk? Currencies he buys may fall; currencies he sells may rise. The work? Because he buys and sells in nervous markets, he constantly feels under strain. His paperwork takes several hours a week. He reads economic reports, trade figures, and forecasts.

You'll have to decide how much risk makes sense for you. But bare-bones retirees need to have a special feeling about risk and financial security. I admit to being security-conscious. I insisted on arranging my affairs so that I'd never have to return to work. After I retired in 1984, economic factors turned against me. Interest rates fell, the value of the dollar fell, and the dollar cost of living in Argentina went up. Yet, in spite of the bad breaks, our net worth has increased by more than inflation. That's the advantage of "normal" retirement with $400,000 or $500,000 in the bank. Even if rates go against you, you can continue to live well and increase your net worth.

But if you retire with $100,000 you'll have to find financial security in yourself, in your ability to innovate, rather than in a fistful of CDs. I think Vicki has the right attitude for bare-bones retirement. She shares none of my security hangups. She feels optimistic about all aspects of our lives, including finances. As I mentioned in chapter 4, she handles our investments and controls our spending, and she does it without worrying. She knows we can figure a way to deal with any financial problems that come up. We'll go back to work part-time, adopt a new investment strategy, move to a cheaper country, or whatever.

FOCUS ON SPENDING PRIORITIES

The retired couple living on $50 a day makes very few sacrifices. They may live in a smaller house and drive a station car rather than a Mercedes. But they go where they want and spend what they want. With just a bit of creativity they enjoy the comforts that most highly paid executives feel they have to work for.

But when you retire on a bare-bones program you've got to scrimp a bit. Not much. You still live well, especially if you move to the Third World. You have money to lunch at the club, play golf three times a week, and take cooking class. But you have less financial security. You have to keep your eyes open for ways to earn a few bucks. At times, you may long for your former life.

But remember why you retired. Was it because you preferred a simpler life? Because you burned out working in an intense job? Because you were going out of your mind with hurry and stress? Because you wanted to do something different with your life? Whatever your reason for retiring on $743 a month, you need to have it set clearly in your mind. On bad days after you retire you'll wish you had enough money to live like you used to. But that's when you need to remember the energy you expended on the job every day, how exhausted you were, how quickly you got mad, and how busy you felt. You also need to remember what you wanted out of retirement. That will help you:

Focus on spending priorities

When you spend only $743 a month, you don't scrimp on everything you do. Rather, you focus on those few things that can make a difference in your life. When major expenses come up, if you know your spending priorities, you can afford them. It's easier to buy a car, for example, if you know that all you need is a station car. It's easier to choose a hotel if you know you can live without an elevator.

You like to live in a large home? Great. You can house-sit, move to the Third World, or live with others in a rambling farm house. You can decide to live in a smaller place that has some of the features you associate with a big house. For example, I like big, well-lit rooms. It's not so much the size of my house but the size of the room I'm in that affects my state of being. So Vicki and I bought an apartment with a large living room and high ceilings. The living room looks out onto a patio that doubles our sense of space. Large windows let in light, and we installed fluorescent lamps in the ceiling to add even more. The result is a large, pleasant living area that accommodates parties of six, gives me a sense of space, and keeps us from feeling cramped.

You love to travel? On $743 a month you can move to a new country every year. That eliminates airfare and hotels, the two biggest travel costs. Tired of moving? Travel to low-cost countries. To study the Hapsburgs, go to Budapest rather than Vienna. To learn French, go to one of the former French colonies rather than Paris. Visit Hong Kong or Singapore rather than Tokyo, the Dominican Republic rather than Barbados, and Yugoslavia rather than Italy. And travel off-season, when you get better airfares and cheaper hotels. Drop into Rio during *Carnaval* and you'll spend a fortune. Go the month before or the month after, and you'll never be able to spend $743.

You like to go to expensive restaurants? Why? If it's the

food, you can learn to do gourmet cooking at home. When you're retired you'll have plenty of time, and you can get others to share the fun with you. If it's the service, you can hire a teenager to come over and serve. If it's the ambience, you can search for out-of-the-way little places that offer the atmosphere without the cost.

You have a tough time living without financial security—like me? You can work on it. Try yoga, TM, or other Eastern meditation to help you transcend the physical. Read Thoreau and try to think more clearly about life's basics. Spend time at the ocean, near the waves. Some believe that the air around a pounding surf has a higher percentage of negative ions. Those ions may have a calming effect. In any event, you'll find less of a need for financial security once you discover you can live without a paycheck.

The Rules

Chapter 1 presents the three-part formula for very early retirement:

Do your arithmetic
Do some soul-searching
Do what you want

First, *do your arithmetic* to figure out how much net worth you have. Unless you opt for bare-bones retirement (chapter 11), before you retire you should have $400,000 to $500,000 of net worth, including equity in your home. To retire:

Turn hard assets into cash (chapter 1)
Convert home equity to cash (chapter 4)
Convert other assets to cash (chapter 4)

With the proceeds:

Buy one-year insured CDs (chapters 1, 4)

The CDs will throw off enough money for you to:

220

Live on $50 a day (chapters 1, 8)

provided you:

Cut down your infrastructure (chapter 8)

Cutting down your infrastructure means you:

Move (chapter 5)
Sell your vehicles (chapter 8)

If you retire in the United States:

Go south (chapter 5)
Live where the jobs aren't (chapter 5)

Once you set up your U.S. base, you may want to:

Try living abroad for three to six months (chapter 5)

The best way to live abroad, whether for some or all of the year, is to:

Keep calm; you can always return to the United States (chapter 5)
Live like a resident, not like a tourist (chapter 5)
Rent, don't buy (chapter 5)
Choose hotels that offer what you need and nothing more (chapter 8)
Learn the language (chapter 5)
Go with the flow (chapter 5)
Don't criticize, complain, or compare (chapter 5)

Once you're retired, you:

Spend on yourself, not on your assets (chapter 8)
Spend more than $50 a day if you must (chapter 8)
Remember the Coin Toss Law: Less is more (chapter 8)

Do some soul-searching to decide when retirement makes sense for you. The idea is to:

Enjoy your career and then move on (chapter 2)

No matter where you are on your personal career path, you'll want to:

Look for meaning in yourself, not in your job (chapter 2)
Take the two-year test (chapter 6)

At some point you'll take the two-year test and see retirement in your future. That's when you:

Talk to others (chapter 6)

Talk to your spouse to make sure he or she wants to retire with you. Talk to your friends and consider what they say, but:

Don't expect a little help from your friends (chapter 6)

When retirement day comes:

Manage the change (chapter 6)

During the first months of transition, managing the change means you:

Fill your new days with old activities (chapter 6)

After a transition period, *do what you want* with your new retired life. The rule is:

Do what you wish, but you must do something (chapter 3)

To get started:

Make a to-do list (chapter 3)

At times your new life will seem unimportant. But you'll feel better if you:

Remember that work was just talking on the phone (chapter 3)

When you retire, you:

Modify your work ethic (chapter 3)
Live without guilt (chapter 3)

To keep from doing something stupid:

Make a clean break (chapter 7)

from your old job, and:

Avoid major purchases for two years (chapter 7)

After the transition period:

Go back to work if you feel like it (chapter 7)

If you retire with kids (chapter 9), you need more than $400,000 to $500,000 of net worth. How much more depends on how many kids you have and how old they are. To raise a child costs about $4,000 a year.

If you don't have enough money to retire (chapter 10), you need to work to build your net worth. You should:

Manage your career (chapter 10)
Control your spending (chapter 10)
Set up a savings routine (chapter 10)
Start a high-risk/low-risk investment program (chapter 10)

If you opt for bare-bones retirement (chapter 11), with a net worth of $100,000 or so, you should:

Live overseas or live in the United States like a student (chapter 11)
Search out moneymaking sidelines (chapter 11)
Focus on spending priorities (chapter 11)

Norman M. Lobsenz, in a September 14, 1986, *Parade* article, says that during Edward Kennedy's first campaign for the Senate, he "was jeeringly described by an opponent as a man who never worked a day in his life. Next morning, when Kennedy solicited votes at a factory, one man shook his hand and referred to the jibe, saying, 'Don't worry, Ted. You ain't missed a thing.' "

As of this writing I've been retired for four years. I feel I haven't missed a thing. On the contrary, I still marvel at my good fortune. I have all the money I'll ever need. I have time to visit friends, invite Vicki out to breakfast, and take a siesta. If I want to work a political campaign, enroll in a two-month jazz course, take Vicki on a round-the-world junket, write a book, study

Italy's economy, or build a vacation home, I simply go ahead and do it. I have my limits. I try to do only what I want to do. I won't drink wine coolers that smell like strawberry shortcake, for example, or try a new restaurant on New York's West Side that features a $25 endive salad as a main course. But within reason, if I want to do something I do it.

Without the stress and anxiety I felt on the job, my disposition has improved. I see people in a different way. I think I'm more compassionate, more sympathetic to the needs of others. I growl only at people who truly deserve it, like New York cabdrivers, for example, and customs inspectors and French waiters. And I feel less hurried. Life has become a stroll through the park, with colorful flowers, freshly cut grass, and friendly faces, rather than a rush to get through the day's agenda.

What did I do to deserve my good life? I followed the rules in this book. But beyond the rules, I happened to have been born at the right time. I grew up and went to work during the most sustained, spectacular boom in economic history. That boom continues, in spite of the debt crisis, government deficits, competition from Japan, and shortages of Cabbage Patch dolls.

According to the Census Bureau, as reported in the January 1987 *Journal of Accountancy*, the U.S. standard of living has doubled in the past thirty-five years. We work less and less to earn our goods and services. On average we now earn enough in six minutes to buy a dozen eggs, down from thirteen minutes in 1960. We earn enough in two hours to buy a toaster, down from six hours in 1960. We earn enough in seventeen minutes to buy a six-pack of beer, down from thirty minutes in 1960.

Those are averages. Many of us earn more than the average. In a decade or two we may earn enough to keep us in eggs, toasters, and beer for the rest of our lives. Not to mention plane tickets, hotels, personal computers, hair spray, and microwave popcorn that butters itself.

Our new wealth means we have more options than ever before. Many people choose to ignore those options. They stay on the job, pushing the accelerator as hard as ever. They want to live on $500 a day, not $50 a day. They echo John L. Lewis's cry for "More, *More, MORE!*" They already have a pile. But they figure another pile wouldn't hurt.

Many others choose to downscale. Srully Blotnick, in *Ambi-*

tious Men: Their Drives, Dreams, and Delusions (The Viking Press, 1987), reports that almost 40 percent of successful men make a midlife switch to lower-level careers. According to Blotnick, those men tend to enjoy their new careers. They long for their old jobs about as much as a West Texas Bible preacher longs to march in San Francisco's Polk Street Halloween parade.

Still others choose to retire. According to an October 13, 1986, *New York Times* article by Steven Greenhouse, the Bureau of Labor Statistics reports that one in three men aged 55 to 64 is no longer working. If present trends continue, only one in two American men in that age group will be in the labor force in two decades. The bureau reports that more younger men are retiring as well, although not in such high numbers.

Are the young retirees happy in their new lives? The Bureau of Labor Statistics isn't telling. The bureau measures income, net worth, and numbers of new jobs. Ask them to check on happiness, pride, dignity, and the like, and they get bogged down in methodology.

I, however, have no such hangups. I simply go out and ask retirees whether they're happy with their lives. Over the past three years I've talked with hundreds of young retirees, men and women in their 40s, 50s, and early 60s. And I've found that many of them don't like their retirement lives one bit.

The problem, in a word, is boredom. Unhappy retirees long for "something to do," an "office to go to," or "a way to keep busy." They feel stale and restless. I can understand why. On a typical day they watch TV and, for real fun, go to a brokerage office. I suppose they try to decide whether the stock quotation screen is more or less exciting than, say, *Perry Mason* reruns.

So it's possible to hate retirement. But I've also met retirees who love their retired lives. The difference seems to be almost wholly one of attitude. Happy retirees believe they retired to *do* something rather than to *stop* doing something. They view retirement as one of life's phases, like childhood, adolescence, going to school, working, raising a family, and getting cable TV installed. Retirement can be better or worse than the phases that preceded it, depending on what one makes of it.

Happy retirees lead active, programmed lives. They learn new basic skills, in activities that have many facets. They know that hobbies don't quite cut it. It's fun to play golf, garden, and knit. But when they do those things all day every day, they get restless. Happy retirees insist on meatier pursuits. They write screenplays, learn to sail, follow a baseball team around the country, make speeches, or study the law. And whatever they do, they do it with a spirit of adventure and sense of humor.

In the end, although this book is about retiring young, it's more about retiring well. Whether you're 35, 55, or 75 when you retire, the idea is to enjoy yourself. To contribute and learn rather than feel you're killing time. To grow and develop rather than sit in front of a TV. To love and cherish rather than become bitter and sad. To recognize that retirement can be life's exciting dessert—whatever your age when you start it.